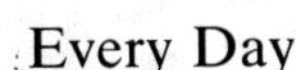
Every Day

# *Every Day*
# *The Story of Joe Williams*

Leslie Gourse

Quartet Books
London Melbourne New York

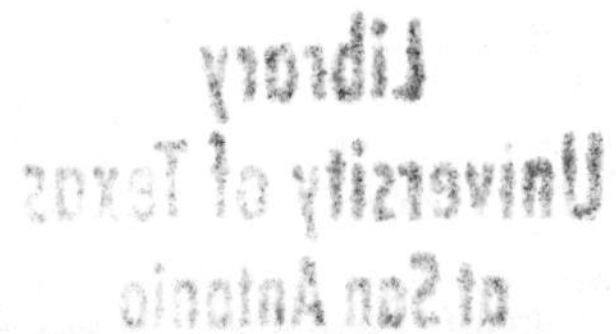

First published by Quartet Books Limited 1985
A member of the Namara Group
27/29 Goodge Street, London W1P 1FD



British Library Cataloguing in Publication Data

Gourse, Leslie
Every day: the story of Joe Williams.
1. Williams, Joe 2. Singers—United States—Biography
I. Title
784.5 ML420.W55/

ISBN 0-7043-2466-0

Typeset by MC Typeset, Chatham, Kent
Printed and bound in Great Britain
by Mackays of Chatham Ltd, Kent

# *Contents*

*Acknowledgements*

The author would like to thank the following for their kind assistance in the preparation of material for this book:

The Toronto Star Syndicate for reviews of Joe Williams concerts, reprinted with permission, the Toronto Star Syndicate; *Variety; Playboy;* the *New York Times* for John Wilson's excerpts, copyright 1962, 1967, 1972, 1974 by the New York Times Company, reprinted by permission; the Urban Research Institute Inc, Chicago; Helen McNamara, the *Toronto Telegram;* Toronto *Daily Star;* CBS Songs; Frederick Music Inc.

Illustrations courtesy of: Lonnie Simmons; Institute of Jazz Studies, Rutgers University; Raymond Ross; Caesar's Palace; Frank Foster; Jackie Gilson Alper; Jill Freedman; MGM; Dr Milan Schijatschky; Clark Terry; Nancy Miller Elliott and Joe Williams.

Extracts from songs by kind permission of the following:

'Kinda Blue', © 1960 Jazz Horn Music Corporation; 'Goin' to Chicago Blues', © 1941 (renewed) Warner Bros Inc, all rights reserved; 'Every Day I Have the Blues', © 1952, 1980 Arc Music Corporation, New York NY, all rights reserved; 'Dimples', © 1956, 1968 Conrad Music, a division of Arc Music Corporation, all rights reserved; 'Somebody', © 1960 Famous Music Corporation; 'Everything Must Change', © 1974/ASCAP Almo Music Corporation, all rights reserved – international copyright secured; 'Changes', © 1980 Bromley Music/ASCAP; 'I Had Somebody Else Before I Had You', © 1925 Harry Harris Music Publishing Co/ASCAP; 'Come Sunday', © 1974 Tempo Music; 'In the Beginning', © 1966 Tempo Music; 'Sad Tune', © 1973 Upam Music, a division of Gopam Enterprises Inc; 'Who She Do', © 1972 Jillean Music; 'Rocks in My Bed', © 1941, renewed 1969 by Robbins Music Corporation – rights assigned to CBS Catalogue Partnership – all rights controlled and administered by CBS Robbins Catalogue Inc, all rights reserved, international copyright secured; 'The Comeback', © 1953 Frederick Music Inc; 'Roll 'em Pete', © 1941, 1963 MCA Music, a division of MCA Inc New York, NY, all rights reserved; 'This is no Shit', © 1953 words and music by Cliff Norton; 'When Sunny Gets Blue', © 1956 Marvin Music Co, 1 Time Square Plaza New York NY 10036.

In memory of Sydney Jane Gourse and Maureen Percelay Zusy, with special thanks to Joe Williams for his unflagging support, co-operation and good will, and to Dan Morgenstern for his generous guidance.

Leslie Gourse

For all the musicians with whom I have worked and who have played a pretty chord, a nice change, beginning with my piano teacher, my mother, and on to Count Basie and beyond.

Joe Williams

# *Chronology*

1918: Joe Williams is born, christened Joseph Goreed, in Cordele, Ga., a Southern lumber town, 12 December.

1921: Joseph Goreed travels by train to Chicago with his grandmother, Mittie Gilbert, to live with his mother, Anne Gilbert, and her sister Juanita.

1921–34: Anne Gilbert meets James Mason, who becomes her lifelong companion, and takes Joe to many musical events in Chicago.

1934: As a teenager, Joe has a year-long bout of tuberculosis, but he recovers and finds he can sing well again. With a background of church singing, Joe steps into a high-school show to perform as part of a trio. That same year he leaves school to start earning money, singing for tips in a downtown Chicago club. His family has a kitchen-table conference and chooses 'Williams' as an appropriate name for the aspiring singer.

1935: Joe Williams moves into his own room on Chicago's South Side and goes home to his mother's apartment for dinners. He works with the band of his friend, Chicago trumpeter Johnny Long, and has a wonderful time hanging out on the scene, going to theatres in the afternoon, working or learning in clubs at night.

1937: He tours the South with the band of Chicago musician Jimmie Noone, then goes home to play on the South Side with the Noone band.

1939: Joe begins broadcasting coast to coast on CBS every night from a club. He is singing all around Chicago's North and South Sides.

1941: At the Regal Theatre, manager Ken Blewett hires Joe as stage-door manager, a job in which Joe gets to meet thousands of entertainers, including Ella Fitzgerald, Fats Waller, Lionel Hampton and Count Basie, to name a few. Joe's singing catches the attention of Kansas City bandleader Andy Kirk; Joe begins working occasionally with Kirk. Singing at the Cabin Inn, Joe sees famous people ringside – actor John Barrymore for one. More importantly for the young singer, legendary tenor saxophonist Coleman Hawkins, back from Europe, leading his own band during World War II, hears Joe and invites him to tour with the band.

1943: Ken Blewett, impressed with Joe's voice and his warm relationship with his mother, recommends Joe to Lionel Hampton as a temporary replacement for Hampton's regular bandsinger, Rubell Blakely. Joe works with Dinah Washington in the Hampton band, on a long tour. That year, too, at age twenty, Joe marries his first wife, Wilma Cole, nineteen, and soon finds out that his marriage is troubled because Wilma had no respect for her father and she was extremely attached to her mother. The same theme will run through Joe's second and third marriages. He and Wilma get divorced in 1946.

1946: Joe marries his second wife, Ann Kirksey. Still a struggling singer, he's popular in the South Side clubs and the Midwest region.

1947: Joe's grandmother dies. The struggles of trying to build a career and a life on the South Side take their toll. Joe, nearly thirty, has a nervous breakdown and goes to a hospital. Recovering, he decides to become a singer seriously, artistically, not just for the money. He practises in the park, singing to the birds. Some of the songs, he will later record.

1950: Working as a Fuller Cosmetics Salesman door-to-door, he also begins singing at the Club DeLisa, the most popular club with musicians on the South Side. And Joe is the most popular entertainer there, a star in his regional circle. In this period, Ann Kirksey asks for a divorce, which Joe arranges through his lawyer. Joe makes his first recording of 'In the Evening' with Red Saunders, bandleader at the DeLisa. The song will become one of Joe's hits. This year, too, Joe sits in for the first time with Count Basie during the Count's summer-long engagement at Chicago's Brass Rail. Joe makes his first recording of 'Every Day' with King Kolax, bandleader at the Regal Theatre. And Joe marries again, to Lemma Reid, and keeps working around Chicago and the Midwest, occasionally seeing Count Basie on the Kate Smith show on television.

1952: Lemma becomes pregnant with the couple's daughter JoAnn.

1953: JoAnn is born on 19 January, 1953. By then the marriage is already troubled. And Lemma on occasion goes back to live with her mother in Cincinnati.

1954: Disconsolate over the turmoil in his third marriage, Joe throws all his best efforts into singing. On a break during his show at Chicago's Cotton Club, he hurries to the Trianon, where Count Basie is appearing. Joe sits in with the band. Count Basie is so impressed that he hires Joe to sing with the band and sends him a money order to pay for the trip from Chicago to New York.

1954: Joe flies to join Basie. (25 December) The bus picks up drummer Sonny Payne for the first time, too, and heads South for a tour. Then the band makes its way up the East Coast, honing its blues-based repertoire, including 'Every Day'. When the popular Basie band reaches New York City for its traditional springtime engagement at Birdland, Joe becomes an 'overnight' star in the jazz world's pre-eminent club.

1955: Joe's first recording with Basie, including 'Every Day', 'Alright, Okay, You Win', 'Roll 'em Pete', 'In the Evening', 'Teach Me Tonight', 'Send Me Someone to Love', and Joe's own tune, 'My Baby Upsets Me', becomes an international hit. (July) That year, too, Joe wins his first *Down Beat* polls as the best new male singer deserving of wider recognition and as the best male bandsinger. Joe makes his first appearance at the Newport Jazz Festival in RI and the first of several Birdland tours with the Basie band; other tours follow in 1956 and '57. And on 29 November 1955, Joe Jr is born.

1955–7: Joe Williams becomes enamoured of golf, learning

from his bandmates, especially guitarist Freddie Green. Golf becomes still another bone of contention between Joe and Lemma, who wants him to spend less time on golf courses during their reunions.

1957: Joe meets a beautiful Englishwoman, Jillean Hughes-D'Aeth, born 22 November, 1921, an enthusiastic amateur golfer. The couple meets for the first time after Joe performs at the Waldorf-Astoria's Starlight Roof – the first time a black band has performed there. Sarah Vaughan and her trio have appeared on the same bill, too. Joe takes Jillean to Birdland, likes her very much – and doesn't call her. Jillean, working in the New York office of a British firm temporarily, takes a tour of the US and goes home to London.

1959: While touring Europe with Basie, Joe meets Jillean again after a Southampton performance. A romance begins. Jillean accompanies the Basie band to the Continent. In Holland, Joe gives her two dozen roses, flies to Los Angeles with the band, and begins calling London from every payphone he can find along the route of a Western tour. At a payphone in Des Moines, Iowa, he is finally successful in reaching Jillean at her London flat. Jillean is transferred back to the New York office of her firm. The romance continues. Joe records an album, *That Kind of Woman,* with the tune, 'Here's to My Lady', as he looks at Jillean visiting the studio. She sends the album to her family in England, particularly to her cousin Andrew Heath, a traditional jazz fan. Apparently oblivious to the interracial aspects of her romance, she finds that she gets no adverse comments from her family.

1960: Joe and Jillean find an apartment on Central Park West and move in together, while Joe's lawyers begin arranging a divorce settlement for Lemma and Joe's two children. Joe begins planning to leave the Basie band to go out as leader of his own group. Basie and his manager, Willard Alexander, assist Joe, hiring the Harry 'Sweets' Edison Quintet and other personnel to travel with Joe, and set up six months of bookings. *Billboard* magazine's DJ poll calls Joe the favourite male vocalist.

1961: Joe does his last performance as the official Basie

band-singer at the Apollo Theatre in Harlem (12 January). The next day Joe and Count Basie take a train together to Boston, where Joe sees the marquee at Storyville 'Count Basie Presents JOE WILLIAMS'. Basie travels back to New York alone. That year, Joe works more weeks than he has ever done before in one year in his life.

1962–4: After the quintet, Joe hires the Junior Mance trio; manager John Levy, a friend since Chicago days; New York City accountant and lawyer Godfrey Murrain. And Jillean is record keeper at home, maintaining a liaison with Levy and Murrain for business affairs. Joe makes his first solo appearance on the Johnny Carson show, booked by Bruce Cooper, a fan and friend since Joe's Basie days.

1964: Joe begins travelling with a pianist only, simplifying the road life. He follows itineraries planned by himself with John Levy at Christmastime, when Joe normally takes a vacation from the road.

1964: Joe and Lemma are legally divorced (10 September).

1965: Joe and Jillean are legally married, with Godfrey Murrain as witness, at the Bronx County Courthouse (7 January).

1967: Disenchanted with the inconveniences and hardships of Manhattan's lifestyle, Joe decides to buy a house. Jillean suggests Las Vegas, which Joe likes, too; they buy a house next to a golf course.

1968: Joe's mother dies (3 April). The next day the Rev Martin Luther King Jr is assassinated. Joe, appearing in Texas, is devastated. He flies to Chicago where he meets Jillean for his mother's funeral on 7 April, 1968, then goes on television to try to help quell the riots in the wake of King's funeral. That year, settled in Las Vegas, Joe begins travelling again, with Ellis Larkins as pianist. They tour the world.

1974: Joe wins *Down Beat's* International Critics' Poll as best male vocalist – and wins nearly every year thereafter. Jazz begins to undergo a renaissance, after rock eclipsed jazz in the 1960s. Reviewers become more engaged than ever by Joe's voice and style. John S. Wilson of the *New York Times* notes that Joe has become so skilful 'that he could bring life to any bit of musical dross'.

1983: Joe's star is added next to Count Basie's on the Walk of the Stars in Hollywood, California. John S. Wilson notes that, in his reunion concerts with Count Basie, by then a longstanding tradition, Joe has become the dominating, vitalizing force. Basie is nearly eighty years old.

1984: Count Basie dies. Joe sings, in a quavering voice, the Ellington blues, 'Come Sunday', at Basie's funeral in Harlem's First Abyssinian Baptist Church. Afterwards Joe's car is besieged by Harlem fans.

# *Prelude*
# *The Excitement of Joe Williams and Count Basie*

Blues singer Memphis Slim leaves East Memphis and drifts on to Beale Street in Memphis, Tennessee as a teenager. He wants to be where the music is. Tall, slender, with a rich, brown-umber complexion, he meets an older woman, Annette, a prostitute who lives near a laundry. She befriends him and gives him space in her bed. He lies there, naked, while she takes his clothes, washes them and presses them – and sings, 'Every day . . . every day I have the blues,' he recalls. 'She never finished it. But it stuck in my mind. And when I went up to Chicago, I finished it for her.'

Memphis Slim and another blues singer recorded the song, 'Every Day', in the 1940s. By 1950, Joe Williams, who was a popular singer in the Midwest and especially on the South Side of Chicago, learned it. Memphis Slim liked to hear Joe start the Club DeLisa set swinging in the Blue Monday breakfast shows on the South Side. The song was a great crowd-pleaser and so was Joe, a tall, rugged man with a vibrant stage presence and a rhapsodic baritone voice.

By the 1950s Memphis Slim toured the South with his group, the House Rockers, and took them into a Louisiana club. He felt homesick for his wife and started to play the piano and sing, 'I know my baby's going to jump and shout.' When he got back to Chicago, he recorded that one with a full set of lyrics: 'The Comeback'. Joe Williams liked it and learned that one, too, later taking the two songs into Count Basie's band. And he and the band had a wild, international success with a blues-based repertoire.

During and after the Basie years, Williams went on to win many honours. *Down Beat's* International Critics' Poll has chosen him as 'best male vocalist' for every year from 1974 until 1984, except 1979. His star, made of metal, embedded in the sidewalk and encircling his name, was added (next to Count Basie's) to the Walk of the Stars on Hollywood Boulevard. He was called *the* living male vocalist by the Establishment in the music world, whether he was singing his old blues hits, Ellington songs or any ballads in clubs or at Canegie Hall. And at his reunion performances with Count Basie, as the legendary bandleader grew older Williams, the vitalizing force, seemed to loom larger than the band on the stage – dominating it, mesmerizing audiences. 'One, two, you know what to do . . . ' he said, leaning and pointing towards the band. And the band did it.

The recordings of 'Every Day', 'The Comeback' and other blues tunes that Joe and the Count made in 1955 are still selling nearly thirty years later, and are regularly broadcast on the radio.

In 1983, Joe Williams eats in his favourite Manhattan restaurant, La Scala, not far from where Birdland used to stand. He has his usual dinner of Saltimbocca and arrugala salad, with a couple of glasses of dry red wine, waves 'goodbye' to the staff, and hails a cab outside. A young black driver of a yellow cab, recognizing Joe, slams on his brakes, looks around and tries to figure out a way to back up. But cars block his path. With other cars honking at him, the cabbie inches forward reluctantly, grudgingly losing the treasured fare. Smiling, Joe hails another cab and rides down Fifth Avenue to Greenwich Village, where a crowd of people is waiting to hear him sing in a club.

On the bandstand, the spotlights catch the mother-of-pearl iridescence of his tie, the gleam of a very wide gold-and-diamond wedding band and the brightness of his pearl-grey slacks. And he begins the first of twenty-two one-hour sets scheduled for a week and a half's engagement. He juxtaposes the blues written by the country's poorest people with ballads popularized or written by the country's eminent composers and lyricists, among them Big Joe Turner, Cole Porter and Duke Ellington. He holds the two worlds together craftily with an easy charm and a vast vocal range. The constant shifting from the blues of the black culture to the popular music of the whole American culture gives scope and variety, ebb and flow, to his performance. If he doesn't get around much any more, as he sings in one standard, then at least he has quite clearly been to all the places. He encompasses them; his physical size, six-foot-one and over two hundred pounds, adds to the impact. And he tells about the landscapes of his life in intimate detail. He makes sure to include his audience in the intelligence that John Lee Hooker wrote 'Dimples', so that Hooker and the Chicago blues scene seem more real, if the audience have no personal recollection of it.

'I love the way you walk, I love the way you walk, I've got my eyes on you, I *love* it when you switch,' 'love' on a falsetto tone; then he talks: 'When your hips change gears you have my undivided attention. I've got my eyes on you. You've got dimples in your jaws . . .'

Joe's pianist plays with a lot of blues feeling for a while, and Joe comes back in: 'I love the way you walk, Crazy about your walk, Crazy about your walk, Crazy about your walk, You're my baby, Got my eyes on you. I laaaaaaaaaaaaak it when you switch, I've got my eyes on you, Every day.'

# 1 Goin' to Chicago

Route I–75 runs through Cordele, Georgia and intersects with Highway 280. That takes you to the house of former President Jimmy Carter in his 'home-taa-own' of Plains, and so 'naa-ow there are ten to tway-elve motels in Cordele', said the City Clerk recently in the accents of the Deep South farming town. In the years before Carter, only a couple of motels existed in Cordele, 150 miles south of Atlanta in the centre of the state. Even now, with tourists adding to the coffers, Cordele's people concern themselves mainly with raising peanuts, cotton and so much watermelon that Cordele calls itself the watermelon capital of the world. Cordele's 12,589 residents, up from about 8,000 recently, with a 50–50 racial split, and a history of total segregation, celebrate their status with an annual summer festival of watermelon.

In 1983, the landmark lumberyard in the middle of town burned down, but within a couple of months the town built a new one. Those who don't farm in Cordele are connected with the lumberyard, which existed when Joe Williams was born.

On 12 December 1918, Anne Beatrice Gilbert, a teenager, gave birth to a boy. Miss Gilbert christened him Joseph Goreed, Joseph for his grand-uncle, Dr Joseph Gilbert, a practising physician in Royston, Georgia. Willie Goreed was the baby's father.

For a short time, Joseph Goreed lived with his mother, Miss Anne, and father in the very small town of Osilla, Georgia, with a population now of 3,500 people. There's no record of Joseph's birth in either Osilla or Cordele, because Georgia didn't keep birth or death records until 1921. Until then, people just put them down in the family Bible and let it go at that. Osilla is almost strictly a farming town, primarily raising peanuts, with some tobacco and soybeans and a few trailer factories, too. In 1918, the main crop was cotton. So it's likely that Willie Goreed did farm work.

Joe Williams, born Joseph Goreed, doesn't recall if anyone on his mother's side of the family farmed or worked in the lumberyard in Georgia. Neither does he recall the hot weather – about 100 degrees normally in summer and half that in winter, in a town built mostly on sand and black soil, far from all but a few traces of the flamboyant orange-red clay in other parts of the state. He left Cordele and travelled to Chicago by train when he was three years old.

'But I have some memories of Cordele,' he said, reminiscing one afternoon in New York City, just before his sixty-fifth birthday, sipping cold milk.

> Mostly I remember the grandmother, Mittie Gilbert, washing clothes in a tin tub filled with heated water and of course bathing in a tin tub. I don't remember if we had running water or if we pumped it. But I remember a house where there was a grandfather, Jose Gilbert, a grandmother, my mother and her sister, Cherry Inez, who changed her name to Juanita when we moved to Chicago. And memories of waiting. One of the most exciting things was waiting for a car that was bringing my grandmother home when she was away or had been someplace to do something. My mother sang a song, 'Here Comes Mama'.
>
> I don't remember my father at all and don't know anything about him. I don't have a clue in the world about where he went or what happened to him. Willie Goreed was never talked about, *never* talked about or mentioned. The only memory I have is my mother told me very explicitly that she never gave the young man who was my father a chance. 'Because I was determined that you wouldn't be brought up in ignorance,' she said.
>
> Her family *loved me* and asked her to bring me home from Osilla to Cordele. She knew what the situation was there.

So he and his mother, who was about seventeen or eighteen when Joe was born, went to live with his grandparents and aunt. His grandparents had enough money to support the family and wanted their daughters to finish school. The family attended St Paul's Colored Methodist Episcopalian Church, which had a connection with Paine College, a small black school in Augusta. That's where Joe's mother and aunt went to school for a while. 'Which I guess is one reason why we didn't have a dese dem and dose type family; everybody could read,' Joe reflected. 'And both girls played the piano.'

He always took particular pride in his family. In those days it was difficult and exceptional for a black man to become a doctor, yet Joe's grand-uncle, Dr Joseph Gilbert, became one. Years ago he was written about in *Ebony* magazine.

> I was the only child and doted on, I guess, because the male child and that kind of thing. My grandfather had grown up sleeping in the same bed, practically, with a white family called Herd, with their son. Later on I heard stories that my grandfather would take the truck on orders for the Herd family to go to the railroad yard to pick up provisions and things that were being brought in. He worked for the Herds. So we always had plenty of food, all kinds of food. I'm not exactly sure of the spelling of the Herd family name. Their names are forgotten as quickly as ours.

Joe's earliest remembrances of Sunday particularly were of going to church, where there was a bellows organ that needed to be pumped up. Afterwards the minister – and other ministers from other churches – went to Joe's house for dinner. He remembered:

> There was always a feast – a big spread. I would churn the ice cream by hand. I was a strong, very big, big child, at age three. The ice cream would finally get so stiff until I couldn't turn it any longer. Then one of the grown-ups would take it. And I remember looking up and saying how marvellous and strong they must be, with those big brown arms, black arms.

As a little boy, he thought his relatives were the strongest-looking people in the world. And the women had:

> great dignity and soft voices. And they could turn it. And as a reward for having turned it, I was allowed to lick what was called the dasher; a spangled wheel like a fan, which would move what had been put in. That of course had been real, fresh, tasty Georgia peaches and cream and vanilla and other ingredients. We had peach trees, as I remember.

Williams said this with his easeful bass-baritone voice, conjuring up the smooth texture of the blended peaches.

He also recalled another use for the family's peach tree. His grandmother used green branches from the tree to punish Joe's cousin with at least once. Part of the punishment was having to fetch the switch from the peach tree and give it to Miss Mittie.

For his third birthday, two weeks before Christmas, the family gave him a velocipede, a tricycle with pedals attached to the front wheel – 'A three-wheeled bike was what it was really, as opposed to a kiddie car,' he laughed, mentally comparing the early bicycle with the 'hydromatic kiddie car' that his 'baby' was going to buy him, and which he would sing about joyously in a hit blues tune, 'Roll 'Em Pete'. 'We had guests; one of them must have been a girl who was possibly older than I was. I remember she pushed me over the edge of the porch, which didn't have a railing on it.' He landed under the house, where the family, as so many others did in those days, planted flowers and other things in cans. 'Things would always get under the house, which in those days were built up. Being little, of course, you would always see all those things as opposed to seeing things that were higher up,' he recalled.

'In the South, too, there were certain things that happened so that I can understand now, much later, why other things happened. An older woman, who supposedly sold soap, used to stop at the house. The kindest way to put it is that she looked like a witch almost, what the caricatures are of a witch, with blonde, scraggly hair.' When Joe was about two or three years old, his grandmother, who was five foot three with copper-coloured skin from Seminole Indian ancestry, used to say, 'If you're not good, I'm going to sell you to this older woman, and she'll make lye out of you and sell you for soap.' Joe was terrified:

> The lady didn't look clean; she looked unkempt. I'd never seen a witch, an all-hallows-eve-type witch, a bad witch of the West. I was well aware of lye, soap, watching my grandmother at the tin tub. Well aware of what soap was like. So when I would see the lady, of course, I would almost hide – and watch and wow and say: 'Is she gone yet?' before I would come out. Hide under the house or anything. She couldn't get me there. And I can see why that might have been done to a small black boy in the South, so you would have a built-in mechanism that would protect you from some of the (segregationist) thinking that was going on there at that time. That's what that was.

Joe couldn't remember any details about the house in Cordele, had no recollection of where anybody slept. He hadn't had enough awareness about Georgia to know whether he liked it or not.

> You play and try not to get in the way, and you observe a lot. I do remember very well singing and entertaining myself with the music from church. I would pretend that I was the choir marching in and singing, I would conduct the choir and try to sing all the parts.
>
> And I remember oddly enough something about being told that I mustn't cross the tracks. But I don't remember *ever* seeing a train go by or anything like that. Or even hearing a train in the night. [Though Cordele had had a railroad since the 1880's, on which Joe took a train away from the South and out of the woods for ever.] If my mother worked at all, she worked to get enough money to go to Chicago, where we had friends. Reverend Jay, who had been in our home for dinner many times, had a son and two daughters. One was named Dorothy, I remember, because she was my first babysitter in Chicago.
>
> It was my mother's dream to raise herself up by going to Chicago – and to lift the rest of us, too. One rises only to lift

> someone else. So she went to Chicago and stayed with the Jays at 59th and State Street, got a job and saved money to send for my aunt, who was in Paine College. Then my mother sent for my grandmother and me, too. My aunt enrolled in Englewood High School, as I remember, and graduated from there and later from Crane College, both about ninety per cent white. I went to the graduation exercises, a little boy, having a great time, seeing all those caps and gowns. My grandfather felt safe and secure in Cordele, so he stayed behind. But my mother put her dream into action, and that dream is still 'a-borning' for black people all over this country.

After living with the Jays, Joe's family moved to 57th and State. 'We had *many* residences in Chicago,' he recalled. In one residence, he had the lesson taught him about the witchlike woman in Georgia amended. In a building he lived in at 6133 Indiana, the janitor was white. He performed services for that sixteen or thirty-two-unit flat complex; his family had the apartment closest to the boiler. Joe wound up being protector of the janitor's children, not letting anyone in the neighbourhood fight with them, in return for the janitor's service. 'So naturally I wound up on the porch with his daughter, Hilda.' She and Joe compared hands. Hilda wanted to know why she and Joe had the same colour hands on one side but Joe's were a different colour on the other side. He said he didn't know and went home and asked his grandmother. She said, 'I don't know either, darling.' Which prompted Miss Anne his mother to tell him, 'Anyone that likes you, bring them home.' And for him and any of his friends, Miss Anne was always prepared to serve meals, exactly as she had done in Georgia, never letting people go hungry, despite the scantiness of her own budget.

In all the areas that Joe lived in on the South Side, he collected acquaintances who later said that they had grown up with him. Many people, 'because especially after you start school at age six or seven, you really start meeting people. We started at the Carter grammar school,' Joe said. Then the family moved again northwards but still on the South Side, and eventually settled on 50th and Forestville.

> Much happened, oh God, so much happened in that area. I think my first real fight took place with a boy who lived in the building. And after having had the fight, I became part of the group and accepted, at about eight or nine. Not only was I an only child and a bit of a loner, but I was a late bloomer, I guess, too, because people said, 'You didn't get into a fight until you were eight or nine?'

The family lived there a couple of years, until about 1928 or 1929, when the Regal Theatre was built in Chicago. 'That was super. I used to walk across a vacant lot on my way to church. Then they built the South Center and the Savoy Ballroom and the office complex above.'

To the outside observer, the South Side may have looked like a crowded black ghetto. Blacks, called 'coloured' in those days, had to live either there or in a few other Chicago neighbourhoods. And nobody on the South Side lived east of Cottage Grove or south of 63rd Street. Joe became intimately familiar with the daily news that a rat had bitten a baby's toe. He watched the elevated train that came from downtown and ran between Calumet and Prairie Avenues over the back alleys of the South Side, giving the neighbourhood a grim demeanour. He saw people ride the train to work in the stockyards, the steel mills, the post offices; his mother went to the kitchens of the wealthier whites and then rode home at night. But within the confines of the South Side, there were houses in good repair, some owned by financially comfortable blacks, with well-tended lawns, as well as run-down, neglected houses. And Joe learned his way around the more heart-warming sights – people dressed in high style, going to dances in private clubs or into the first-class Rhum Boogie nightclub on 55th Street and the vibrant DeLisa's on State.

He saw all kinds of shops: for barbecue, chicken; and Kiah's restaurant where black musicians 'hung out' after work and ate their dinners at dawn – hamhocks with mustard greens, hot biscuits, bacon and eggs. The self-contained world of the South Side had its own ministers, doctors and dentists, who had graduated from Howard and Meharry Universities. Compared with the segregation of the South, 'Chicago was more or less heaven', a childhood friend of Joe's recalled. He and Joe and thousands of others could escape there from the constant undercurrent of prejudice they felt besieged them in the whites' neighbourhoods.

Joe's mother brought home discarded magazines – *Life, Liberty,* and *National Geographic* – from her employers' houses. Joe liked to lie on the floor and read the captions under the pictures. What he didn't understand, his mother would try to make clear.

He attended the predominantly white Austin Otis Sexton Grammar School with 1,800 students, where, in the seventh grade, he was appointed 'head marshall'. He was supposed to anticipate semi-officially any fights or difficulties going on. And the principal, a man named Johnson, particularly assigned Joe to take care of the fifth-graders. Johnson told Joe, 'Anything that you can't handle, you're to come to us, and we'll take care of it.' Johnson's thinking, Joe surmised, was, 'Joe will keep the discipline; he won't let them get away with anything.'

Joe, who eventually finished the eighth grade in the top ten per cent of his class, was impressed with being chosen for the role of protector. 'I was big. But I wasn't so aware of being big.' His voice rose to a high falsetto. 'I thought that I was one of them! I was one of the little kids! I shot marbles! I used to shoot marbles and do other things that kids did. But I was Model A, so they sent me to take care of the class. The whites would be afraid of me, and the blacks would respect me; that was the thinking.'

But while people were relying on Joe for protection, when he was still a little boy himself, he had his own fears:

> For instance, My God, will I ever kiss a girl? Or will a girl ever kiss me the way I see people kiss on the screen? I said, my gosh, that must be wonderful. It was the thing to do, obviously the thing to do. And when is it going to happen to me? I was afraid that it might not ever happen to me. There were times that you would grab a girl – not really grab a girl. I was too big, always a big kid and strong, too. There was no sense in my grabbing. And who wanted to grab a girl and try to kiss her and have her turn her head away? So I would kiss

> her on the cheek and let her go. But will it ever happen to me? There was always that fear of rejection. No one would ever want to kiss me the way romance was portrayed to me visually on the screen. It will not happen to me. And of course when it did, I fell irrevocably in love.'

He walked a girl named Dorothy Allen home from grammar school, to the back door of her house, where he moved a little to kiss her. She said, 'yes'. He closed his eyes. And as he started for her cheek, she kissed him 'dead on the lips', he could recall years later. He opened his eyes to find her with a big smile on her face. And there he stood, a gawky boy suddenly transformed into a budding young man, very warm from the top of his head to his toes, he recalls.

He had an after-school job, sacking potatoes, counting stock and delivering groceries for special customers in an A&P grocery store. And he walked to work in a dream: 'You know, like wow, *wow.* All I have to do is wait. Somebody's gonna do it to me. I don't have to grab.'

Not very much later, when he was twelve or thirteen, in a movie theatre, he started what he recalled as his first relationship with a girl.

> Some young lady in the theatre was *miserable* because some young man didn't like her or was with somebody else; she was crying her heart out – and really causing a *disturbance* in the theatre. I wanted to see the motion picture. So I walked over to where she was sitting – she was my age or a little older. I said to her: 'Move over.' And I sat down beside her and said, 'Listen, you probably were miserable about something last year, and it wasn't him. And what you were miserable about then isn't important now. And I promise you that what you think is important now will not be important. You just give yourself a chance.

They became involved with each other – constant companions. 'Oh, God, we used to kiss for ever, it seemed to me. I've wondered myself, how did I get to that point for that to come through me at that tender age?' And he thought that the lesson taught to him by Dorothy Allen had helped. 'I think that's why I was able to talk to the other girl in the theatre and tell her, 'Hey, don't worry about it. I don't think it's worth it.'

At home he was well taken care of, but, by himself, he took care of his qualms about his acceptability, lovability and his destiny; more aptly he found that sooner or later, some matters took care of themselves naturally, without his straining. And occasionally life's thorny problems were simply taken care of 'magically' by women.

'So even before I left home, I found out that women were magic. Women would take care of me. They're the magic in your life.' (Later in life, he would try to impress upon his own son, Joe Jr the same thing and advise him: 'Put your dirty clothes in one place and eat what's put on your table. So many things happen as if by magic – and understand and respect it.') 'Women would bathe your face in the morning, ask you what you wanted, tell you to go to sleep and when you woke up, it would be ready, it would be ready for you. Oh, yeah, I found that out, which was a revelation by itself.'

Money, however, did not take care of itself magically. Joe's family had about $200 a month income. Not very long after moving to Chicago, his mother met a man, James Mason, who became her lifelong friend. 'He was the man who helped out,' Joe recalled, referring to him as his mother's husband, though he didn't live in the house with the family, when Joe was a boy. 'So she could bring all her money home.' On Sundays, after church, in the 1920s, the three went to hear Erskine Tate's band playing, with Louis Armstrong hitting those crowd-pleasing high Cs in the pit at the Vendome Theatre. Right away the virility of Armstrong's sound impressed Joe. Sometimes Joe's mother took him alone to the Vendome or to Grant Park, where the Chicago Symphony Orchestra conducted by Dr Frederick Stock put on free concerts. 'Soloists were Rosa Ponselle, Lawrence Tibbett and Lily Pons, folks like that.'

There was always music in the house. Joe remembered parties with music and dancing, nights when his grandmother would take a shot of bourbon and ask Joe to stir some sugar in it for her. Miss Anne set out food in front of Joe's friends, before they mentioned they were hungry. 'She was a beautiful woman, like the mother I wish that I'd had,' one of Joe's friends from Chicago later recalled. Joe was very dark, growing tall and rugged, while his mother was a small, round woman about five foot three, as her own mother was. And both women were coppery-coloured. But Joe resembled his mother, friends recalled, in the impression of warmth that she exuded. And all of them recalled her as a very tall woman, because of an authority in her demeanour.

Joe's mother and aunt, who was also short but dark as her father was, played the piano. Joe learned to pick out melodies with the help of a beginner's primer, so that he could do a little sightreading. His mother sang in church, too. After church services ended, Joe could still hear all the choir parts and sang them, playing church. 'I always heard the music. I could have played an instrument as well as I sing, whichever one called to me. But singing isn't something you do. It's really more something that comes through you.' In saying this, Joe is echoing legions of other musicians, who believe that music, which touches the spirit, springs from a mystical source, over which they have no power. They can only direct it. And they are the voices of a higher spiritual force outside themselves.

Nobody encouraged Joe especially to sing; he did it because he liked to sing, to entertain himself and others. His mother was his first music teacher. From a child's lesson book he learned to sing a few exercises that he could still sing years later. But his main teacher, when he was a child, was the radio. He heard Duke Ellington and Ethel Waters, whose phrasing – the sense of the lyrics that she imparted by her delivery, with an exceptionally clean-cut enunciation and a clear tone, particularly enchanted him. And Ellington's music was glorious, broadcast from the Cotton Club in New York City in the 1930s. Joe discovered that Earl 'Fatha' Hines broadcast from Chicago's Grand Terrace Ballroom. Joe was allowed to stay up and listen and, as soon as the broadcast finished, got a kiss from his mother and went to sleep. As a teenager, he also loved to listen to Milton Cross, the announcer for the Metropolitan Opera, and was thrilled by the sound of his speaking voice reading libretti. '*La Boheme, Butterfly, Carmen* were very popular; *Aida* and all those goodies.' Radio brought him some of his first encounters with the voices of Roland Hayes and Paul Robeson. 'And then there were the Marian Anderson junkies, of course.'

Early in life, he gravitated to popular music, not feeling the gospel influence as strongly as Aretha Franklin, Nat Cole or Dinah Washington did. Joe did, however, join a quartet called the Jubilee Boys named for the Jubilee Temple, a CME church, that the boys belonged to. They sang primarily at white and black church functions, and for a while may have given Joe's mother the idea that Joe could be heading for the ministry. But he was intrigued by other, more exciting tempi.

Chicago was full of music, with scores of clubs of all kinds, from strip joints to elegant supper clubs. From post-World War I days until the 1950s, Chicagoans could hear not only the great bands that passed through but fine musicians who had been born or worked there for years; Ahmad Jamal, singers Dakota Staton and Anita O'Day, drummer Gene Krupa, bandleader Cab Calloway and all the good musicians in the band, and trumpeters and singers Jabbo Smith and Louis Armstrong, Nat Cole and his brothers and hundreds more. The especially popular Club DeLisa had Blue Monday performances, breakfast shows on Monday mornings for all the night people who entertained at the weekends.

Even street sounds impressed Joe as a musical experience. Of his several odd jobs, selling newspapers, making deliveries, he would remember best the musical aspect of being an ice-carrier. With youthful energy, he climbed several flights of stairs in Chicago for an older iceman, who paid him about fifty cents. Joe liked the lilt of the iceman's call: 'Iceman here', three notes – one high, two low and the same tone – and began the habit of drawing upon all the noises around him and transforming them for musical improvisation.

When he was fifteen, however, something interfered with his odd jobs, his musical and all other experiences. Doctors discovered a spot on his left lung: tuberculosis. They recommended pneumothorax treatment and stuck needles in between Joe's ribs, punctured his lung, put gas in and collapsed it so it could rest and heal. It developed scar tissue from the treatment, for which he went to a doctor twice a week for almost a year. Later the lung became fully expanded again. Although he was in Reserve Officers Training Corps (ROTC) in Englewood High School, his bout with pneumothorax kept him out of military service.

However, he *could* sing. And he did enjoy singing, though he didn't plan to make a career of it. For fun, in high school, he performed in a school show. One of the singers in an assembly trio backed out of the show at the last minute. So Joe stepped in to sing harmony on 'Blue Moon' – and loved it.

Even more alluring than music in those days were sports. He played handball, soccer, baseball: 'I used to run like the wind, and I could throw a ball for ever', and touch tackle. 'But I thought it was much more clever to elude someone than to knock him over. That's the way I grew up – a sports nut.' Chicago friends thought that he was a better-than-average athlete in his early teens. Because he was so dark, he was sometimes the butt of prejudice among black families. Some parents told their daughters to bring home only light-skinned men. Joe didn't qualify. Nevertheless his sandlot baseball team during his high-school years elected him as coach. He wasn't oblivious to the prejudice; he simply didn't slow down to listen acceptingly. And he followed the careers of Bill Tilden, Jack Kramer, Pancho Gonzalez, Lou Gehrig, Babe Ruth – and could possibly have become a professional athlete. 'In fact, I was an athlete,' he recalled. 'I just got sidetracked into singing, because some older musicians asked me to sing. The grown musicians liked what the kid did.'

## 2 *Moving on to the Scene*

From his mid-teens into his twenties, a baritone with a high range, he sang downtown and in churches, at weddings, even at funerals on the South Side, with the Jubilee Boys. And Joe acquired the view that the South Side was very sophisticated, as he moved around, observing the music scene, looking for places to sing:

> There were many private clubs; people would get together and say, 'hey, let's form a club'. So there would be a group from 35th to 39th Streets or maybe 43rd Street. They would have regular club meetings, parties, and decide what they they wanted to do. There were twenty to thirty of these clubs. One was called the Post Office 500, whose members were well-to-do blacks, who lived in the Rosenwald complex. I wasn't a member of a club. The only one in Chicago that I was a member of was the Collegiate Oldtimers. But these other clubs would sponsor dances and hire orchestras. I was singing with the orchestras.
>
> In summer they would have a formal dance, which meant white dinner jackets and tuxedo trousers for the men. The women wore gorgeous gowns – lime-green, soft sky-blue, and white; they carried elegant bags. And the clubs would have their winter formals, at which the men wore white tie and tails. And again the women wore elegant gowns and furs. And there were two semi-formal dances in spring and fall. You just wore a tie, no formal dress. Almost every club had these dances. So there was plenty of work.
>
> The musicians earned only, say, seven dollars a night. The

> leader would ask the musicians to kick in a quarter apiece for the singer. I was never on the contract. I was getting only five dollars a night tops. The singer would just sing a chorus of the tune, the vocal refrain, the chorus and a half. You rarely sang the end of the song. I sang the popular tunes of the day in the thirties and forties; that was the thing there then.

When he was sixteen, it became clear that he was going to sing for a living. So he dropped out of high school to work. And his aunt, mother and grandmother sat down at the kitchen table and decided to do something about his name. They didn't like the ring of 'Goreed' for a professional singer. Juanita, his aunt, whom he still called Inez sometimes, had always taken an affectionate but bossy attitude towards him, since she had often been left in charge of him. She disapproved of much of what he did, he thought, possibly even of his decision to become a singer. But he didn't pay much attention. He thought of her as an older sister whose real interests were in meeting the men he played ball with. She went to watch his games occasionally. When he brought his friends back to the house, he thought they may have come to visit her. 'She's really looking for a husband,' Joe thought, watching her flirt with them. But she was of course included in the family conference about his welfare. He had nothing to do with choosing the name Williams and didn't know what inspired the women. He never even thought about changing his name. Once they decided upon Williams, he simply began using it, though he didn't change the name legally until he was living in New York City several decades later.

At first, he sang in a downtown Chicago place called Kitty Davis's, bringing in the biggest paychecks the family had ever seen, earning twenty to thirty dollars a night in tips. To do it, however, he cleaned the latrines in the club and, as payment, was allowed to sing for the tips.

> I suddenly felt that I was helping out. Until that point, the family had supported me . . . I don't think in my whole life I had ever saved more than fifty-five dollars. But thirty dollars a night! It was fun to bring it home. In fact my mother said that my grandmother had told her: 'He's such a good boy, I

hope when he grows up that he has a lot of money.

He gave his money to his mother. 'It was part of the spirit of dealing with those who love us. You have to have someone who wishes you well. Then I asked my mother for the several cents to go to work the next night,' he recalled.

About a year later, he moved out of the apartment, deciding that it was time to go. There was something about living at home that was a little bit as if he hadn't grown up, he thought. In those days the style for men was to grease their hair a lot – rub oil through it, to 'process' it. Some men used their mother's stockings and wore them like stocking-caps to make the hair lie close to the skull. Other men used to brush their hair for a long time until they got the same effect. Duke Ellington kept the hairstyle for nearly his entire life. Joe Williams oiled his hair when he took a shower and then quickly rubbed most of the grease out with a steaming hot towel. 'I didn't want to get grease on anyone's pillow,' he recalled. 'There, that's the real reason I moved out of the house.'

Processing his hair with a light touch was his way of repaying women who cooked for him and loved him – gave him, as they say in the street 'the old feed 'em and fuck 'em routine'. 'Ooooo, that's a trap, what a trap that is. You walk in, and it smells so good. The food is heaven. What are you going to do?' he asked himself.

At that time, his mother and James Mason took their own apartment together, leaving Joe, his aunt and grandmother together. Joe could have gone with his mother or stayed with his grandmother, but he decided that total freedom would be the best arrangement for him. So on his own, he rented an apartment on the third floor, in the back, in a house on 43rd Street at 4325 South Parkway, which later became Dr Martin Luther King Drive. He could walk out of the door to his apartment, take two steps, open the door to a flight of stairs and go down and out into an alley behind the house. Garbage trucks, which could drive two abreast because the alleys were so wide, made their pick-ups there. Joe paid $4.50 a week for a private room and bath. 'So if I had a job that paid five dollars, OK, rent's paid. Or if you worked three times a week, Sunday,

Friday and Saturday – or Thursday, Saturday and Sunday, and you had the rent paid, it was really easy.'

Ordinarily he liked to walk everywhere. Some friends had cars and gave him rides. Sometimes he worked for his friend, trumpeter and bandleader Johnny Long, who picked Joe up and took him to gigs. Johnny's mother lived in the building next door to Joe. So Johnny ran up the stairs to Joe's door, knocked and shouted, 'Hey, Joe, got a job at such and such a time!' Joe said, 'OK.' Johnny said, 'I'll pick you up!' 'All right.' Joe earned some of his first money, starting with fifty cents a night, working his way up to five dollars, for singing in the 1930s with Long's band. And occasionally, after Long, Joe found encouragement from Erskine Tate, who led the band at the Savoy Ballroom and paid Joe $1.50 to sing.

He got home from singing or from hanging out in the wee hours of the morning or sometimes not until other people were having lunch. He slept until noon and then, awaking, smoked part of a joint, got up and went to a theatre for the show that started at 1 p.m. Afterwards he smoked a little more of the joint, drank some milk, and went to his mother's house for dinner. Because of his mother, he didn't need a kitchenette or even a hot plate in his own room. Throughout his life, he would discover, he would never have to learn to cook for himself, because women would always do it for him and find him appreciative, thanking them in the prettiest of voices. He could always make 'Thank you so much' sound like 'Adeste Fideles' with chimes. His mother's house remained an oasis. For him, his mother would buy fillet steak, have it ground and take it home to make hamburgers.

'The blood blisters, the meat on the plate with the butter and blood in the middle of the potatoes and the salad looked so good,' he recalled. 'Once I asked Mother if there were any bread. She said, "You don't eat bread and potatoes, son." "Thank you," I said. I didn't have any idea. It just looked so good. I wanted to take some bread and slip it in that juice.' She brought him up, he thought, as if she expected him to finish dinner and then go outside and play croquet on the front lawn.

He left her house to get ready for work, smoked the rest of the joint, and worked all night. After work he 'hung out', smoked more and drank some. And it was very exciting on the scene. Sometimes he went to dances. He especially admired a young piano player, Nat Coles, his real name until the late 1930s, who had his own band for dances and clubs. Nat hired a 'boy' singer, as male band singers were called then, named Hicks, to do the vocal work.

And Joe's private life was hectic. If you wanted to get into the music business, you had to be there where it was happening, he learned fast. You had to go to all the shows and be a part of the audience. In those early days in Chicago, though, he never dreamed of becoming an international star. The routine was simply to work and hang out. 'Stardom wasn't the object of the exercise. I was just enjoying the company of people who were producing great music,' he recalled. 'Because music is like bathing. It bathes you, washes you, cleanses you, transports you.'

# 3 Changes and Choices

The legend and lore of the jazz world says that John Hammond, visiting Chicago in the late 1930s, was listening to a short-wave radio broadcast. On it, he heard the new, dynamic Basie band playing in a club in Kansas City. Hammond told agent Willard Alexander, who was lured by the sound to fly to Kansas City and sign the band to a contract. Alexander also directed Jimmy Rushing, who had been singing ballads, to switch to the blues. Then, to publicize an upcoming tour of the South, the band made some records, featuring the vocalist. Joe Williams, learning and honing his craft in Chicago, first heard the Basie band on those records. By that time Joe was becoming known professionally. He was singing upstairs in the ballroom of the Vincent Hotel with Johnny Long's band, when the much more prominent band of Jimmie Noone, a New Orleans-born clarinettist, was playing downstairs in the hotel's cabaret. Told about the young baritone, the chubby, smartly-dressed Noone went upstairs to hear Joe and asked him to sing with the band.

In Chicago, Joe and the Noone band went into Swingland, formerly called Dave's Cafe, another well-known South Side club, and broadcast by remote most nights over WBBM, a local CBS station, in 1938. It was the big-band era; remote broadcasts brought the sound of the bands into people's houses. When the bands toured, people came out in droves. By 1939, Joe and the Noone band moved to the Platinum Lounge and the Cabin Inn, where Joe sang over CBS coast to coast nightly. He loved the broadcast experience, which taught him about singing for the audience's ear, to be heard once and only once and make a lingering impression. (Noone, a great clarinet stylist, had built a very influential band, with pianist Earl Hines in the group. Joe was proud to be singing with Noone, aware that Benny Goodman had gone to the Apex Club in the late 1920s and studied Noone's music.)

Keeping his repertoire *au courant,* Joe went downtown, got stock arrangements from publishers and sang pretty ballads: 'The Dreamer in Me,' 'The Lamp is Low', and 'Always and Always I'll Go on Adoring the Wonder and Beauty of You'. 'I'd get hot and do five choruses of "Back in Nagasaki",' he recalled. Noone led his band in 'Big John Special', 'I Know that You Know' and other popular tunes of the thirties, rearranging stock arrangements. Electronics were minimal; orchestras played softly for the singers. For broadcasts, he simply used the microphones from the studios. In 1939 and 1940, too, he toured the Midwest with the Les Hite band, then went back to Chicago, and Noone.

Joe used to see many famous faces in his audiences. John Barrymore, travelling with the road company of *My Dear Children* in 1939 'came to see us almost every night at the Cabin Inn'. The police may have actually come looking for Barrymore there, since he had a habit of missing his own curtain calls. Johnny Desmond and Anita O'Day visited; they were singing with Gene Krupa in a Chicago club. And Krupa, too, came by; so did Lana Turner. Saxophonist Coleman Hawkins of everlasting fame for his classic recording of 'Body and Soul', back from Europe and leading a band, used to sit and listen to Joe every night at Cafe Society in Chicago in 1941. Joe was earning forty dollars a week then, singing with Jimmy Wood, a pianist from New York City. 'We did everything we knew and liked – mostly ballads, low and soft,' Joe recalled. A dancer named Foster Johnson also played piano for Joe sometimes.

Hawkins offered Joe eighty dollars a week to go on the road with his big band and sing the ballads. Joe said, 'I'm your man.' He was in Memphis, Tennessee with Hawkins when Pearl Harbor was bombed on 7 December 1941.

The first luxury Joe gave himself was a tailor-made suit of white tie and tails, done by tailor Scotty Piper. As Joe sang, dressed in the tails, popping his fingers, the women walked right across the floor and brought him money. 'Well, they've got to show off their outfits, too,' he thought, amused.

Joe's grandmother, 'who had seen her mother in a slave line', Joe has said,* never went to nightclubs. So he modelled the white tie and tails for her in the family's South Side apartment. She purred: 'The boy looks like he was melted and poured in it.'

In 1941, too, Joe caught the attention of Andy Kirk, a stylish bandleader from Kansas City. He had taken his Kansas-spawned band into a theatre in downtown Chicago and afterwards, tipped off by another jazz musician, went around the corner to a little club to hear Joe sing. He went to the tables and sang intimately to the customers. He stood six foot one, trim at about 170 pounds, very dark and imposing, with a large head, big features and fleshy hands fine for passing a football or swinging a bat – the image of an athlete. His buoyant voice was electrified by youthful energy and passion. He sang 'Laura', Kirk recalled years later: 'He knocked me out. I'll always remember his phrasing. He sang the first line, then he hummed. I almost cried.'

Joe himself was held in thrall by other singers on Chicago's music scene. Big Joe Turner from Kansas City had such a robust voice that he could sing without a microphone for hours and not tire. Joe could understand the lyrics that Turner sang, while the dialects of the rural blues singers were incomprehensible. Joe felt as if he hadn't really been singing the blues, until he heard Turner sing-shout about what was happening and not happening and what he wanted and dreamed of. Once, when Turner was unable to make a gig with Pete Johnson and Albert Ammons, Joe sat in for six weeks – the first $150-a-week gig that Joe ever had. He was influenced by all the great, rich-voiced blues singers in town – Roosevelt Sykes, John Lee Hooker, Big Bill Broonzy, Memphis Slim – even Walter Brown, who had 'a cute little style', Joe said in that era. Brown sang 'Hootie Blues' and 'Confessing the Blues' with pianist Jay McShann's Kansas City band; at one time, it included Charlie Parker. And Joe heard others, whose graphic, often raunchy lyrics his mother disapproved of.

Once she went to a club and heard him singing 'Cherry Red',

*Figuratively speaking; actually his grandmother had been born in about 1880 written by Big Joe Turner, in which the singer says he knows he may be inviting a fight to the death by craving sex with a certain pretty 'Mama' in her big brass bed. Joe's mother wanted to know how Joe ever learned such a bawdy song. He explained that he was simply 'all ears'!

In those vital, early days of his career, Joe became a stage-door guard at Balaban and Katz's Regal Theatre for a while. Theatre manager Ken Blewett, a soft-spoken man, who was deeply in love with beautiful music, talent and show business, approached Joe to do the job; Blewett didn't have anyone he coud trust with that assignment backstage. Essentially Joe had to make sure that the wives and girlfriends of the entertainers didn't meet face to face. 'That's what that was,' he recalled with a laugh. Joe liked the job because, for forty-two dollars a week, he met hundreds of entertainers. He did the job six nights a week, except on Tuesdays, when he sang next door at the Savoy Roller Rink with a series of intermission organists – first Tiny Parham (a bandleader and arranger who recorded hot jazz in the twenties), then Bill Davis and last Sterling Todd.

Joe also met Ella Fitzgerald at the Regal, leading a band she had inherited from her mentor, drummer Chick Webb; bandleader Lucky Millinder; Herb Jeffries sang 'Flamingo' and 'My Little Brown Book' with Duke Ellington; Charlie Barnet, Buddy Rich, Jimmie Lunceford with his ballad singers Henry Wells and later Dan Grissom; Joe met Cab Calloway and the musicians in his band; and the great, wiry little drummer Papa Jo Jones, a former dancer; and even Count Basie. And a Chicago-born bassist, John Levy, a rangy man with glasses and a soft voice, met Joe backstage, heard him sing, and recommended him as a bandsinger to Duke Ellington to replace Herb Jeffries in 1942. But Ellington hired other singers, including Al Hibbler, instead.

One night Fats Waller called Joe to the stage to do three tunes. The audience kept yelling 'Encore'. And afterwards Ken Blewett told Lionel Hampton about Joe. Hampton, playing four or five shows a day at the Regal, had already hired Dinah Washington, who had been singing at the Garrick Bar every Sunday with Sally Martin, who also had a gospel singing group. Hampton listened to Joe sing and asked him to appear with the band for most of its shows at the Regal. Blewett was happy that he could help Joe, because he saw how close Joe and his mother were. She came to many shows, stopped backstage, sometimes brought fresh-cooked, rich soul food for Joe and other performers, sampled it herself, and at showtime slipped into the audience to see Joe perform. The affection between the rugged singer and the conservatively-dressed woman, who liked her own cooking and offered it proudly, and whom Blewett thought Joe resembled, touched Blewett. He was reminded of a homily told to him by his mother: 'If a man looks like his mother, he's marked for success.' Blewett wanted to give nature a little, courtly boost.

Eventually Hampton took Dinah Washington along on a tour with his 'boy' singer, Rubel Blakey. Then Rubel decided to leave the band for a while. And Hampton put in a distress call to Ken Blewett. He approached Joe and asked if he would like to step into the Hampton band. It would pay eleven dollars a night. 'Sure,' Joe said, and took the train to Boston. Hampton liked Joe's singing so much that he asked him to tour. Hampton, who always had a good ear for fresh, young talent, thought the new musical pairing of Dinah and Joe, who did some singing together, was splendid. In Boston, too, Joe had his first experience living in a downtown hotel. It was near the old Tic Toc Club. For several months he toured with Hampton, playing in the Howard Theatre in Washington, the Royal in Baltimore, the Stanley in Pittsburgh, Loew's State in New York City, the Auditorium in Kansas City, the Palace in Cleveland, Ohio with Billie Holiday singing on the same bill; in 1943 she had signed a contract to do a few shows with the band.

Backstage it was cramped. But Billie, then a great attraction, didn't pull any star rank; she moved right into Joe's dressing-room with him and said, 'You sure know how to sing pretty, baby. Now why don't you learn how to zip up a gown some kind of way?' 'The first time she ever sang "Porgy" was in that elegant Palace dressing-room, with posh leather sofas and private bathing facilities for the performers,' Joe recalled. Trumpeter Joe Newman, who was travelling with Hampton, too, and comedian Willie Lewis heard that private performance.

Joe rode the train with Hampton, shopped with his wife Gladys in Wanamaker's, and became close friends with Dinah, who called herself 'Queen of the Blues' and gave away fur coats and gowns as presents to other women musicians. Joe called Dinah his 'baby' in affectionate friendship. Officially Hampton assigned the blues to Dinah, later probably the most colourful figure who ever lived in the jazz world; sometimes she carried a gun under her fur stole on to the stage. And: 'If you can't teach old dogs new tricks, get new dogs,' she explained about why she changed husbands so frequently. Hampton gave Joe the ballads – 'Skylark', for one. And Joe took over an arrangement written by Milt Buckner, the band's pianist, of a medley for Rubel Blakey: 'Brazil', 'So Nice to Come Home to', and 'Easy to Love'. Joe had the ballads as part of the usual division of work between the 'boy' and 'girl' singers in the big-band era, but he may have sung some blues with the band, too.

Those were, in a way, fine days, despite the legendary rigours of travelling. Segregation compounded the dangers and hardships for black musicians. They never knew if they would be able to find a place to sleep and often had to buy food and cook it in a hotel, because they weren't welcomed in restaurants. Sometimes they were lucky and found a black family who invited them to their dining-tables or gave them some place to sleep in.

Then there were the great distances between gigs; a band might travel from California to Texas in a day. Some musicians fought the tedium, homesickness and muscle-soreness with alcohol or drugs to get themselves 'up' to play after the long jumps by bus, car or train. The drinks and drugs were often supplied by fans or anyone else concerned with getting musicians revived to play. Some people wanted to make money from musicians or simply have a party with them.

But Joe didn't mind the road life; he loved it: the sense of freedom and adventure; the sight of new places and strange faces. He slept a great deal on the long trips between gigs, advised to do that by other musicians, and awoke to go to the dining-car and drink and dine. There was something magical in the miles covered. He felt that musicians were magicians; music was the other magic in his life. And later he would look back on the train travel as having been romantic, despite the grind and uncertainty underlying the entire lifestyle.

Joe worked with Hampton in the Regal and Oriental Theatres – everywhere until Rubel Blakey returned to the band. And Joe worked at the very popular Savoy Ballroom a centre of social life, and at the Regal with trumpeter King Kolax. He later became an official with the Chicago Musicians' Union. Joe left town only to work on the road. It never occurred to him to leave Chicago permanently. In 1943, he seemed to become even more attached to the city.

He married for the first time to Wilma Cole, a Chicago woman whom he had met four years earlier, when he was twenty and she was nineteen. From the start, Wilma aroused the protector's instinct in him, because she was such a small, fragile-looking woman. Five feet four and a half, she may have weighed as much as 110 pounds when she was pregnant, though she never had the children. The couple got married during a sidetrip to Detroit, where Joe had a gig; then they moved into a flat in the house in Chicago where her mother lived.

'I wasn't ready for marriage, I guess, emotionally,' Joe recalled. Several times he and Wilma discussed moving out of the house, so close to Wilma's mother, and establishing their own place, staking out their own territory. 'I tried to leave the house once,' Joe recalled. He found another place within a block of where her mother lived. 'So I thought I had it figured out,' he said, laughing. Wilma had seen the place and made the commitment with him to move. But when the moment arrived, she said 'no', she didn't think so, Joe found another place to move to. 'She asked me if I wanted her to go with me. I said "no" to her for the first time. If I had to do it all over again, I don't think I would have said "no",' he mused years later.

Legally the marriage lasted until 1946. After the divorce, they had a brief encounter once. Wilma asked him, 'Joseph, did you get what you wanted?' And then Joe didn't see Wilma for some years. He had never considered her to be physically hardy. And so somehow he was not astounded when the news reached him that she had died young. He never learned exactly what she had died of. But he had thought instinctively, from the start, that she would never make 'old bones'.

Eventually he did feel that he could understand what had gone wrong with that marriage – and several more marriages to follow – 'at least two, at least,' he said with a trace of wryness years later. 'I didn't handle the first marriage very well. I was dealing with a young lady that used to refer to her father as a dog. But she was a gentle person. She didn't say anything worse, you dig? She was a strong-willed woman, but she had no respect for her father.'

By 1946, he was married to Ann Kirksey, another Chicago woman, a pretty girl with chiselled features and caramel-coloured skin. 'She had a very sophisticated, even arrogant air about her – the air of a little goddess,' recalled Daddy-O Daylie, a Chicago disc jockey who was working as a bartender in a club where Joe sang in those days. 'Though she was polite and sweet.' While Daddy-O Daylie was busy admiring Joe's eye for pretty women, Joe felt that he had fallen into the same trap with his second marriage that he had with his first and attributed the trouble to Ann Kirksey's disrespect for her father, too.

Early in his relationship with Ann, when the marriage seemed very happy, Joe was working as a singer and master of ceremonies at El Grotto. Ann used to go to the club to see Joe. 'They're little sweethearts,' Daddy-O Daylie observed from his position behind the bar. 'We're struggling through, though we don't have much money – that kind of couple.' Joe particularly liked working in El Grotto, because it was owned by blacks, as many other 'swellegant, elegant' clubs that he worked in were not.

El Grotto had waiter service and candles on the tables. The owners paid $5,200 a week for shows with ten chorus girls culled from the country's prettiest women by a roaming producer who found them and sent them to Chicago. In a back room, gamblers played blackjack. And the highrollers and those in the fast lane used to ask the club owners to change chorus girls every five weeks. The club was rated one of the top ten in town. Earl Hines and his orchestra played there. So did Georgie Auld, dancers Honi Coles and Cholly Atkins; comedians Moke and Poke, Paterson and Jackson, Redd Foxx, Slappy White and Willie Lewis; all big names in the black entertainment world.

And Gerald Wilson's orchestra; Ivie Anderson and Pearl Bailey sang there, too. Timmie Rogers, a comedian, dancer and singer, entertained. And Joe admired a marvellous dancer named Kelly and the entertainer Marie Bryant who later taught Marilyn Monroe to dance. Joe was the singer and MC off and on for years. When the comedians worked as MCs, Joe simply did the singing. But he felt that the MC job taught him a great deal about stagecraft; he even played straightman, learning the timing of comedy from a very popular comedian Dusty Fletcher. Daddy-O Daylie married the daughter of one of the owners, Harry Fields. Whenever Daddy-O's wife walked in, Joe sang, 'I'll Always be in Love with You' – her favorite tune in the forties. After hours, Harry Fields, who was particularly fond of Joe, treated himself to some of his own liquor and asked Joe to serenade him. Joe even sang Irving Berlin's 'Always', arranged, he thought, by Chicagoan Marl Young, and may also have entranced Harry Fields with 'If You are but a Dream, I Hope I Never Waken' and 'The Sunshine of Your Smile'.

At El Grotto, which became the Beige Room in the late 1940s, the bar often stayed open until 5 a.m. for showpeople after work. On summer days, Daddy-O and Joe walked from the club, located in the Pershing Hotel at 64th Street and Cottage, toward 47th Street. They talked about their dreams. Daddy-O wanted to be a disc jockey on radio. Joe dreamed of becoming one of the world's greatest singers. It was hard for him to keep his mind on the dream, as he rushed from the shows at El Grotto to other clubs and even to benefits, one at the Gardner General Hospital to entertain the veterans of World War II in particular. The shock victims were screaming. As Joe was getting set to sing with Johnny Long's band, a nurse wheeled out a small crib, or basket, containing a blond-haired, blue-eyed veteran; his arms and legs had been blown off. Upset at the sight, Joe saw the nurse waiting expectantly for him to sing. And with those blue eyes looking up at him, Joe thought, 'Oh, God, who's doing penance here? And I'm supposed to sing?' And he sang. That was as nerve-wracking as the performance he had given, in the late thirties, with Jimmie Noone's band in a jail at 26th and California. As the gates were lifted, Joe and some dancing girls were mobbed by prisoners.

The walks at dawn with Daddy-O Daylie were more peaceful – a few minutes when it was possible to dream. They went to Walgreen's at 47th Street and South Park Boulevard, near the Regal Theatre, and had breakfast with other show people, who liked to stop and chat there, too.

By 1948, Daddy-O began a radio show on WAIT from 1 to 5 p.m. and talked about Joe on the air. On South Park, from 67th to 31st Streets, Chicago had a lot of jitneys. People could ride a long distance for a dime. The jitneys on South Park tuned their radios into Daddy-O's jazz show.

One day he announced that if Joe Williams were listening, Jay Burkhardt and his band had a gig for him at the Nob Hill that Monday night. When Daddy-O walked into the Nob Hill, he found Joe singing with Burkhardt.

Another day during those years, Daddy-O went to get his hair cut by a barber at 46th Street and South Park, near the Manor House Hotel. Count Basie used to stay there when he was in town and have his hair cut at the same shop, the Metropolitan. It was near the Regal Theatre, the Savoy Ballroom, and the Groove Record Shop, very popular places with entertainers. At the Groove especially, where you could find the offbeat jazz labels, musicians were always stopping in to have a party; those who weren't working and others who dropped by after their gigs. Joe liked to go there. In the barber shop nearby, Basie, who knew Daddy-O as a bartender, chatted with him, saying, 'Hey, Daddy-O, I'm looking for a blues singer.' Daddy-O replied, 'OK, I've got just the guy.' But Count Basie left town. Daddy-O didn't see him for several years.

With Burkhardt's band, Joe worked in many places in Chicago: the Club Silhouette, local ballrooms, the Regal Theatre. Burkhardt's personnel included Gene Ammons and Joe Daley, guitarist Jimmy Gorley, Gale Brockman, pianist John Young, drummer and arranger Tiny Kahn. While with Burkhardt, Joe met George Shearing, who was the headliner at the Regal Theatre when Joe sang there with the band. Miles Davis played at the Regal, too, when Joe was singing there with Burkhardt's band; Miles was so impressed by the band that he sat down, wrote two arrangements on the spot and played them with the band. Joe kept working in Chicago throughout the forties and heard many singers who never recorded or gained national recognition. Others were headed for prominence, even stardom. 'Elmo Tanner would whistle or sing, just – right. Perry Como with Ted Weems, wow, so right, I just took it in. I was overpowered by a lot of great singers,' Joe recalled.

If Andy Kirk were impressed with Joe's singing, Joe returned the compliment by admiring June Richmond, who sang with Kirk and then went with Jimmy Dorsey, and especially Kirk's talented ballad singer, Pha Terrell. The tough, dapper little man had been working as a bouncer in a Kansas City Saloon, when Kirk discovered him and hired him to emote the ballads with the band. 'Until the Real Thing Comes Along', 'Just Fooling Myself', and 'What Will I Tell My Heart?' – Terrell made the women swoon with those ballads, even though the critics groaned. Billy Eckstine as well as Joe counted among the many musicians who heard something special, mightily impressed by Terrell.

By 1943, Joe became an admirer of Eckstine's singing, too. Early one morning, Joe stopped in the Club 65 on Wabash and heard Eckstine, who was travelling with Earl Hines's band, sing 'South of the Border' in a lilting, high, straightforward baritone in those days. The vibrato, which would seduce a nation, came later. But Joe loved Eckstine's beautiful young voice and would recall it for ever afterwards. Joe saw no reason, however, to try to sound like the Other Baritone, who was already having a strong effect on younger singers. There could only be one Eckstine, as there could have been only one Louis Armstrong. Joe did assimilate the Eckstine style, though, and filled up with musical impressions of the many fine singers he heard. He knew that first he imitated, then assimilated, then innovated, as trumpeter Clark Terry, teaching in schools many years later, would define the process by which Joe and others became musicians.

Instrumentalists had an enormous impact on Joe, too, Art Tatum was exciting at Cafe Society. First it had been a Chinese restaurant called the Golden Lily, then White's Emporium for its owner Ed White ('a very big man and a very black man, and it made him look even bigger to be that black', Joe thought).

Tatum's piano playing was so spellbinding there that it once caused someone to be arrested. Tatum had a regular gig downtown at the Three Deuces. Afterwards he went to Cafe Society, arriving at 2 to 2.30 a.m. and played spontaneously, whatever he pleased, until dawn.

One morning at about 5 a.m., he took a break and sat on the piano bench, sipping a beer. Someone slipped a nickel into the jukebox. Immediately a black detective arrested him. The detective didn't take the man to the precinct. He simply called the station to have other policemen come to do that part of the job. He wasn't going to miss the music himself; Joe thought that was so amusing. Some of the musicians hanging out asked what the charge was. The detective said 'disturbing the peace'. The musicians laughed, imagining what might have happened if Tatum had actually been playing. 'The detective probably saved the guy's life,' Joe thought. 'It happens to you in Chicago.'

Joe stayed there as usual until dawn with the hip people who went to listen to music, after their own gigs had finished. Classically trained pianist, singer and entertainer Rozelle Gayle, Joe's best friend, was hanging out with Joe that night. Rozelle also had a resonant, deep voice and worked as an intermission pianist in North Side clubs – the Tailspin, the Argyle Show Lounge. They featured eminent jazz musicians such as Howard McGhee, or Charlie Parker with his band: Miles Davis, Max Roach, Tommy Potter on bass and Duke Jordan on piano, Lester Young, Jackie Cain and Roy Kral (not yet singing together). Sometimes Rozelle, who liked to buy a new car each year, would pick Joe up at his house and take him to the North Side gigs, in white neighbourhoods and white audiences. Joe occasionally worked on the North Side. And afterwards he and Rozelle would stop at Joe's house, or Rozelle's, or go to eat Soul food at Kiah's.

Rozelle called Joe 'big brother' because Joe was two months older. But actually Rozelle was 'big brother' in another way. Six foot four, about 220 pounds in his twenties, Rozelle looked like a football player, with broad shoulders, a fifty inch chest and a squarish face with heavy eyebrows that he thought gave him an impressive satanic expression. He actually dwarfed Joe, who, seen alone, was of imposing proportions. But Rozelle and Joe shared size-thirteen-and-a-half, triple-E shoes. So in those days they literally and figuratively began to know what it felt like to walk in each other's shoes.

Many nights after working or hanging out, they sat in Rozelle's car beside the lake, listened to music – strings and French horns – and watched the sun come up. They wondered if they would ever get a chance to realize their ambitions. Joe hoped that he might get to look increasingly like Caesar Romero. More seriously, Joe told Rozelle that he wanted to sing with strings one day and get the support given to other performers, all of whom were white, Joe noted. Rozelle wanted to sing in the mainstream of the opera world.

With only three months of vocal training in 1938, he had won a scholarship against hundreds of white singers in the City College System of Chicago. But afterwards he couldn't buck the colour line in the white-run opera world. So he kept entertaining on the North Side. He could play standing up, jump high and land on the correct chords without missing a beat. To amuse himself in the after-hours clubs, he performed other unique tricks. With his tongue he could snatch a cherry from a cocktail pick held four inches away from his mouth; he could also touch his tie with his tongue. Joe thought Rozelle was hilarious. And Daddy-O Daylie, watching from behind a bar, noticed that Rozelle never lacked company. Women became fascinated with Rozelle's prowess. But it was music and not a jive trick that bound Joe and Rozelle together as friends. They could do critiques of each other's work – a support system that would last all of their lives.

Once Rozelle, stopping to hear Joe at the Beige Club, didn't like the way Joe was singing a top note and showed him how to reach for it more easily – one of the thousands of technical tips that Joe recalled were offered to him by singers and musicians.

Rozelle was also one of the few people who saw how uneasy Joe was becoming in the late forties. He was very busy working, learning, perhaps too busy. Because he had always been so big, people had frequently turned to him for protection and advice; and he could give that to them. Lonnie Simmons, a baby-faced saxophonist with a wide smile, five years older than Joe, used to hang out with Joe, call him 'Mr Anthony' and confide his problems with women. Joe's hectic life, his own and others' problems, a collection of distresses, began to take their toll on him. Daddy-O, who had thought that Joe had been very happy with Ann, noticed a change in the relationship. Exactly what happened, Daddy-O doesn't know; Joe doesn't mention it, if indeed anything special happened. But Andy Kirk, with whom Joe began working in 1947, noticed Joe's marriage was troubled. Joe appeared to be getting tired and depressed.

One night he and a friend got very stoned on pot and Scotch. As Joe was sitting at a bar, he discovered that he was literally paralysed. 'I can't move,' he told his friend.

Years later Joe surmised that the mercurial, erratic music business and its finances overwhelmed him; the pace; perhaps the Scotch and marijuana (which at worst can make a person feel paranoid and even hallucinate); the uncertainty of a musician's life, combined with the demand for a constant output of energy; and the inhuman burden of dealing with race prejudice; plus his marital difficulties.

There was a public-image problem, too. Women – black women as well as anyone else – liked a man to be pretty if he were going to sing ballads. Joe was big, black and muscular, always attractive in a rugged way. And according to a poll taken personally by Rozelle Gayle, 'so sexy'; that was the essence of all the female comments. More than anything else, Joe wanted to sing ballads. And he was singing beautifully in those days. But he simply wasn't one of the pretty boys. Rozelle Gayle never heard Joe sing the blues until he recorded 'Every Day' with Count Basie in the 1950s. And pianist Hank Jones thought Joe was strictly a ballad singer, when their paths crossed in Cleveland, Ohio, in 1943, where Joe had a gig at the Lindsay Sky Bar, with a good trio. He sang Ellington songs – always among his favourites – as well as he ever did in his life, Jones thought. He was working in a little club called the Cedar Garden. And the two up-and-coming musicians had a little informal chat about how they might work together one day. But Joe sang the blues a lot, by request of club owners and audiences, because he didn't look like their idea of the quintessential balladeer. And, like all the black male singers who wanted to sing ballads, Joe had to fight for the chance to do them. 'It broke his heart, I think,' recalled Daddy-O Daylie years later. 'I watched him in clubs and knew he wanted to sing ballads. Joe was always warm. Lyrics were always important to him. He wanted to get inside a lyric and sing pretty tunes. Anyone who calls him a blues singer doen't have ears.'

The rude, depressing prejudice against anyone but pretty boys singing the ballads was so great that when Lucky Millinder's ballad singer, 'Bull Moose' Jackson, who unfortunately earned his nickname because of his appearance, came on stage to sing his hit tune, 'I Love You, Yes I Do', women booed the man with a rich, easy baritone.

For Joe, nearly thirty, his daily routine – the precariousness, the dangers and disappointments – overtaxed his physical stamina and inner resources. His patience ran out.

Years later Joe would draw upon his sense of humour to express his attitude about being called a blues singer. 'Just call me. Ha ha.' But the label always annoyed him because it usually signified that a singer was black no matter what kind of music he or she was singing, whether a twelve-bar blues or 'Blue Skies'. Once he saw a story identifying Sarah Vaughan as a blues singer. Actually she had never sung the blues in her life. So he threw the misnomer out – out of his mind. 'Duke Ellington and his jungle music' was another nutty phrase that Joe once saw and dismissed by saying, 'The most sophisticated jungle music I ever heard in my life.' Eventually Joe would get the chance to state to the public with equanimity: 'I do popular music as opposed to European classical music.' But for years he had to live with the absurdity that people called him a blues singer because they couldn't just say 'Joe Williams, singer'.

In 1948, too, he had an especially great loss. His grandmother, Mittie Gilbert, who had shepherded him during their migration north, died. She was between sixty-five to seventy years old when she died – 'of old age and loneliness', Joe speculated – a woman who, in middle age, had left her husband behind for ever in Cordele, Georgia, where he felt safe and sane. But she had opted to take her small grandson to Chicago; he might find an opportunity there. And she had never turned back. After her death, Joe's Aunt Juanita lived on her own. Joe didn't see her very often, except in church, if he happened to go on Sunday mornings to St Paul's CME on Dearborn, the family's choice.

One night with Andy Kirk's band, Joe sang 'O Danny Boy'. The audience went wild with enthusiasm, Kirk remembered, 'because Joe, a black man, had sung that particular song and interpreted it so well'. However, Joe wouldn't go back to take a bow. 'It seemed as if he just didn't want to be bothered,' Kirk recalled.

Another time Joe cancelled a date with Kirk, pleading illness. And a third time, Joe travelled to another city to keep a date with Kirk's band but, in the afternoon at rehearsal at the club, felt a little feisty, in no mood to work. He wanted a fight with Kirk, made motions to start one, then backed down. Kirk called Joe's wife to come and pick him up. For a while he went to a hospital – 'a gloomy period', Kirk recalled. A record that Joe made that year with Kirk was never released, because Joe couldn't become involved in the promotion.

He recalled being filled with 'happy juice'. But one day a psychiatrist asked him about his mother. 'What it literally boiled down to as far as I was concerned was who was my mother sleeping with,' Joe recalled.

> And it was just as if the doctor hadn't given me any medication or anything that would have made me feel happy. Because whatever he used to give me that made me feel like wow, oh, man, well, it's beautiful and wonderful, it was as if he hadn't given me anything. 'And what did you say?' No matter how much they fill you full of, you still react to some things. That was none of his business. I never thought about it. And certainly I don't understand why he would ask. As far as I know, my mother was with one man for forty years, James Mason, till she died in 1968. She went to work everyday and came home at night.

Joe's entire upbringing rebelled against the doctor's invasion of Joe's mother's privacy. 'Hell, he hadn't even asked me who I was sleeping with.'

Some days from a window, Joe watched the doctor.

He couldn't get across the street by himself hardly. He started, and then he came back, and he would stand by himself. He would start across the street again and then turn around and come back. I used to see him. And he is going to tell me what is and what is not? And he can't get from this side of the street to the other side of the street. He can't make up his own mind? He couldn't get his shit together.

There were many things besides my not getting along with my wife. I needed to straighten many things out in my head. Financially, I was probably doing better and had better prospects in 1947 than ever before. But there were many extenuating things that I was able to get together in the time I was in and out of the hospital, until finally I was released. He essentially isn't going to hurt anybody, maybe not even himself, you dig?

I guess the hospital thing was a blessing, because I discovered a lot of things that I hadn't even considered or thought about before. My relationship with the rest of the world, with other people.

For one thing, Joe had been regarding himself as 'a bit of a sacrificial lamb'. He had wanted to help everyone and had even found that, during the war, he couldn't pray for the pain and suffering only of American soldiers. He prayed for Germans and Japanese, too. 'That was hard. *Hard!* To pray for the alleviation of all suffering. Because if one were in pain, it diminished all of us, didn't it?' he felt.

And then he reflected upon 'those goodies' that his mother had preached to him. 'You're your own best friend.' And he had time to think about how people had walked up to him and told him how much his performing had become a part of their lives and what had happened to them because they happened to have heard him sing. 'Like the first kiss. And now we're married. A fellow said: "my wife never even kissed me until she heard you sing 'Stardust' at the Regal Theatre; now we're married and going to have our first child." And I realized that what I did helped bring people together.'

And he would be able to look back on it continuing that way from the comfortable vantage point of stardom years later, as he sipped milk in the afternoon, quietly, waiting for the hour to go out and face another club filled with fans. He would even get letters from people saying that his singing had helped them respond in mental hospitals where they hadn't responded before. And couples in their forties would tell him that his records had helped keep their marriages going, when they themselves were at a loss for words and needed the lift of the music. Women would say: 'Oh, Joe Williams, I put your records on on Saturday mornings, baby, and it's a breeze. I got through my housework and didn't even know it.' He would even have a man come up to him years later in Birdland and put a baby in his arms. The man would say: 'Mother, you're responsible for this,' with his wife standing aside, 'blushing, guilty.' He laughed.

In the hospital Joe made up his mind that he was going to be a singer instead of simply someone who got paid to sing:

> That's what I had been doing. But I made up my mind that singing was what I was going to do for a career. If there was any special encouragement to feel better, it was that I wanted to get the fuck out of the hospital. Either you participate in life or not. You have the choice. In there, they take care of you completely. Feed you, give you a place to sleep. You don't have to do anything for yourself. And outside, all of life is going on. I decided to participate. Maybe someone will be helped by my talking about this. It's a do-it-yourself thing, is what it is. If I can help my fellow man, let it be by inference and example.

Joe himself was always mystified about what exactly caused the breakdown and thought, in retrospect, that the music business gave him the *coup de grace* at that point in his career. And if there were other causes, he either never really knew them or else never divulged them publicly. The mere passage of time, he thinks, may have helped him. And when he came out of the hospital, he could light a joint for someone and simply hand it to another person without smoking it. And he also noticed that alcohol had a very powerful effect on him; little amounts made him high quickly. So he decided it would be better if he didn't try to develop a reputation as a big drinker, either, because he would not be awake to enjoy it.

The marriage to Ann Kirksey, whom Joe had left in April 1948, foundered during that period, too. Sometime in the early fifties, she asked Joe if she could use his lawyer to get a divorce. She was planning to marry a man named Julian, who had offered to pay legal fees. Joe called his Chicago lawyer, Levi Morris, and told him that the charge was desertion. 'Of course we've had a good relationship since,' he laughed. 'Before, during and since. You know, one of those things. We're good friends,' he reflected.

Joe never met Julian and went his own way 'without becoming nosy' about Ann's affairs. Anyway Joe had his own life to rebuild at the time. And he was mindful of a saying he had learned in childhood: 'Drink hearty, stay with your party, and watch your qs.' 'And life is pretty much like that. You deal with people that like you, black or white, no matter who. You choose your friends for yourself, choose the ones that like you. And if you have champagne tastes, there's no sense in trying to hang out with the beer boys.'

Determined to seek his own level, Williams started to find his way back to the music scene. And when it seemed to him that things weren't going anywhere, he practised. 'I would sing to the point of getting tired. And I told myself: "Don't strain." Probably some of my greatest performances were heard just by me and a few birds in Washington Park. You can just scream to your heart's delight.'

Much later he recorded some of those songs.

# 4 *Rekindling the Trianon Connection*

To make money, in the early fifties, Joe became a Fuller Cosmetics salesman door to door for a while – as arduous a job as he may ever have had. He told Al Duckett, a writer for *Tan* magazine, in 1956:

> When you're a salesman door to door, and you really work at it, you're pretty beat at night. I used to get home and say, 'I'll lie across the bed for a few minutes to rest and then I'll get up and eat and do this or that.' I'd wake up the next morning in the clothes I'd laid down in. Then I'd start out on the same routine and try to keep a calm, even disposition when the lady on Langley, second floor front, who had been so insistent that I come back to make a sale, cooed at me sweetly, 'Oh, Mr Williams, I forgot all about you today.' Customers: I loved 'em 'cause they kept me eating. But many a day they almost broke my heart.

During those lean days, a policeman guarding the Civic Opera House took Joe backstage, so he could hear a Duke Ellington performance free of charge. While Johnny Hodges was playing a solo, Duke spotted Joe in the wings, slipped offstage and hugged him, saying, 'How nice of you to come! How are things going for you, man?'

Joe was so touched that Ellington remembered him from the days backstage at the Regal in the early forties; Duke was a great gentleman, Joe thought.

Joe wasn't aware of him, but a small, bright-eyed, quiet teenage pianist, Norman Simmons, first heard Joe at DeLisa's.

Later to become a leader of a trio that worked with Joe in the 1970s and 1980s, and a close friend and *de facto* musical director, Norman was beginning to work professionally in Chicago then. Most musicians worked at the weekends, until 4 a.m. on Monday mornings, collected their salaries, ate in restaurants such as Kiah's, and then drifted into the Club DeLisa for the breakfast show. The club presented the show so that entertainers, waiters and night people could enjoy some music and unwind. DeLisa's usually had the greatest shows, because entertainers knew they were performing for the hippest audiences in town.

For the first and only time professionally, Joe sang an aria from *Pagliacci,* wearing a clown suit as part of a show. He knew what he was singing and even years later recalled 'smear you face with powder . . . the people pay you . . . and they must have their fun, laugh, clown, Pagliacci, and they will say well done . . . '

Joe did it at the request of Sammy Dyer, the show's producer, who had always wanted to hear a baritone do the aria written for a tenor. Armed with a smattering of high-school Spanish and sheet music with the Italian libretto and an English translation, Joe disappeared into a room at the Hotel Ritz in Chicago to study. His accompaniment that night was provided by a young woman. So he didn't do his music homework right away. But in the morning, he left behind 'a full bed, once again the bed is warm', he mused, and went into the bathroom to study the libretto and an arrangement by a Chicagoan, Johnny Pate.

Joe's aria impressed Norman Simmons so much that afterwards he went to DeLisa's especially to hear Joe. Many other musicians did, too – pianist Junior Mance, for one, who was also working in clubs at that time and would later lead a trio for Joe.

And a great blues singer on the Chicago scene, Memphis Slim, admired the way Joe was singing 'Every Day' all the time by audience request. The song was a great crowd-pleaser for all of Joe's fans except for his mother.

One night Miss Anne went to the DeLisa and heard him sing the unhappy blues that his audience loved. He screamed, wailed, yodelled – even brayed the song with his magnificant baritone:

Nobody loves me, nobody seems to care,
Speaking of bad luck and trouble,
Well you know I've had my share.
Every day, Every day, Every day
I have the blues . . .

It made his mother figuratively wring her hands. 'Life isn't that bad, son,' she told him afterwards, when he joined her at a table. 'There are people who love you. You know I do!'

But Joe knew better about that song. He liked it. Furthermore, he couldn't get away from it, because people requested it all the time. Eventually it would become a rare event to hear Memphis Slim sing it, while Joe would find himself performing it nearly every night of his professional life.

At the DeLisa, from the 4 p.m. cocktails on Sunday until the 6 a.m. breakfast show on Mondays, musicians barely left the bandstand. Nat Jones, a reeds player in the Saunders band, recalled that Joe would arrive at work on Sunday afternoons wearing sports clothes, a big man in Bermuda shorts. Otherwise the next morning he would attract stares, walking down the street at noon, leaving the club in a tuxedo.

The DeLisa, which opened in 1941, was actually the New Club DeLisa, at 5521 South State Street, by the time Joe worked there. The original DeLisa had burned down across the street. According to Dempsey J. Travis's book *An Autobiography of Black Jazz,*

> The new club cost $300,000, seated 1,000 people comfortably, and could actually seat 1,500 in a pinch. [The original club squeezed 500 people into a space for 300 on Saturday nights. Customers sometimes sat through four shows without drinks, because they couldn't get the attention of the rushing waitresses.]
>
> It also had a gas-fired furnace and central air conditioning. The lighting was mellow red fluorescent, so mellow that your eyes took a few seconds to adjust to it. The bandstand was at

the east end of the room; the dance floor in front of it could be raised hydraulically for shows. the stage area was equipped with vari-coloured floodlights. And people on the scene regarded Joe as the biggest star at the DeLisa, where out-of-town musicians always stopped after their jobs. So he was a local celebrity.

When Joe started singing 'Every Day', the house literally went wild – screaming, whistling, applauding, and beating on the tables with souvenir table knockers provided by the owners. The audience would join in with a rhythmic beat when he began to sing: 'Every day, every day I have the blues . . . ' Chicks would yell, 'Yeah, yeah, yeah'. Joe sang: 'Nobody loves me, nobody seems to care . . . '

A white groupie sitting at ringside jumped up, shouting, 'I will take care of you, you sweet black mother!'

The beat continued with the drunks and coke drinkers pounding on the tables with their knockers, as Joe wailed: 'Speaking of bad luck and trouble, you know I've had my share . . . '

Joe began to shout louder, as he did a half 'trucking' step across the stage with an empty travel bag in his hand.

> I am going to pack my suitcase
> And move on down the line,
> Where there ain't nobody worried, and
> There ain't nobody crying.

Several teasing brown chicks sitting near the stage exit on the north side of the room yelled, 'Oooooooooh! Don't leave now, Joe baby, don't leave!'

And with a steady beat, the show closed with everybody getting into the act.

Stepping outside of his regional circle, Joe went to hear Nat Cole, already nationally known, at the Downtown Theatre. Although Nat and Joe were approximately the same age, they had never become close friends on the Chicago scene. Nat had left Chicago as a teenager to go on the road with a show. But they knew each other. And between performances, Nat sat down in the basement of the Downtown Theatre, where Joe had gone to say 'hello'. Nat played a new tune that someone had handed him the sheet music for: 'Candy', which had been a hit in 1944 – and heard something that struck a generous personal and professional chord in him, 'Here, you should sing this,' he said to Joe and handed him the music. Joe liked it a lot – and tucked it away for a while into his growing repertoire.

Bandleader King Kolax was also impressed with Joe at the time. Kolax, with whom Joe worked at the Regal, shared the general opinion that Joe was a quiet loner who would finish singing and go into his dressing-room to relax by himself with a Cola-Cola. And Kolax was struck by Joe's demeanour – his walk, his manner of speaking with people, his carriage – 'as if he were the most beautiful person on earth', Kolax thought. Although aloof, even remote, he could nevertheless be extremely friendly. Never a heavy drinker, he liked to hang out in clubs to talk to people. But he also liked to sit alone, think about music, about life, about organizing his career somehow; he liked to walk around Chicago and look in windows on his own.

Kolax led the house band at the 1,500-capacity Regal, which 'had a centre dome made up of 69,000 small crystals that emitted enough dazzling light to illuminate a small park on a dark night.'* Kolax asked Joe to record a few songs. And in 1951, Kolax and Williams made Joe's first recording of 'Every Day' on Leonard Chess's label, which would also have its rights taken on by Savoy/Regent. That record was first released in 1954, too, eventually becoming a collector's item, nearly impossible to find. Joe's sunny, easeful voice was lilting and clear on the ballad, 'I'm Always on the Blue Side'. He did a more ornate and dramatic interpretation of 'They'll Never Believe Me' than he ever would present on ballads in the future. On 'Every Day', his voice was overdubbed with a wonderful boogie-woogie pianist, Prentice McCarey very much in evidence in the accompanying group. This 'Every Day' began as a muted version, on which Joe built to a rousing end.

And so Joe stayed busy in the early fifties, singing all over the

'*An Autobiography of Black Jazz*' by Dempsey J. Travis

South Side, occasionally on the North Side again. At about the same time, Daddy-O Daylie needed another haircut and went back to the Metropolitan barber shop near the Regal Theatre. Count Basie needed a haircut that day, too, and said to Daddy-O, 'I'm looking for a blues singer.' Daddy-O said, 'I've got just the guy for you.'

He took his new Hudson to pick Joe up, he recounted, and drove Joe downtown to the Brass Rail at Clark and Randolph Street, Basie was appearing there. On the way, Daddy-O said to Joe: 'Basie wants a blues singer. Sing what the man wants. When you make it, you can sing what you want to.'

At DeLisa's, Joe used to excite audiences with 'Stop Pretty Baby Stop' as well as 'Every Day'.

'Sing those songs for the Count,' Daddy-O told Joe.

He did.

'The Count looked at me and winked,' goes Daddy-O's tale, when Joe sang 'Stop Pretty Baby Stop'. Then Joe sang 'Every Day' with the Count's full attention upon him.

In Basie's septet in those post-war years, Buddy De Franco played clarinet; Clark Terry played trumpet; Bob Graf, tenor saxophone, Gus Johnson, drums, Jimmy Lewis bass, and Basie on piano. And for a two-month gig at the Brass Rail, Joe was the singer. Joe learned to listen for Basie to play five notes – 'Ping ping, ping ping ping' – with his show-stopping, single-note piano style, the perfect light touch to contrast with his brass and rhythm. Joe knew the notes were his cue to step up on to the bandstand near the bar. As described by one habitué of that club, observed during a gig other than Basie's,

> The Brass Rail, which opened in 1941, was a well-laid-out spot, with a balcony all around the place, over which customers could drool and listen to the music, but from the standpoint of the boys in the band, who felt like sardines, only a colossal optimist would say the club had a bandstand . . . The trombonist had to stand with one foot on the stairway leading down from behind the bar or else he had to choose between the leader's or bartender's neck to jab his slide into.

But it was a fine little club musically. One night Basie started playing 'Solitude' for Joe to sing. Then they did 'Ain't Misbehavin'', 'Honeysuckle Rose' and other standards. Basie paid Joe $50 a week out of his own pocket, because he liked the singing so much. Joe still had no idea that his future lay with Basie and thought the man simply had one of the great bands for anyone to be singing with.

Joe struck up a friendship with trumpeter Clark Terry during that gig and made a little bet that Ezzard Charles would beat Joe Louis in a fight. Clark Terry said it would never happen. After the night's performance, they heard the news. Louis had lost; Terry had lost. Joe had an 'I told you so' expression written all over his expansive, smiling face. He would have been much less likely to bet on his coming fame with Basie. Terry didn't mind losing to a fellow Sagittarian and was happy when their paths crossed again in St Louis soon afterwards. Joe was probably singing with Gerald Wilson's band at the Club Plantation, while Terry was working with Basie. And after work, Joe and Terry went to a park and played baseball. Ella Fitzgerald, who was passing through town, went to bat balls and run bases until dawn, calming down after the night's work, too. One night Joe slid into home plate and hurt himself so badly that little Clark Terry picked him up and rushed him away for medical attention. Then Terry went off with Basie, and Joe went back to Chicago to establish himself further.

He sometimes saw Count Basie as a guest on Kate Smith's television show. She'd say: 'BILL!' Joe thought it was a godsend to Basie to have that kind of visibility. 'To be on God Bless America's show. Regularly!' Joe laughed. 'What could be better than that?' And without a crystal ball to augment his television tube, Joe kept working hard in Chicago. By 1951, still there, he married again, this time to Lemma Reid, a light-skinned woman with a lazing smile and a figure that Joe liked to photograph, it was so fine. She had also been born in Georgia, moved to Cincinnati with her family and married a musician named Reid.

She and Joe were living in a tiny apartment on the South Side, with no space for a baby. So Joe found a bigger place, at a higher rent than he could easily pay, and told his landlords, Mr and Mrs Townsend that he and Lemma would be leaving soon, because of the baby coming. The Townsends said they were sorry to see him go: 'And if you run into difficulties, let us know,' offering to loan him money to keep going. Joe was astounded. At DeLisa's, Red Saunders said, 'If it gets heavy about the goodness, let me know,' offering a loan, too. Lonnie Simmons, a saxophonist and organist, with his cherubic smile offered help. Five years older than Joe, but used to unburdening himself about his troubles with women to him, Lonnie invited the young singer for grits one morning at Chili Mac's, picked up the bill, and said, 'Bub, if you need anything, let me know.' Joe knew that Lonnie always had money in his pocket. But he didn't borrow anything.

He told Lemma, though, about the offers. 'To have three people offer when you're setting out with your life, your wife and child, cutting ties, that gives you an inner strength so you can do it.' Lemma wasn't so sure. By that time, the marriage had already become stormy.

Their daughter, JoAnn, was born 19 January 1953. Joe took her to show her off at the DeLisa one afternoon. Lonnie Simmons, a camera buff, put her in a big camera case, arranged her with her head sticking out, one foot, too, and a hand holding up the lid. He took a photograph, which later appeared in *Ebony* magazine with headquarters in Chicago, where Lonnie had friends on the staff.

But the marriage was fraught with arguments. 'Her big hero was her mother,' Joe learned about Lemma. And his third wife, as his first two wives had done, admired men but didn't have any real respect for them. Lemma went back to live with her mother in Cincinnati and had tense reunions with Joe from time to time. He found his wife very strong-willed, pulling in her direction, saying things that were demeaning to him, while he was pulling hard in another direction, unintentionally pulling, doing the best he could for the family. He had to hang out on the scene; he worked there, and he loved it. It was important fun for him to be there, listening hard, loving the sounds, and laughing with other musicians.

He had scores of escapades, while he studied the music, absorbing its inspiration, flirting with the girls who liked to hang out, too. Composer, musicologist, French horn player, musical taste-maker-to-be Gunther Schuller packed his bags one night in Chicago, ready to leave town and join the Metropolitan Opera the next day. Then he went out for his last night in town with Joe, hanging out in the jazz clubs, drinking a little, until way past dawn. At 8 a.m., Schuller, bound for New York City, left Joe in a club, saying, 'Next time I see you, I want to hear you singing at the Met.' Joe laughed, knowing the legitimacy of that music would never suit him. And then he went home, feeling dejected, even disgusted, that still another marriage wasn't working out, though he knew that he had always felt protective towards women.

No longer living in any nest, he threw his energies into singing. With music as his primary impetus, he took the few minutes' intermission from his show with Dr Jo Jo Adams, who was known for his flamboyant taste in tails made for him in bright colours, to slip into the Trianon Ballroom, where Count Basie was working in Chicago. Basie's biographer, Albert Murray, has written that Reunald Jones, one of Basie's musicians, told Basie about a wonderful singer working nearby. Basie asked Jones to bring the kid by the Trianon. Joe Williams showed up for Basie; when Basie saw him, he remembered him as the same young singer who had sat in with the group a few years earlier at the Brass Rail. Basie told his biographer that as soon as he heard Joe sing, the decision was made; he knew he would be asking Joe to go along with the band. 'And that's how that marriage got started,' Basie told him. At the Trianon, Joe obliged Basie with 'Roll 'em Pete', about his sweet, counter-culture mama with eyes like diamonds and teeth that shone like Fort Knox gold, written by Kansas City blues shouter Big Joe Turner. Then Joe Williams hurried back to his own gig.

Afterwards Basie called Joe to his hotel room and said that he should think about going on the road with the Basie band and see how people all around the country liked his singing. He was already the premier singer in the Midwest. But there was no handshake, no date set for Joe to join the band. Joe wasn't sure the job would materialize.

Then, in December, he received a $50 money order from Basie, with instructions to meet the band in New York City. Joe flew on Christmas morning, 1954, from Midway Airport in Chicago to LaGuardia in an old-fashioned piston-propeller plane. From the airport. he went directly to the Alvin Hotel, in midtown, near the clubs and theatres, where he reported to Marshall Royal, an alto saxophonist and musical director of the band. Royal told Joe to get himself a room at the President Hotel, where Basie was staying. And Joe was about to get on the bus.

# 5 *With the Basie Machine*

In the 1930s, the men in the Basie band called their bus the Blue Goose, probably because it was a funny-looking blue bus common in the era, with spare tyres on the back and shaped, to someone's imaginative eye, like a goose. By the 1950s, the Basie band travelled in updated style. Basie had Greyhound coaches with washrooms. They weren't funny, but they could become quite funky-looking buses after the band members rode in them, eating and sleeping for thirteen hours at a clip. So the men sometimes chided each other: 'Hey, get that bottle out of there,' and tried to keep the bus in good shape, though few of them could be called a bundle of domesticity.

Within a few years, this Basie band would do a command performance for the Queen of England and then play at the Kennedy Inaugural. Although less ornate and more brassy, the band would rank musically with Duke Ellington's as one of the greatest, longest-lived big bands in the world. And Basie's complicated, emotional and dedicated musicians perceived their collective entity as larger than the sum of its parts. Basie's musicians thought the band, itself a unique musical instrument, was the greatest thing that ever happened to them.

Trombonist Benny Powell, only twenty-two when he joined in 1951, called the bus an 'iron lung', the greatest support system he could imagine, going down the road. And though the bus kept the men cooped up, it nurtured them in a way. Each man could retreat into his own little world. Guitarist Freddie Green studied arranging in his seat. Saxophone player Billy Mitchell would eventually come aboard with books about the uses of hypnosis in childbirth and dentistry. Joe Williams brought cameras and manuals; he had become fascinated with photography. The bassist, Eddie Jones, a graduate of Howard University, studied calculus. Later he would become an IBM systems executive. And Benny Powell, who shared a love of photography with Joe, felt confident and secure, because the men on the bus had their own interests, as well as their own jokes and complicated natures. If Benny got bored sitting in his seat, he could talk to Joe about photography. Or Joe passed Benny magazine articles.

Once Joe told Benny about how Miss Anne had found an article with her son's name in it. A critic had praised his singing. She had told Joe how pleased she was. When somebody wrote about you that way, she said, you had clearly done something of value and proved you weren't on earth simply to breathe air that somebody else might have put to better use.

From seemingly casual conversation, Benny got the impression that Miss Anne's respect for cultural achievement had given Joe vision. He had taken in her vision by osmosis; her attitude was responsible for his presence on the bus, a few seats behind Benny. Benny felt that he shared with Joe the background of an idealistic mother. And both men felt the pride of having been invited to join an illustrious big band with a tradition of clean suits and clean sounds. It was simply because the men needed a creative sense of humour, if they were going to survive by rolling around the country in a bus, that they called the bus many things besides the Blue Goose.

On Christmas Day, 1954, Joe boarded one of these good grey buses and joined 'twenty nuts', as tenor saxophonist Frank Wess typified the eighteen talented individualists of the Basie entourage. Taking the steps up to his new seat, Joe doubled his income from $75 to $150 a week. And the bus headed south to Washington, DC, and picked up drummer Sonny Payne, who was also embarking on his first day with Basie.

Musically the men on the bus were still tightening their soloistic work to forge one entity – a blues-based swing machine that Basie had originally conceived of in Kansas City. There, in the mid-thirties, he organized a band with a spare, lighter-than-air swing, with explorers Jo Jones, drummer, and Walter Page, bassist. Add to that innovative horn players improvising in the band – saxophonist Lester Young, trumpeters Buck Clayton and Hot Lips Page, trombonist Dickie Wells and the pianist Mr Basie, who had fallen under the spell of stride piano in the era of Harlem rent parties.* The left hand produced the rhythmic feeling of someone striding down the street.

From 1949 to 1952, for financial reasons primarily, Basie disbanded and toured with a lively, seven-piece group. But by the early fifties, Basie began building a big band again, drawing the talent into his bus as he moved along. Step in here, Frank Wess, and sit down there, Frank Foster.

Foster, just discharged from service in Korea, still wearing his army uniform on his first day back in Detroit, went to audition at a club where Basie was playing. On the street the word was out that Count was looking for a tenor saxophonist. A few months later, Foster received a money order and the message to meet Basie in New York. It was the same system that Basie used to hire Joe and most of the others, not conducting interviews but simply listening and observing the musicians as they played and mingled with each other. Somehow Basie could tell which men had the character and talent to fit in with his plans and demands. No matter how young you were: 'Once you were in Basie's band, you were a man,' Benny Powell quickly learned. 'It wasn't a job for kids. Basie didn't hire kids.' And the best and the brightest wanted to go along with Basie.*

Basie had 'a streak of the pixie' in him, as Benny Powell called it, that kept Basie impervious to the men's varied

*According to Albert Murray, also passing through the band in those years were: Buster Smith, alto saxophonist and clarinettist; Jack Washington, alto and baritone saxophonist; and George Rabbit Hunt, trombonist; Joe Keyes and Tatti Smith, trumpeters.

*In the band on Christmas Day, 1954, were trumpeters Wendell Culley, Reunald Jones, Thad Jones and Joe Newman; trombonists Henry Coker, Bill Hughes and Benny Powell; Marshall Royal and Ernie Wilkins on alto saxophones; Wess and Frank Foster, tenor saxophonists, and Wess on flute, too; Charlie Fowlkes on baritone saxophone; Eddie Jones, the bassist; Freddie Green, guitarist, who had joined the first Basie band in New York City in the 1930s. Sonny Payne also joined on Christmas Day, 1954. After that, others who passed through the band during Joe's tenure were Eddie 'Lockjaw' Davis, tenor saxophonist; Lenny Johnson, trumpeter; from time to time Harry 'Sweets' Edison, trumpeter; Billy Mitchell, tenor saxophonist; Al Grey, trombonist.

temperaments and needs, artistic and otherwise. Powell, an alumnus of the Hampton band, auditioned for Basie and was called to do a concert on 10 October 1951 in Boston. After the show, Benny sidled up to the round-faced Basie, who had heavy-lidded, profoundly penetrating eyes and an easy smile. Benny asked, 'Trombone sound all right to you?' Basie said, 'All right.' Benny said, 'Am I doing the job that's pleasing you?' Basie said, 'You're here, aren't you, kid?' Benny thought: yes, but how long will I be here? A week later, he went to Holyoke. Mass., called by Basie for an afternoon gig in a water tower. Afterwards Benny said, 'Mr Basie, everything all right?' 'Yeah, fine, Benny.' 'Is the band going to be working?' 'Yeah, we have a few things coming up.' 'Well, am I going to be with it?' Benny asked. 'Well, you're here, aren't you kid?' This routine went on for about three years.

Joe Williams was a different case; he knew he was here, wherever that turned out to be. Older than Benny by twelve years, Joe simply slipped his paycheck deep into his pocket. For one thing, the Basie band had become a much more certain entity by the time Joe joined it. And the men on the bus before Christmas Day 1954 knew that they almost had the music right. Some felt that they hadn't done as well as they would have liked to in the Bandbox that year in New York City, following Duke Ellington's band. They were ready for the infusion of drummer Sonny Payne and Joe, the new blues singer.

By their first stop, a naval base in Virgina, Joe made it immediately clear that he was a professional with a great deal of stage presence; a musician who didn't get upset by little things going wrong. He came prepared with Memphis Slim's 'Every Day' and 'The Comeback'. And Big Joe Turner's 'Cherry Red' and 'Roll 'em Pete', and 'Shake Rattle and Roll' and 'In the Evening'. Basie asked Joe to sing 'Boogie Woogie Blues', which Joe's predecessor, Jimmy Rushing, had done so effectively, in his rougher, more plaintive register in his younger days. But Williams didn't know any of Rushing's material (and didn't want to learn it and seek out comparisons with the simpler, more pristine Rushing; his habits and temperament kept him closer to his roots than Joe had stayed to his. Actually, with his ear, Joe could hear a song once and know it. Years later, when he finally did some Rushing songs, Joe joked that he never got them right.)

The band headed further south and spent New Year's Eve in Orlando, Florida. Then New Year's Day in Miami, with Joe Louis in the audience. Williams matched Louis foot for foot. That is, both men wore size 13½ Triple-E shoes. And Williams showed off his size to audiences by wearing patent-leather shoes on stage. They caught the light, adding subtly to the glamour he was striving for. Cab Calloway's band was performing in town at the same time, impressing Williams especially; Calloway with his gracefully flying white tails and his rakishly tossed long black hair. And Sonny Payne made an everlasting impression on his new roomate, Joe Williams, too.

Small and dapper and loath to go to sleep for fear of missing something, Sonny Payne stayed up to have a party all the time. One night in Miami, at the Sir John Hotel, then called the Lord Calvert, Sonny outlasted nearly everybody, including Joe Williams. Joe left the jam session in the wee hours, leaving behind the gorgeous girls at the pool and the hip whites hanging out with the Basie band at the black hotel, and went to bed. In the middle of the night, he awakened suddenly to see Sonny Payne walking into the closet, about to urinate, confused by all the refreshments of the night.

'Hey, mother, what do you think you're doing?' Joe shouted. Oh, God, the suits! he thought.

'Get out of there, mother!' Joe shouted, and steering Sonny towards the bathroom, told the befuddled drummer: 'Oh, *that would have been awful, mother!'*

After Miami, the tour's stops included the Two Spot Club in Jacksonville. Audiences cheered for the fresh, exciting sound. And somewhere along the way between Florida, Washington, DC, and Baltimore and all the other southern states, cities and towns, with their halls and clubs that the band played in, as the bus made its way back up the east coast, the musicians got the sound exactly right. For 'Every Day', Frank Wess played a riff; Thad Jones added another one on trumpet. Then Ernie Wilkins, an alto saxophonist, wrote an introduction, primarily the same thing that the band was already playing and Joe was singing. But the blues became slicker and swifter in the hands of the great Basie machine than it had been when Joe had sung it on the Chicago recording. Wilkins also arranged 'Five o'Clock in the Morning', written by Joe, and 'Teach Me Tonight'. 'Roll 'em Pete' was a head arrangement by the whole band. Frank Foster, who arranged about half the Basie band's music, did 'My Baby Upsets Me' for Joe – another tune that Joe wrote 'about not being able to get it right for someone you care about. No matter what you do, you just can't get it right,' Joe said was his inspiration for writing that tune in his Chicago days. And Foster arranged 'The Comback', too. Joe dictated a couple of the lines, and suggested a couple of the licks, as he and Basie often did for the arrangers. And Joe began his habit of introducing Frank Foster to people as 'my prearranger'.

Joe impressed the band members by the way that he could sing ballads, blues, scat, jazz, even gospel. He felt comfortable doing it all. As few singers ever could, Joe seduced the instrumentalist with his 'big pipes': a strong enough voice to soar over the bursts and flares of the Basie band, not a soul of whom could quiet down or lose momentum for a singer who couldn't sing, or simply because the singer's turn to come on stage had arrived.

Joe never showed the slightest bit of strain, singing with a powerhouse behind him. Instead, buoyancy and sweetness tempered his force. He could take a note and improvise wildly on the changes, never losing the beat, and twirl a tune around so fast that an audience could never track the course of its notes. He could suddenly scream like a huge, wounded banshee, without inhibitions. Or he could make a melody skip along smoothly, much the way it was written, with a sunny tone, sounding as happy as a kid at a ballgame. At such times, his voice was full of home runs. In short, he carried off dramatic, vocal acrobatics with a lilt. All the while he stayed out of the band's way, never competing with it, never letting it overwhelm him either. And by turns he took command, with his sound and his feeling for the lyrics – or made space for the soloists and the ensemble; he could ride with them, fly above them, dive through them – and withdraw. And he was as brazen as brass to do it all, forcefully, without seeming to be anything but natural.

A streamlined Basie band, without any excess complications

in the arrangements, arrived in New York City for an engagement at Birdland. At first there was a little hitch behind the scenes. Birdland's owners didn't want Joe Williams to sing, because they didn't want to pay extra for the sweet fillip of featuring a singer. They thought Basie's instrumentalists would draw sufficient attention to the club. But, on the brightly lit bandstand, as the people who left their seats and stood up in the Peanut Gallery alongside the bar shoved each other to get a better view, Basie played the usual introduction to 'Every Day'. Afterwards, Joe sang the one ballad that Basie had approved for the night, 'Teach Me Tonight', and then 'Roll 'em Pete' about Joe's supergal who was going to buy him a hydromatic kiddie car, and several other songs. And the musical powerhouse had Birdland's audience screaming.

'They melted,' Frank Foster noted, looking out at them. 'First they screamed and shouted, then they melted.' And trumpeter Thad Jones watched, spellbound himself, as the audiences fell silent when Joe began singing 'Every Day', then screamed wildly afterwards. Thad Jones thought that Joe Williams was the greatest blues singer of his time. 'He lent dignity to the blues with his voice, with an intensity generated from within and projected masterfully,' Jones recalled years later. And Joe was able to fit in with the Basie Band's style; at the same time, he could dominate the band and enhance its originality. He wanted to sing more ballads, but they were overwhelmed by the excitement generated by his blues repertoire. So Basie kept him to the directive: sing the blues. And Joe made an electrifying impression on some very important New Yorkers in Birdland. Lines formed around the corner in the snow, as the saying goes. A nostalgic Frank Wess recalled: 'The newspapers said "Basie's back". They didn't even have to say where.' Joe, at age thirty-seven, was the new kid in town. Birdland was the most important place in the jazz world to be cheered in. After his first night there, somebody said, 'Who's got his contract?' Basie said, 'I do.'

Later, the band went into a Philadelphia room, where the owners didn't want to pay the extra money for a singer with the Basie band. But again Basie took Joe into the performance. And afterwards, there was talk about extending the engagement – for Joe, with no mention of the Basie band!

In *Down Beat* magazine, Leonard Feather caught the spirit of Joe's blues singing:

> Joe is a spellbinding artist to watch. Much of the time he stands very still, hands in front of him, with fingers touching, as if in prayer. Sometimes he throws a syllable away as casually as an old-time blues singer who can't hold a note; at other times, he grasps a tone and bends the syllable into half a dozen different notes for a wild, dramatic effect. And on one or two numbers he just takes a note, sung falsetto, and holds on to it for an entire twelve-bar blues chorus, while the band builds up tremendous intensity behind him. Again he will take a simple phrase like 'Oh, well, oh well' and repeat it like some magic incantation throughout the twelve-bars.

About his clasped hands and quiet stance, Joe thought: 'In general it behoves you to do as little as possible to distract from the singing, especially if you're singing well.' And when he had the chance to see Frank Sinatra in live performance, Joe studied the singer's physical movements – not to imitate them, simply to watch and teach himself what to leave out. 'How many gestures are there anyway?' he asked himself.

When the band reached Boston, Basie and Joe, playing at Storyville, stopped in the RKO Palace. Buddy Johnson's band was playing there. featuring Buddy's sister Ella as singer. She did a tune that didn't impress Joe very much: 'Alright, Okay, You Win'. It wasn't his cup of tea. Basie said to Joe: 'You should sing that song.' Joe didn't think so. Basie said, 'Kid, you're going to need that song one day.' Joe still didn't tumble. Basie added, 'I'll bet you can't sing that song as well as that bitch.' That piqued Joe's interest, wrote one critic. 'That made him mad. Lawd,' Joe told a friend, with a chuckle, as the counterpoint for the slight drawl he occasionally lapsed into.

'So I got together with Frank Foster,' Joe later told jazz critic Stanley Dance, 'and he made an arrangement. I wasn't going to do it the way Ella Johnson did it. It suited her with her little cutesy ways, but it wasn't ballsy, and so far as I was concerned it didn't suit a male vocalist. So I changed it.' To the point where authors Sid Wyche and Mamie Watts recalled the sheet music and rewrote the song the way Joe had revamped it. And it was always done his way with jump blues feeling after that.

And after Thad Jones arranged 'Ain't No Use' and a couple of other tunes for Joe, Jones noted that Joe always created the shape of music written for him, guided by 'faith, harmonics and faith', Joe explained as his approach. The band deferred to his interpretations of the arrangements.

Joe had no idea that his first record with Basie in 1955 would be such a terrific hit. He had heard people cheering, as the band gained momentum. Then he watched, fascinated and joyful, as people began buying the record and asking disc jockeys to play it. 'Yeaaaaaaaah, that's it,' he sized up their reaction. He kept snoozing on the bus, while the disc jockeys played the records: Joe Adams in California; Daddy-O Daylie, Marty Faye and Eddie Arnesty in Chicago. Symphony Sid Torin broadcast from Birdland over WEVD in New York City, with a voice as deep as a bass fiddle, cared for with cognac and Camel cigarettes, and supplied the people at home with the news that Joe Williams was singing with Count Basie. The commercial stations kept playing the songs all the time. Joe slept on the bus and headed to the bandstands in scores of cities to find that he had become the Glitter, the *pièce de résistance,* in his Basie uniform, as he had not been in years past, when he had done his job in a Lionel Hampton band uniform with a red jacket and dark pants. Whenever Joe turned the radio on, he heard disc jockeys playing those songs. He listened and studied how he might sing better next time. He usually had to wait several months before he could decide whether he liked what he did.

'Every Day' was five minutes and twenty seconds long in the first version, at a time when everyone else was making three-minute-and-twenty-one-second records. 'The Comeback' ran over five minutes, too. Joe decided that the sheer length of the records enticed the disc jockeys to play them, because the long tracks gave them a chance to go to the bathroom. And nobody could quarrel with them, because the music was so good. 'And they're still playing those records and still getting that long break,' Joe noted years later.

Joe watched while the Music Business Machinery went to

work on the Basie band's karma. Willard Alexander booked the band on a Birdland tour in 1955, beginning in White Plains, NY, taking along pianist Erroll Garner, tenor saxophonist Lester Young, who had played with the pre-1949 Basie band, which had a looser, less polished sound than the Basie band in the 1950s; and Stan Getz, Sarah Vaughan and pianist Bud Powell. 'Beaucoup de people,' Joe counted to have fun with on the bus.

They went into Peps on South and Broad Streets in Philadelphia, from which city Basie and Joe took a train without the band into New York to do Joe's first network television show, 'Music '55' on CBS, produced and directed by Jackie Gleason. Joe and Count Basie stayed overnight at the Count's house in St Albans, Queens. Then the next afternoon, in the Manhattan television studio, Basie played piano while Joe sang 'Well, Alright, Okay, You Win' with Stan Kenton leading an orchestra. They did some Harold Arlen tunes, too. Joe found the show so exciting, working with Kathryn Grayson 'who had been appearing with Mario Lanza, folks like that', Joe recalled about the days when his professional life was first touched by magic, and 'Julie Wilson, a fine singer with great feeling, and Sarah Vaughan stood us all on our collective ears; she's such a fine musician', his face alight, ethereally pensive, as it always seems to be when he engages in reverie. And then he went back to Philadelphia to rejoin the tour – and from there to arenas around the country with thousands of people in the audiences. And the next year another Birdland tour took Basie and Joe, his main attraction, along with Sarah Vaughan and soft-toned Lester Young again and the blind singer, Al Hibbler, an original band stylist, who had sung with Ellington and Jay McShann.

The Birdland tours of 1955, 1956 and 1957 took the band to Richmond and Norfolk, Virginia; Charlotte, Raleigh, Fayetteville and Durham, North Carolina; Nashville, Tennessee; Toledo and Cleveland, Ohio; Pottstown, Pennsylvania; Kansas City and Topeka, Kansas; Dallas, Houston, and Fort Worth and Port Arthur, Texas; St Louis, Missouri and Detroit, Michigan, Buffalo, New York; and the Civic Opera House in Chicago, Illinois. And in addition to the Birdland tours, which took about three weeks with one-night stands in each city, there was a tour, with George Shearing and Ruth Brown, that went some place in the South, possibly Memphis. Joe noted with disdain that 'some silly son of a bitch started hollering and yelling', as he introduced the Basie band: 'FOR THE FIRST TIME ON STAGE TOGETHER, COLOURED AND WHITE!' 'Doesn't he think people can see?' Joe thought. 'What does he keep hollering and screaming about?' Joe began observing there and in other cities that many people simply didn't know what to say. But the Basie band played its music and, on an independent schedule, too, kept moving constantly, playing in every state except for Wyoming and the Dakotas. The Newport Jazz Festival became a regular stop, every summer, for Joe with the band, beginning in 1955. He would only miss the years, later on, when there were disturbances.

Now for Joe with the band there were countless benefits, in hospitals as well as jails. The band stopped in a Virginia jail for a show produced by a priest named Father Brightfellow, who tended an incarcerated flock – a happy-faced, smiling, benevolent-looking priest. Joe wondered how the prisoners could stand to look at that cheery face, while they were closed in, behind bars. It was so incongruous to see that face in a jail. Maybe it was nice to have someone to talk to who looked that good, the Basie bandmen thought. You could at least hear a different opinion, Joe thought, from a man with that face. But none of the musicians would have been able to stand being locked up and seeing someone so happy looking, the musicians joked after that benefit, grateful for their freedom, riding on the high note of the band's career.

The band stopped for a three-week engagement at the Paramount Theatre in New York City, doing fifty-seven shows, with Nat Cole, Ella Fitzgerald, Marty Allen and Mitch De Wood, and on another trip to New York moved into the Apollo Theatre to share the bill with dancers Cholly Atkins and Honi Coles.

By that time Andy Kirk was living in New York City, with a family-run florist shop near Harlem Hospital. During a break between shows at the Apollo, Joe took a walk uptown and told Kirk: 'I'm sorry.' 'Sorry for what?' Kirk said. 'Oh, I know, I know,' Joe said with a great, wide smile, recalling the disturbance years ago, when he had disrupted Kirk's rehearsal and gone to hospital. But Kirk, who had thought that Joe had simply become deeply tired, felt particularly happy to see him in fine shape. Kirk had always really liked the young singer personally and professionally.

# 6 All That Happiness

The 'kid' could really generate excitement, Peter Long, an assistant manager at the Apollo, noticed. Long was such an ubiquitous jazz promoter that he found himself publicizing shows at the Brooklyn Paramount, too. On one bill, he had Miles Davis, Count Basie, George Shearing, a comedian and Joe to work with – 'a really big, hot show,' he assessed it. Basie had injured his neck a little. Although it did hurt, it wasn't a catastrophic injury. Long asked Basie to agree to the publicity that he had broken his neck but would play anyway. Basie agreed. The theatre had two stages, one stationary, one movable. As Joe was singing 'Every Day', his last, rousing number in Basie's set on the stationary stage, with the curtains closing, Miles Davis came up on the other stage, noodling on his horn, as if accompanying Joe. That kind of segue made the shows even more exciting; people stood up and screamed. And Joe was ready for all that happiness.

The first Basie–Williams record went to Europe in 1955, the year that Joe won *Down Beat* magazine's New Star Award. By 1956, Willard Alexander booked two wildly successful tours in Europe for Basie and Joe – and again in 1957 and twice in 1959. Joe watched happily how people did a lot of promotion for those tours. 'And,' he smiled, 'they made a lot of money.'

Maybe the Spanish lessons in high school helped, and the go-around with the aria in the Hotel Ritz bathroom, too. Most likely it was Joe's sensitive musical ear that allowed him to have such a great time with his lyrics in Europe.

The first stop on the forty-two-day tour in 1956 was Sweden, where Joe, armed with a Fielding guide book, ordered *frukost:*

breakfast. He got the inflection exactly right, sweeping up and down wildly, exaggeratedly on each vowel and even on the consonants. He made the words sound like the sight of a seagull flapping its wings. If he thought the Swedish word for breakfast was funny, he found it hilarious to sing, in Swedish, 'fifty chicks under twenty-two', as part of the lyrics for 'Alright, Okay, You Win'. *'Femti,'* he began, his inflections soaring. And when he got to Germany, it became *'Fiftsik Fraulein unter Tsvei und Tsvansek',* with the more dolorous German intonation. He was off and running amok in languages, as he matriculated in an educational experience of the world, with a rapidly changing but transporting curriculum. And the world began serving as a university for him, as it had for many other jazz musicians – men who may have given up on formal classes in schools but went on to tutor themselves, becoming familiar, through practical experience, with international cultures, social systems, laws and politics. And they could talk to anybody with charm, which was part of the job and one of its great side benefits.

In London the Basie band's first performance was at the Royal Festival Hall. For the first concert, Princess Margaret, came with the Queen's cousin and returned for the second concert, sitting in the royal box.

Back in the US, the band was so popular, it had many engagements where it could 'sit down' in a town for a couple of weeks or a month, welcomed for long bookings in clubs. Basie usually brought the band into Birdland for four weeks at Christmastime and two at Eastertime, in summer and sometime in fall, Joe recalled years later. On Easter Sundays, the jazz community gathered in Birdland for Basie's band performances, gala social as well as musical events for the in-crowd. Dinah Washington descended the stairs, dressed to the nines, with jewels in her high-heeled shoes, greeting everyone, reminding people that she was Queen of the Blues. She inspired repartee from another singer, plump Sylvia Syms, a masterful storyteller with wonderful intonation: 'No, Dinah, I'm the Queen, and I'm not dead yet.' Dinah howled. And the Basie band celebrated itself.

Sarah Vaughan, who had sung a duet in Boston with Joe in an after-hours club on the night he first heard 'Alright, Okay, You

Win', sometimes stopped into Birdland and sang a duet with him – a precious blend, those two beautiful voices. The crowds cheered. In Joe's audiences, too, sat Dorothy Kilgallen, the anaemic-looking but sharp-witted journalist with a tiny smile; Tommy Dorsey, the trombonist, who had his eye on Ernie Wilkins to do arrangements for the Dorsey band, also showed up frequently. Lena Horne sat in the front row, 'popping her fingers', as the saying goes, encouraging Joe by calling out, 'Sing it baby, sing it baby,' and not only Joe but the rest of the audience was mesmerized by Lena's beautiful face. Watching her, Joe hit his stride. Hazel Scott called Joe 'Daddy', as did Billie Holiday. 'Daddy', Joe would say, imitating Billie's small, soft, high voice that sounded, when she talked, as if she had a champagne bubble caught in her throat. 'It sure makes a man melt when a woman calls you "Daddy" like that,' he thought. Sinatra and sloe-eyed Ava Gardner, simply dressed in a yellow silk shirt and wool skirt, ravishingly beautiful, showed up separately.

Miss Anne began a summer tradition of going to New York City to stay at the Taft Hotel, where Vincent Lopez led his orchestra. And Joe could chirp a nasal imitation at the ultra-fast speed of old Movietone newsreels, to his mother's great amusement: 'Good evening everybody, Lopez speaking.' Proudly Miss Anne and her girlfriend Carrie Johnson went nightly to Birdland to hear the 'kid'.

The band loved its two-week stays in Chicago, too. Those long engagements gave arrangers a chance to write – not something they could manage very well while constantly moving and playing. Record producers often hired studio arrangers because the bandmen, exhausted by the stop-start of the road life, were inconsistent, slow producers, despite their brilliance. Joe still didn't mind the road life; he actually enjoyed it, much preferring it to life in a domestic nest – in his case, all too often a mare's nest. His tumultuous renunions with his wife, Lemma, continued. In 1955, she had become pregnant with his son, Joe Jr, born 29 November. She had named their daughter after Joe and his mother, and now had a son named after him too. Joe thought that Lemma loved his mother and guessed that Lemma loved him, too, 'in her lucid moments.' But she didn't have many of those, he thought. He prided himself upon being a 'street animal', as he called himself, and enjoyed the movement. (Of course his idea of a good street had come to be Fifth Avenue, Savile Row, and the rue de Rivoli.) But the arrangers needed quiet rooms where they could linger and do their best work.

Basie's own arrangers knew all the band's idiosyncrasies and strengths. So a Frank Foster–Ernie Wilkins-arranged album such as *Count Basie Swings, Joe Williams Sings* was no accident. Wilkins and Foster had been able to write arrangements for that album and have Joe and the band hone the work over a long period of time. However, for another album, *Just the Blues*, Frank Foster should have had plenty of time to write during a two-week Chicago engagement. But he completed only seven of eight songs assigned to him. All were blues for Joe with the band.

Fans had interfered. Socializing happily in Chicago, Joe introduced his 'prearranger', Foster, around. 'And everyone in the band had almost a harem in Chicago,' noted Foster, who was no exception. He tried to settle down to do the writing in a hotel suite. 'But I was doing some heavy petting at the time,' he recalled. 'I'd be in the front room, writing, while a woman was waiting for me in the bedroom. It's a good thing I had a suite, or I wouldn't have gotten those seven tunes written.'

On the East Coast Teddy Reig, who produced many of the Basie albums, got the word that a tune was missing and said to Foster: 'What? We'll be the laughing stock of the whole music world!'

Foster hadn't fallen short through any disregard for Joe, whom he 'revered as a perfect singer'. They usually worked quickly to get the proper range, the proper key. Joe would give a few suggestions about the introductions, about how he wanted a song to sound, about a cadenza – details that he felt were important, and then told Foster to do what he felt. Foster simply didn't feel like doing the eighth tune. The record was done with some tracks brought in from another recording date.

In Chicago, the Basie band always played either in the Blue Note or the Civic Opera House. And Joe's mother took the opportunity to remind him of his roots. She brought pots full of food to the Blue Note, where the band played matinées, or to the Opera House. She made a ritual feast for the whole band each time it stopped in Chicago. Fried chicken, ham, collard greens, corn bread, sweet potato and apple pies: Southern cooking, soul food that the men thought of simply as food, the really good stuff. And after the rich feast, Joe took some musicians to his mother's house, on the trail of a further, seductive invitation which Miss Anne extended to Joe: 'Martini's in the fridge, darling.'

The long engagements served as mini-vacations from the gruelling tours on the road. If musicians didn't stay in hotel suites, they rented studio apartments, even houses, so they didn't have to jump up in the mornings and run out to buy breakfast. They got to know people at dances; sometimes a woman, sometimes a man and wife who invited them to dinner or for a drink. The fans became friends to call the next time the band passed through town. And people gave many parties for the Basie band.

Pretty women liked Joe, and Joe liked pretty women. They threw themselves at him, jumped into his lap backstage and left long, shimmering strands of blonde, red, brunette and black hair on the couches in his hotel rooms – 'and sometimes even nightgowns in the hotel drawers', he noted.

'It's something in the women's minds. It has nothing to do with Joe Williams,' observed one musician. 'He's a man who acts like a man.'

One young woman sitting in a theatre with him once, backstage, suddenly surprised him by saying, 'Sit there on your throne, because the woman who is going to hurt you hasn't been born. Her mother flushed her down the toilet.'

'Now that's someone who's making love to me,' he mused, feeling whipped, rather like a little boy who had been put in his place.

So he said to her, 'Oh, there's a difference between making love and being made love to. There is a difference.' And he sang the words a little, picking a few high, light notes. 'You see, making love and being made love to. Ha ha.'

'Would you like to define that difference?' the woman asked.

'I think it loses much, God, if you had to define it. The name of the game is don't try to explain it to yourself, just enjoy it. Oh, people can make love to you without stripping you and taking your clothes off.'

'Right,' the woman said.

'And taking you to bed,' he said.

'All the time,' she said.

'Oh, sure there are many ways to do that thing,' he said.

'Mmmmhmmmmm,' she said.

'You can look into each others' eyes and know that you are together, and it doesn't matter which way you go from there,' he said.

'Mmmm. Yes,' she said.

He laughed.

Frank Wess at this time gave Joe musical pointers. Wess told Joe to push the diaphragm in, so that he would come in on pitch, as opposed to being just the slightest bit out of tune flat. Sometimes, too, Joe learned, when he was sharp, he could tuck his head down to get a note out correctly. And he began to appreciate what a good, intent listener he was, how excellent his ear was, and how important it was to hear himself. The more he listened, the better he became at hearing. He could usually hear everything the instrumentalists were playing and felt very lucky that he could do that, because the music was usually going by very fast. Sometimes Joe heard himself in his mind, not objectively, and was glad that recordings let him listen, much later. The distance let him analyse his work and enjoy some good things. He bought a tape recorder, taped his performances with Basie and listened critically to himself in bed the morning after, often resolving to jettison aspects of his work which displeased him.

Basie himself never told him how to sing and simply required that all musicians stay sober. If they didn't, he said nothing but played all their features. Then they kept tripping over their own feet to the microphone to solo, in bad form. So they didn't show up drunk twice for work. Basie also liked his musicians to be healthy to do their gigs, not always the easiest assignment because of the exhilarating high life in the big cities. And sleep-time on the road was sometimes interrupted by special disaster.

One morning the band left Lyons, France by a two-engine plane 'that could hardly make it over the hill', recalled Frank Wess, to get to Lisbon, Portugal. The plane didn't make it over one of the hills and had to stop for repairs *en route*. Altogether the band was delayed for fifteen hours. By the time it arrived in Lisbon, taxis were waiting to take the men directly to the gig, with no time to eat or wash. People wanted to dance. So the band played for the opening hour and a half before anybody got a chance to give himself any care.

Joe loved to smoke gritty, unfiltered cigarettes and sometimes smoked heavily. But he cut it out whenever he thought smoking was affecting his voice. 'Once I told Basie that my throat was terrible, just awful! He told me,' Joe recalled, hunching over and imitating a pianist fingering his instrument, 'Don't tell me, kid. I play piano.' 'I got to the bottom of that,' Joe reminisced. 'He took care of his hands, and I had to take care of my voice. At first I was hurt that he didn't care. He was supposed to care. But I learned from it.'

He acquired a reputation for liking the good life – rich pastas, exotic salad dressings and sauces, creative Chinese dishes and seafood and wine. He took blind pianist George Shearing's advice literally, when Shearing said that he had to taste his way around the world because he couldn't see it. Joe decided to taste it even though he could see it. And it was primarily the rigours of the road life that kept his weight from soaring. Furthermore, he took a tennis racket along, looking for opportunities to exercise by hitting balls against theatre walls.

He regarded the men in the band as a group of people with 'very, very special human qualities, everyone in that band'. And they kept an eye on each other's humanity. And so it came about that they thought they had finally caught Joe with his humanity showing with flagrant dereliction once in London. The band was playing in a theatre in the West End that Joe had never seen before. He didn't find out in advance of the performance about how to get from the backstage to the stage. And then he couldn't find his way. Ordinarily he heard his introduction and entered from the opposite side of the stage where Basie sat at the piano. Simple etiquette, Joe recalled, always kept him from crossing in front of the leader. But this time the small stage was very crowded. Joe's usual entrance route was blocked. He had to run all the way around backstage and fumble a long time, listening to his introduction being played repeatedly, before he found his way to the bright lights. It ran through his mind: 'They're thinking: I've been delayed in a bedroom. I might not show up at all for once.' When he made it, they gave him a look that signalled: Old Slick Joe always gets it right. He had promised himself that no matter what was going on in his life, he would never miss a cue: 'Wine and women must never delay the song,' he told himself.

He tried to take care of his body, which was his total musical instrument, sleeping as much as he could between gigs. He had learned, years before he had become even a gleam in Basie's eye, that he could become sick if he were in weakened condition from too much high life. And those musicians who lived wild lives, letting the traps take their energy, were dying in their thirties, he noted.

In the US, he was placing high on the *Down Beat* polls every year, during his Basie days. In 1955, he won *Down Beat's* international critics' poll for best new male singer deserving of wider recognitions; *Down Beat's* readers' poll chose him as the best male band singer in 1955. In 1958, after Sinatra, with 2,868 votes, Joe came second with 645 as the best male vocalist. Rushing was third with 267. On the rhythm and blues charts, Joe followed Ray Charles, the leader there. *Billboard* magazine's DJ poll voted him the favourite male vocalist in 1959.* Joe was looking wonderful.

One day, Freddie Green, practising his guitar, told Joe: 'Take some and leave some,' as Joe was drooping under the weight of over-indulgence in wine and cooking. Joe instantly heard the wisdom of that advice and tried to stay alert to the point where he could guess how many people, at one glance, were in a hall, within about fifteeen people – a trick common with musicians and especially valuable if they were working for a percentage of the door admissions. Joe had learned well in

*See *Prelude* for other *Down Beat* awards won by Joe

Chicago that he couldn't be stoned, taken advantage of and survive in the music business. A tense business, yes, but he didn't have to unwind all the way. He might not get wound up again. Things did not upset him that much any more anyway. Even the reviews in England, which for several years ended with the comment that though the great Basie band had a good singer, Joe Williams, he was no Jimmy Rushing, didn't aggravate him particularly. Joe attributed the critics' taste to a fondness for traditionalism then – and let it go at that.

However, he began to feel a continuous pain in his stomach that convinced him he was terribly sick. He actually went to a doctor – not something he or anybody he had grown up with did at the drop of a hat. Stopping in Chicago for a gig, he obeyed the warning signal and visited a Dr Plummer, who told Joe: 'You have gas.'

'How exotic,' Joe laughed. And went on a diet that was not gas-producing. No raw vegetables, only chicken, fish, veal – preferably from young animals. On the bus he carried a supply of tuna fish packed in oil in cans. One day, sitting near Frank Foster, Frank Wess and Benny Powell, Joe took the lid off a can of tuna. Possibly the bus hit a bump. Anyway, the can slipped out of his hand, flew up in the air, and landed upside down on top of Joe's head. He sat there with the oil running down his face. And they were not near the rest stop.

Perhaps the greatest boon to his health happened to him on the Basie bus, too. He noticed that Freddie Green carried golf clubs with him, practised shots and went out on a course at every possible chance. Early one morning in Kansas City, Joe tagged along to the golf course, even though the Good Life According to Freddie Green, a far less sociable man, ordinarily diverged widely from Joe's concept. But Joe liked walking around behind the little ball; he liked to keep his eye on the dimples. From that time on, he, alto player Marshall Royal, Henry Snodgrass, the road manager, and Freddie Green played golf together all the time – 'and probably saved my life', Joe guessed, because he had thought that he was going to wind up like Frank Foster, 'very much like Frank Foster', succumbing to too much heavy petting in hotel rooms.

Furthermore the whole game fitted in with his comprehension of what life was all about. When he had been in a Chicago hospital, a few years earlier, a doctor had told him to give up tennis and play golf. At the time, Joe demurred, explaining that he never rushed the net anyway. And if his opponent got a great drop shot, Joe just said, 'Great shot.' But golf began to appeal, because no one else in the band played tennis, and because 'golf was never the same, and never went quite the way you wanted it to go. Though a lot of things went the way you wanted them to go or even better than you could have imagined.'

Some days he found that the game went better than other days – but it was always very humbling. He had days when it didn't even come close to what he would have liked. He could *depend* on it; he could *rely* on golf going like that. Winston Churchill said that it was a game invented by the devil and perpetrated with instruments incapable of performing the task, Joe learned. It was quite a game, really, never ending, always different. Joe liked not having to compete with anyone except for himself and the golf course. 'It's a matter of discipline and of thinking; Arnold Palmer said that golf is ninety per cent above the shoulders.' Joe liked the subtle, inner discipline.

Many times he hit the ball with no target in mind, simply out there on the course to enjoy himself and have some exercise. But he had much more fun once he began studying the game and developing a discipline so that each time he swung the club, he had a specific target in mind. He tried to get a picture in his mind of how the ball was going to look going from one place to another. Then he tried to execute the shot. And when he did that, he did enjoy the game more because he came close. And he was thrilled at being able to come close. It amused him. All he had to do was concentrate.

# 7 *Growing with Basie*

When Lemma and Joe reunited at various places, including Las Vegas, Lemma didn't like finding Joe firmly addicted to golf. She wanted him to spend more time with her. And she never learned to play golf. By 1957, the reunions were foundering badly. Joe and Lemma couldn't get along. And although Joe didn't realize it, another woman whom he met that year, a golfer who touched his life briefly for an evening in New York City, would become a much better, easier friend than he had ever had before. But he didn't want to know much about her at that time, so thoroughly had he become disillusioned about the fruits of romance. And there were so many women chasing after him, they could divert him from being serious.

It was easier for Joe to find a place to play golf in Las Vegas than to live in a hotel there. In those days, all Basie's musicians were black. And Las Vegas hotels had definite restrictions against blacks. Famous performers had their run-ins with the white bosses of Las Vegas. Nat King Cole wasn't allowed to mingle with whites in the casinos. Dinah Washington, according to people who toured with her, dressed in a trailer for black entertainers outside the Sahara. By 1957, Harry Belafonte stayed in the same suite of rooms that comedian Alan King had, without a problem, Joe observed. But the Basie band, during its intermittent engagements in Las Vegas in the fifties, did have its difficulties.

In 1957, staying at a motel on the Strip and playing in another place, the Dunes, the men noticed that their motel pool was drained as soon as they moved in. When they started checking out, the pool began filling up before their very eyes. Nevertheless, Joe threw his weight around only if hotel employees or others supposed to accommodate him didn't give him service. Then he called room service or approached whomever he had to and said, in the strongest speaking voice his bandmates ever heard him use: 'THIS IS JOE WILLIAMS. I WANT TO BE ACCOMMODATED!'

And there were directives given to the band every day, one musician remembered. Don't do this, don't do that. Don't fraternize in the coffee shop or the main dining-room. 'Not only don't fraternize, don't go,' commented Benny Powell. Whatever the men did one day, the management would try to hinder the next day. The men went where they pleased anyway, behaved with casual normalcy, and had no trouble, pushing against the directives by ignoring them.

As a child, Benny Powell had made two words of 'coloured', playing his own game to preserve his sanity. 'Colou-Red. And it became a character to me. Is anyone here Colou-Red? That must apply to them.' Later he did not want to remember that era at all. In Las Vegas, he decided, he didn't have to believe what people told him, either. And so the Basie musicians went into the coffee shop anyway to break down barriers by the sheer force of their presence. For they knew that if they listened to what people told them, they would become a part of the conspiracy. However, if they used their own imagination, sense and courage, they wouldn't have to go along with what people would do to them.

(To help avoid racial incidents, the men usually travelled in pairs. Once in Gettysburgh, Pennsylvania, two of the smaller musicians in the band were refused service in a luncheonette. Then four bigger Basie-ites, all over six feet tall, Joe, Wendell Culley, Henry Coker, and Eddie Jones, a former football player, showed up behind the two smaller men and forced the issue, flexing their muscles a bit and murmuring little nothings in the proprietor's ear about the laws of the land.)

In Las Vegas, Joe ignored the anti-fraternizing edicts, directed, he thought, most especially against any men in the band who might make a pass at a white woman coming in from Hollywood. The band didn't want to be bothered with women arriving in town with other men anyway, Joe thought. In 1959, he performed and afterwards joined singer Jackie Cain, who embraced him in the audience, and sat down with her and her husband, pianist Roy Kral, both white and enormously well-respected musicians. And Joe 'ate strawberries and cream in the coffee shop' when he pleased, he recalled.

Because the racial situation in the motel had really gotten on their nerves in 1957, Joe, Frank Wess and Benny Powell in 1959 rented a three-bedroom house in the black neighbourhood called the Dust Bowl, so called because the streets were unpaved then. On one side of the musicians lived Dr J.B. MacMillan, a dentist. And on the other side, Dr Bucky West and his wife Dotty had a house. Both doctors had pools, which the musicians swam in. 'We moved there so that we could feel comfortable and have our privacy and guests,' Frank Wess recalled. And they rented a car so that they wouldn't have to be bothered by discrimination from taxi drivers.

Joe taught Benny Powell to drive in Las Vegas. After the night's work, Joe went to play golf, from about 5 a.m. to 8 a.m. when the broiling sun came up, and the desert heat started climbing to the 110-degree mark. Woody Herman and Lionel Hampton were in town with their bands, too, and bassist Major Holley and other musicians played golf with Joe. As usual, Joe met hundreds of the most important jazz and popular musicians on the road, people he had performed with or would later sing with: a veritable Who's Who, Who Was and Who Will Be of jazz.

Since Joe had the car in the early mornings, he was asked, on the first day, to buy groceries. He arrived at the house with about $20 worth of nectarines. Benny and Frank didn't let him shop after that, even though Joe tried to impress upon them how he never needed a laxative because of all the fruit he ate.

Wess did most of the cooking – corned beef and cabbage, beans, hamburgers, steaks. Joe actually cooked a few little things, too. Exactly what, nobody can remember. Benny Powell bought a Betty Crocker cookbook with recipes for two people and later recalled the household as 'the odd couple' plus one, though he never figured out exactly who constituted the odd couple. But none of the men had much practice with domestic chores. Fortunately dancer Norma Miller and her group came to town to work and moved into a house near the men, who immediately set out to charm the women into giving cooking lessons by example. Lemma spent a few days in Las Vegas, too, that time, and did some good cooking, but it didn't help the marriage.

Jazz musicians love to gossip among themselves, but some, including Joe, have an aversion to bragging to the public about the wilder side of the troubadour's life. There is one, of course. But music is the reason for musicians getting together to have a wild life, whenever they do. And music counterbalances and outweighs the worldly pleasures for musicians who value longevity and really love the music and the financial rewards enough. Music is what kept Joe from never missing the bus. Although he was rather quiet, things did happen around him; women happened around him, and he could unbend in many ways. But music was what he lived for; he had to be heard more than felt. He couldn't taste or smell it, but he felt that music was his essence and had to come through him. It kept him whole through the changes – the different scenery, the faces he moved past quickly, the years going by. He carried photographs of his two pretty children, JoAnn and Joe Jr, in his wallet. Occasionally Lemma brought them to meet him on the road. And then he got on the bus and left because of the music. Lemma took the children back to Cincinnati.

The Basie band was a perfect vehicle for Joe personally as well as musically. Basie provided a secure salary and absolutely no hassle. Arrangers got paid for what they wrote. Basie made money with a publishing company and included Joe in a partnership. And on the bandstand, Joe loved and respected Basie enormously.

'Basie was the leader. That's who he was. He was the catalyst of the presentation, and I was just one part of it, just one of eighteen voices. That's what that was,' Joe reflected on his Basie years and his own role in the history. Some people said that Basie had been the reason for Joe Williams's sudden fame. Others said that Joe brought Basie a greater stardom. Once, when the band's path crossed Duke Ellington's, Duke put his arm around Joe and said, 'You brought all this good luck to Count Basie.' Observing from the trumpet section, Thad Jones thought that what Joe did for the Basie band and for the blues were what was really important about Joe's career. It really didn't matter who gave whom the credit. Basie had been the star first and undisputedly the mentor; then the blended artistry of the two musicians lifted them to greater heights than either had ever reached before.

'Basie was an international star when I met him,' Joe assessed.

> And in all our performances the band members would strive for their finest peak of excellence. And the most unusual thing about it was that the effort came from self-discipline among the band members, without Basie saying anything to anybody. I attribute that to the men's pride in what they were doing. And the group lived up to being the very best. That was the group collectively led by Mr Basie. If something went very well in a performance, Basie simply gave a little nod of his head as a signal that he was well pleased. The Count said that each one of the musicians was a doctor of music, and he was thrilled that they allowed him to play with them.
>
> He set the tempos. I learned about pacing from him. We'd start a four-hour dance with the Ellington tune 'What Am I Here For?' [Supposedly Count Basie liked to start with that one particularly if a hall's conditions were far from ideal.] And he would move the tempo up a little more and a little more, until the band was in full flight. Then he'd break the tempo in half, and then halve the tempo of what we had just played. I learned programming from the way he presented certain soloists. Basie, like Ellington and Jimmie Lunceford, could make puppets musically of an audience. And now it's time to have a jolly song.' Those bandleaders triggered that thought in an audience. And the audience responded to the clues by feeling that was exactly what they wanted to hear.

Offstage, Joe was in awe of Basie's temperament that allowed him to deal with all the paperwork, the paychecks, and the problems of the men in his band, with their families and individual idiosyncrasies, even blazing eccentricities. Basie was a masterful shepherd keeping musicians together over the miles. Joe never took any problems to the leader and thought that Basie may have liked him in particular, eventually coming to call him 'Number One Son', because Joe was never 'a pain in the ass'. He left Basie alone, never complained, never asked for special treatment, favours or pay advances.

Most singers are expected to have hypersensitive, even testy personalities – primarily from the fright of having no visible instruments, except for their own bodies, to place as a buffer between themselves and audiences. But Joe never exhibited that special egocentricity that normally sets singers apart from instrumentalists. He was for the most part 'one of the fellows' in the Basie band, he thought. And the instrumentalists agreed. He often sounded like a horn to them anyway. Especially in foreign countries, where neither he nor the other musicians spoke the language, they were more likely to spend time together, all equal members of the same group. Before dinner in Europe, Joe had drinks with Frank Wess, Benny Powell, Eddie Jones. Normally Basie was being shepherded around by some person from the country the band was travelling in. So Joe felt conscious of being basically one of the fellows.

Occasionally he walked a fine line between being simply another member of the band and Basie's star singing attraction. Sometimes Basie asked Joe to wake up and take an early train with him, going first class, from one city to another, while the band followed later. Once Basie and the whole band went along on a train from California to Chicago. But it was Joe who spent most of his time with Basie on that trip,

> gambling a little, not cut-throat, just passing the time away, and talking mostly about life and living it. We reminisced a little about how romantic train travel had been in the past, going from Chicago to Milwaukee, or to Cleveland, to New York or to Pittsburgh. I had known most of the waiters on the trains and loved to go to dinner in the dining-car. Train travel in the thirties and forties had made us all feel like Diamond Jim Brady.
>
> And sometimes Count Basie and I hung out together – in the Tic Toc Club in Boston. And once we went to a fabulous place in Philadelphia, where the girls came down the sides of

the stairs. Basie and I were the only two blacks in there, with all the Italians and their wives. They were honouring us and brought out the Johnny Walker Red and the Chinese food. It was the first time that I ever ate Lobster Egg Foo Young. Oh, God, it was delicious.

When they left that restaurant, walking down the street, Basie said, 'I'm getting ready to take some time off, so save yourself some money. I'm going to make some changes.'

'Any time you get ready, go ahead,' Joe said, thinking that he could easily take a couple of months off.

He wasn't wasting his money. He sent some to his family. And he held on to as much of the rest as he could. But he was grateful to Basie for watching out for him. With many subtle personal touches, Count Basie instilled self-confidence in his musicians. They felt that they had his full, paternalistic support.

One day Basie told Joe that he was 'ahead of the game'. 'Basie meant that I could call my own shots. That people might play games with each other, but he wasn't doing that; he backed me up. And when you know the boss backs you up, you don't have to play games.' Other musicians in the Basie band felt they had the same agreement with the leader. He simply never hassled them. Basie's band was a dream job.

Basie talked about music with Joe only when Joe brought up the subject of new music. 'I had to fight to do new music constantly,' he recalled. Joe wanted to do 'It's a Wonderful World' and 'Too Close for Comfort'.

Basie said, 'Oh, you don't need that stuff.'

Joe said, 'What do you mean, I don't need that stuff? We can't keep doing the same things over and over again. We need some new material, man.'

Sometimes Basie said, 'All right, go ahead and talk to Frank.'

Frank Foster did the arrangements. Then Joe went back to Basie, often the same day, and told him the band was going to do a certain song.

'And we'd work on it,' Joe recalled. 'Work out the keys, the key changes, what we were going to do with it. We'd write it down, rehearse it, and present it. And when it went down well, he would smile and nod his head. And that told me in no uncertain terms; if you really believe in something, you had better fight for it.'

Ernie Wilkins, Thad Jones, Foster, Wess and eventually Edgar Sampson usually did the arrangements for Joe – 'God, the guys that wrote for me with that band,' he recalled with his pensive, dreamy look years later.

Joe thought that Basie disliked the expense of having to pay for arrangements. Others thought that Basie wanted to keep Joe singing the blues because Basie had a blues-based band. Furthermore Joe Williams was not a romantic-looking man – at least not in Frank Wess's estimation, as Billy Eckstine, who had become world-famous for his vibrato-rich baritone, was. And so Joe was directed by Basie to stay black and blue. 'When you've got something that works, you lay with it,' Wess thought about the roaring success of Joe as a blues singer. 'Basie's a very smart man; he knows what he's doing.'

At one point, Billy Eckstine, who had become a nationally famous balladeer when Joe, still in Chicago, was dreaming of singing with strings one day, remarked: 'Here comes Joe Williams, singing the ballads and looking like the blues.' That made Joe laugh. 'Only Eckstine could have thought of a witty remark like that,' he thought. Some white audiences had no idea of the problem. Joe was, in effect, a big, black Humphrey Bogart, whose talent, masculinity and machismo animated his features, which Peter Long had thought were 'as primitive as the wind'. 'He wasn't Billy Eckstine-pretty, but not badly made, and Joe used his size to good advantage,' one of his bandmates thought. But Joe assessed himself as someone who looked better and better the later it got and thought it screamingly funny that he should ever try to get by on a pretty face. He simply didn't think he was attractive and decided that Eckstine's witticism was more or less an objective opinion. Joe shared it, when he looked in a mirror or saw himself on TV. And, to corroborate his opinion, he watched himself on many television monitors, beginning with the Jackie Gleason show and on to the shows of Garry Moore, Dinah Shore, Perry Como, and Ed Sullivan (who with his own 'Stoneface' didn't impress Joe as a raving beauty, either). Joe didn't have to worry about his image on Arthur Godfrey's radio show on CBS and simply used all the finesse he had learned broadcasting nightly in his Chicago days.

Joe woke up some days and said, 'Well, gee, it's not as bad today as it has been; it's better today. I've got a pretty good face today.' Although he knew that many women found Bogart attractive, without strikingly regular features, Joe didn't connect the concept with himself. He simply put pressure on Count Basie from time to time to do more ballads, once the band had such solid blues hits.

And the band was always swinging, in a groove that Basie knew would reach people, during one of the most colourful and exciting decades in the music business. Working conditions were so predictably wonderful that some Basie musicians occasionally felt they were being lulled to sleep, not always revved up, challenged, on the bandstand. Some instrumentalists eventually did leave the band to try to play more experimentally, express their individuality, or simply to settle down in one city, raise their families and try their luck as studio musicians, arrangers, freelancers and leaders of their own groups. Some did very well financially and were glad that they had taken the risk. 'You can't be a seventy-year-old teenager,' one encouraged himself, as he considered leaving the band. As early as 1956, *Ebony* magazine, in an interview with Joe, said that he might go out as a solo by the end of the year. He had been with Basie only for a year and a half. There was absolutely no truth to the rumour. Joe attributed it to 'the many divisive forces', which popped up from time to time and tried to get him to leave the band and break up his winning combination with Basie. 'They' liked to 'mess' with that, Joe knew. So did Basie know, and he paid no attention.

During the band years, Joe did make a couple of recordings without Basie, with Jimmy Mundy in 1957, Joe did *A Man ain't Supposed to Cry*, and *Safe, Sane and Single,* and in 1959 with the orchestra of his friend, Jimmy Jones, a Memphis-born pianist and arranger, who spent some time in Chicago before settling in New York, Joe recorded *Joe Williams Sings About You* and *That Kind of Woman* – all ballads or popular songs, including 'Candy', the tune that Nat King Cole had passed along to him in a Chicago theatre. And 'Candy' was one of his better recordings, Joe thought.

But he actually balked at the idea of leading his own group, thinking of the administrative burdens on the Count. Joe didn't give that kind of responsibility serious thought, while he was still embroiled in his third unhappy marriage. And furthermore, he was a star, having a very good time as just another working stiff – 'last of the "boy singers",' he called himself – with celebrity acclaim on one of the nicest and most admired payrolls in the music world.

# 8 *Signifying Joe Williams*

And the men in the Basie band lived a lot of those years, with their private aspirations and public successes, in the most modern bus that the country had built. They looked out through the Scenicruiser-style windows across the dry riverbeds that were filled with pebbles and boulders, dry and white in the sun, and up to the bright skies over the many mountain ranges that they passed. And there wasn't a feeling of a storm coming, because there wasn't one coming usually. So the men did something to liven up their lives. The men settled upon teasing each other and made an art of teasing, which black children call 'signifying'. With a little good signifying, you can build a legend.

Joe Williams, you will recall, dear reader, has large feet. Furthermore he has always liked to wear patent-leather shoes on stage. They catch the light and add a little glitter to the overall impression. Eventually tenor saxophonist Billy Mitchell left the Basie band with the tale that one musician spotted a pair of Joe's new patent-leather shoes atop Joe's hotel dresser and put a sail in them. Frank Wess saw it and asked: 'How many does she sleep, Joe?' That was true.

But there were apocryphal tales. Trumpeter Thad Jones suggested that Joe's feet weren't made of clay. Jones liked to tell friends about how the band was working in Scotland on a very small stage, jammed up against the edge, near the footlights. The instrumentalists could leave only a small space for a singer to stand in, near the piano, in front of the rhythm section. So Joe was told to enter from Basie's side of the stage. Joe was standing downstairs, talking to friends, when he heard

■ Joe Williams, aged three, on his velocipede (FAMILY COLLECTION)

A nineteen-year-old Joe Williams with Jimmie Noone and Maxine Johnson, Chicago, 1937 (LONNIE SIMMONS)

Joe Williams and Count Basie (POPSIE; INSTITUTE OF JAZZ STUDIES, RUTGERS UNIVERSITY)

■ With (**left to right**) Nat King Cole, Count Basie, Ella Fitzgerald, Paramount Theatre, New York, 1957 (JOE & JILLEAN WILLIAMS)

■ Collage of Joe Williams with Carmen McRae and Mort Fega, Apollo Theatre, early sixties (JOE & JILLEAN WILLIAMS)

■ A pensive Joe Williams, 1963 (RAYMOND ROSS)

■ Publicity shot for the Willard Alexander agency, 1963 (RUTGERS UNIVERSITY)

■ Joe Williams with Eddie Condon (**centre**) and bassist Milt Hinton, New York City (RAYMOND ROSS)

■ With George Avakian, jazz promoter and entrepreneur (**left**) and photographer Chuck Stewart, New York City (RAYMOND ROSS)

■ With Loree Frazier (**left**) Petula Clark and comedian George Kirby, Caesar's Palace, 1969 (CAESAR'S PALACE; JOE & JILLEAN WILLIAMS)

■ With (**left to right**) Georgie Auld, Dean Martin, Tony Martin and Nancy Sinatra, Hong Kong Bar, Century Plaza Hotel, LA (JOE & JILLEAN WILLIAMS)

■ With George Shearing, Palm Springs WAIF benefit, late sixties (JOE & JILLEAN WILLIAMS)

■ With Count Basie and Perry Como (FRANK FOSTER)

■ Joe Williams and Jimmy Rushing singing together, Newport Jazz Festival, July, 1962 (JOE ALPER; JACKIE GILSON ALPER)

■ With Count Basie, Bermuda jazz cruise, 1974 (JILL FREEDMAN)

■ With Count Basie, Meadowbrook (RUTGERS UNIVERSITY)

■ Jillean Williams, 1969

■ Joe and Jillean Williams, Newport Jazz Festival, 1967 (RAYMOND ROSS)

■ With Alan Alda during the shooting of **Moonshine War**, 1969 (MGM; JOE & JILLEAN WILLIAMS)

■ On the same set (DR MILAN SCHIJATSCHKY)

■ Clark Terry quintet on their State Department African tour (**left to right**) Charles Fox, piano; Chris Woods, sax; Dave Adams, drums; Victor Sproles, bass; Terry, trumpet; Joe Williams; two friends (CLARK TERRY)

■ Joe Williams dressed in a present on the same tour (CLARK TERRY)

■ In full flight at Basie's eightieth birthday celebration, Greenwich Village, 1983 (RAYMOND ROSS)

■ At the same venue — the 'number one son' (RAYMOND ROSS)

■ Joe Williams being interviewed, Caesar's Palace, 1981 (RAYMOND ROSS)

■ With (**left**) Buck Clayton and Harry 'Sweets' Edison, Washington Square Festival, 1983 (NANCY MILLER ELLIOTT)

his cue for 'Alright, Okay, You Win' and began running to stage left, as usual – across from the rhythm section. He had forgotten his special instructions. And there wasn't any room for him to walk between the band and the footlights. So he crushed all the footlights on his way to the spot near the piano.

And mindful that Joe liked to sing ballads as well as the blues, saxophonist and arranger Frank Foster had his favourite tale (Apocryphal Tale No. 2) about Joe, too. (There must be something about horns.) Joe wanted to sing ballads so intensely that, one night, to evoke the atmosphere of a torch singer in a little café, he decided to go through a particular scenario. He tried to jump up on the piano and missed it. He tried a second time and failed. When he missed on the third jump, everyone in the band started quaking with laughter. The horn players had trouble holding on to their mouthpieces. Joe gave up and sang the song standing up. 'That's how bad he wanted to sing ballads,' recalled Frank Foster.

Actually Joe did start backing up towards the piano a little when he went out on his own as a solo by 1961. But not before. And as the stories began coming to this attention, seeping out for publication, he became convulsed with laughter. As far as he knew, only Helen Morgan had ever sat on a piano to emote. 'Can you imagine me jumping up on Basie's piano?' Joe commented about Apocryphal Tale No. 2.

It wasn't that Joe tried to hide his large feet – or anything else. He had listened to drummer Papa Jo Jones, who said that a performer should never try to show just his good side to the audience but should share his whole presence and establish a rapport. And Joe did insist upon singing ballads, not just the blues. Many people advised him that, if he put his mind totally on the blues, he could outstrip the great blues singer, B.B. King. But Joe didn't want to do it, he didn't want to do it. So he was teased about setting his sights upon becoming a broad-ranging American entertainer. (Eventually Benny Powell saw the wisdom of Joe's drive – as did hundreds of other musicians: 'If he had listened to other people and said, "I'll be a blues singer," he might have made that route work for him, or it might have led to a wall that he would have run into after a while. I much prefer to see the route he took, because he'll go down in history as one of the truly great American artists with no limitations,' said Benny Powell long after they left the Basie band.)

But for years, musicians passed the little Williams stories around among themselves. And as often happens, many people, when their doubts arose about the veracity of tales, supposed that a grain of truth lurked in them. If Joe minded the signifying, he didn't ever show it. After all, he had had a lot of fun in a lot of ways, and he had had relatively few vices to work with.

'Missed on the third jump, later for that,' he said to himself and howled with laughter. 'Well, as blasé as those musicians are and as much as they've seen and as seriously as they take music and life and as difficult as it has been. Well, if they say it's so that I jumped up on Basie's piano, then . . . well, it's marvellous that I can crack them up and make them envision something like that about me. Then, yes, it's true, let them say that about me, the hell with it.' He threw back his head and belted out a long, whooping laugh.

And that's how he dealt with being a signifyee in a big-band family and thereafter.

# 9 *Jillean*

It had been a milestone, Basie's was the first black band to play in the Starlight Roof of the Waldorf-Astoria, for four weeks in August, 1957. Sarah Vaughan sang ballads with Basie for that engagement, while Joe followed a Basie directive to sing the blues. Sarah had her trio with her, too: Jimmy Jones on piano, Richard Davis, a strong, accomplished bassist, and little Roy Haynes, a fast, impish drummer, who sometimes wore attention-getting, beautifully tailored clothes. 'Walking in high cotton,'* Joe joked to himself about Sarah's trio, thrilled with the swells and crests of her voice, the blare of the Basie brass. The glamour of all that talent inspired Joe. And the audience was awed by his smooth and rousing performances and all the entertainers electrifying the nights.

One night a trio of English people in the Starlight Roof invited Count Basie to their table. He accepted a cup of coffee from his hosts, a retired naval officer, who had been stationed in Norfolk for two years, and his wife, and a blonde woman with fine features. The British said that they had previously been to the Embers, a dimly-lit 52nd Street supper club, where they had eaten wonderful roast beef and heard Britain's own George Shearing playing piano on the platform there. They had come to the Waldorf for a few drinks and the great Basie band. The music had been so fine that they wanted to hear more.

* Since picking cotton was back-breaking work in the days before automation, people preferred to work in the plants that grew high. The phrase devloped: walking in high cotton, meaning that things were in pretty good shape, even first-class. Here Joe meant Sarah's trio consisted of excellent musicians.

Where did Count Basie suggest that they go? 'Birdland,' he said.

Basie's band members were staying at the Waldorf, too. After that night's performance, Joe Williams was leaving through a revolving door on the Park Avenue side, the main entrance with a canopy and a doorman in livery hailing cabs and holding limousine doors for suntanned women wearing fashionable blouson and A-line, hip-hugging dresses. But Joe forgot something in his room, turned back from the street and went through the revolving door again. In another compartment, pushing out, was the pretty, short, brightly blonde woman with fine features who had just drunk coffee with Basie. As she whirled past Joe, she said, 'Ah, wow, that's Joe Williams.' So she pushed all the way around, too.

In the lobby, the retired naval officer and his wife shouted: 'Oh, Joe Williams!' Not that they actually knew him, but the night had been so exciting. The pretty blonde watched them collar Joe and introduce themselves, as she approached. And he was turning to walk away, when she reached him. The officer introduced her, Jillean (Milne) Hughes-D'Aeth (pronounced Daith); she had an exquisite figure, pale-green eyes filled with light, and a slight smile playing around her mouth all the time.

'Three English people out on the town for a last fling,' Jillean summed up the spirit of the group. The officer and his wife, friends of her father, Andrew Milne, were heading back to London the next day. Jillean would follow in a few months. For the moment, she was working in the New York office of a British management consulting firm, Mead Carney, in Rockerfeller Center. Mr Carney was a friend of Jillean's father, a well-known figure in London's advertising circles, head of a national advertising association, and publisher of an influential trade publication, *Draper's Record.* A popular speaker at public dinners, where he often received awards, he had a deep, resonant voice and a big laugh – 'one of those all-enveloping characters with warmth', recalled one of Jillean's cousins. Through her father's friendship with Mr Carney, Jillean first applied to work for Mead Carney in the London office, then transferred to New York City. Jillean, as her father did, had a knack for greeting people naturally and warmly.

One thing pleasantly led to another in the cavernous Waldorf lobby with the massive carpet. When the officer said they were going to Birdland at Basie's suggestion, Joe gave them an easy smile: 'May I show you the way?' He and Marshall Royal from the Basie band were going there anyway. And Jillean's eyes were full of light, Joe noted, along with the brightness of her hair. She had a soft, musical voice with an underplayed British accent, a marvellously rounded little British woman all alone in New York City.

Jillean had never called herself a jazz fan. She had always liked music, big bands, some groups and singers, piano players, George Shearing. And an English cousin recalled that her favourite musician in England had been a West Indian pianist and supper club singer, Leslie Hutchinson, known as Hutch – an entertainer with a society following. In America, Jillean found a goldmine of records and even sent some to her teenage cousin, Andrew Heath, studying economics and languages in the north of England. Andrew was trying to build a record collection of traditional early jazz. Jillean didn't know or care if you called her favourite music jazz or not. She would never come to like avant-garde jazz; it would make her white-knucked to have to listen to it. But if Basie's band played jazz, she knew, she loved it.

Joe had his camera with him in the taxi, so Jillean learned right away that he was a camera buff. She also quickly discovered that he liked to play golf as much as she did. Since her father played, she had learned the game early. She played so well that she had even been suggested as an entrant in the British Curtis Cup tournament to play against some American women golfers. But Jillean hadn't wanted to get into that kind of competition. Joe said that he was extremely impressed. At Birdland's door, she was startled and enchanted by the tiny host in a tuxedo with a high-pitched, childlike but tough-drawled shout, Peewee Marquette; he greeted Joe and let the British enter without a word. And Joe imitated Peewee's screech and made Jillean laugh, as they sat at one of the small, dark tables, listening to the exciting music on the distant, bright bandstand. Jillean said, 'We should play golf together some time.' Joe said, 'That would be very nice.' But he said to himself, 'There's a nice girl. Who needs it?'

After the show, he put the British in a taxi, waved 'goodbye', and didn't telephone Jillean. She didn't go back to the Waldorf again during that engagement and was vaguely disappointed that he hadn't called. There had been a sort of message between them. She knew he liked her as well as she liked him. So she wondered.

But she didn't wonder enough to call Joe. Instead, she bought a bus ticket for a couple weeks' vacation and toured the Western US – Los Angeles, Denver, Las Vegas, where she stayed at the Riviera Hotel on the Strip. Las Vegas, then still a relatively small, desert town ringed by pastel-coloured mountains, became her favourite place. She watched the sun come up over Sunrise mountain and also saw it reflect the setting sun in the evening. She liked the thatched wooden roofs of the houses – such impractical fire hazards and so picturesque. A taxi driver charmed by her accent gave her a royal tour. By then she was more in love with Las Vegas than Joe Williams. And when her vacation finished, she went back to work in London again.

In November, however, she noticed an advertisement that the Basie band would do a command performance for the Queen at the Palladium. Command performances always took place there in those days. Joe, who was dressed and present in the wings, never sang, because the Basie band was asked to do only three instrumental numbers, 'April in Paris', and 'Old Man River' featuring a solo by Sonny Payne, and one other. Judy Garland and Mario Lanza represented the US as singers. Jillean wrote a note and sent it backstage to Joe. He tucked it in his pocket and watched the performance from the wings, excited by the spectacle of the Queen in the royal box and all the elegant people in the audience clapping in the European way, with that loose, easy rhythm of a dixieland band. Judy Garland came offstage and hugged him, saying, 'Isn't it exciting? They just don't understand how exciting it is!'

And somehow, trying to keep his clothes orderly while he was travelling, Joe sent his dinner jacket to be cleaned; the suit came back without Jillean's phone number. When the band left town, without Joe having called, Jillean thought, 'Well, it's one of those things. I'll never see him again. But wasn't it fun?' Still, she had been perturbed that he hadn't reacted to the note.

It wasn't until the freezing-cold January of 1959 that they met again. The Basie band was working in a relatively small hall in Newcastle-on-Tyne in the north of England. A musician's union ban that had kept most American musicians out of England had ended. And Jillean's cousin, Andrew Heath, attending Durham University nearby, continued to be a great jazz fan, thrilled that the embargo on American musicians had ended. He went to see the Basie band and, for once forearmed with the knowledge that Joe had met Jillean, decided to use that meeting to open a conversation. Joe came down the stairs backstage after the show. Andrew said that he was Jillean's cousin. Did Joe remember her? Joe said, 'Why, sure, I remember Jill and her pretty blonde loveliness. Easy.' Andrew, stunned, told Joe that Jill and Andrew's sister, Adrienne, nicknamed Liz, were going to sit in the front row when the Basie band played in a Southampton hall in a few days. And the women went backstage to say 'hello'.

'That was a really exciting evening,' Jillean recalled years later.

'We had drinks and went to Liz's house,' Joe recalled, 'then they left the ladies, as the band moved on to work in Paris for awhile. Jillean and Liz decided to follow the band, playing their own arrangement by ear. 'And when I looked up from the stage, there they were, seated in the Paris club.' Wendell Culley befriended Liz and took her for walks in the early mornings along the Seine. 'Then we got on the train, and all of us went to Belgium,' Joe recalled. Jillean had socialized with show people before, had even lived in a house with an actor and his wife for a while in London. But Liz had not. She had become especially friendly with Sonny Payne and thought she was very daring, travelling around Europe with a bandful of strangers. In Brussels, the band and the Englishwomen celebrated Eddie Jones's birthday by walking through the streets, singing 'Happy Birthday' in the afternoon, until they came to a good restaurant, where they ate dinner. Because Liz had dark hair, Count Basie teased her that she wasn't really Jillean's cousin, was she? And Liz liked Basie so much at the time. Then everybody went to Amsterdam, to the Hague, and back to

Amsterdam again, from which the Basie band was scheduled to take a plane to the US.

'And when we left Amsterdam,' Joe recalled, 'suddenly something happened that had never happened before. I was the last one of our group to get on the plane, which was leaving for the States. I stopped and put two dozen roses in Jillean's arms. She was standing on the field, behind the fence. Then I got on the plane. All the fellows stood up and applauded. Jive mothers. And I found myself in Hollywood calling London.'

But there was no answer at Jillean's house in Chelsea, where she was living with two room-mates. Joe kept trying the number every time he could get to a phone. Starlets and other pretty women in his audiences came backstage in the club where he was playing with Basie and tried blocking Joe's pathway to the phones. He kept calling her at every stop along the way between Hollywood and Des Moines, Iowa.

Jillean was very impressed:

> because at that time, I hardly knew where Iowa was. In Amsterdam, it had all been very exciting; I knew that I was in love with him for the moment. It's hard to explain why you fall in love with somebody or why you find somebody more exciting than another. It's just a thing you both know. This person is special. This is going to be exciting.
>
> What I liked about him was that he was much quieter and more dignified than most people I had met in that sort of world. He also wasn't the sort of person who expected you to rush into bed on the first date. And that I found very intriguing. That I liked. When you're single, sometimes people do push right away. I didn't like that. But he was very laid back. And that was attractive to me. He didn't force himself.
>
> I'm laid back in that sort of way. I'm very cool to start with. I don't mean cold. I mean cool: I try not to worry about things too much. And when they left Europe and he gave me the roses, I really had no idea that there would ever be a future. It just didn't cross my mind that this could go on. I thought, well, I'll see them next time they come back to Europe.

But when spring came, Jillean and Joe had a particular stroke of luck. Mr Carney asked her to work in the New York office again for a while. Although she hadn't asked for the assignment, she was very enthusiastic. 'It just fell in my lap. I couldn't believe that I was lucky enough to be sent twice. I was thrilled to bits.'

Jillean's mother, Anna, had died a few years earlier of heart disease, and Jillean's father had no idea that Jillean had become a friend of Joe Williams, a black American music celebrity. It was 1959, at about the time when the US Census first began keeping records of the small number of inter-racial marriages. Before 1950, they were still illegal in some states. In Britain, Andrew Milne had never known any black people well, as far as Jillean knew. He wasn't a particular fan of music, black jazz or any other kind of music. Only Jillean and her mother's side of the family, which included her cousin Andrew Heath, loved music. England had its Indian and West Indian populations. And the British had their own set of racial barriers and class lines that Andrew Milne had probably never crossed.

Andrew Heath, about seventeen years younger than Jillean, raised more humbly than she, in the south of London, was fascinated by her gregarious nature, her conservative, country-tweedy taste in clothes that always looked soignée, her fine features, her pretty, short blonde hair – in essence, her aura of worldliness. All the flash was in her subtlety, good manners, and a lovely, musical voice. Jillean lived in Northwood, Middlesex, a glamorous suburb in those days, north of London, in a one-storey bungalow with a long garden and a rolling lawn that resembled a golf course. The grounds sported a pond, an orchard and pink, red and rose-coloured flowers.

Jillean's mother had been the only daughter in her family of nine surviving children to marry successfully. Anna Milne's six unmarried sisters, four of whom had never married, made a fuss over Jillean and liked to help raise her. But she was too plucky to sit still and have anyone serve her. Once she gave Andrew a ride in her car from her house to his, about the distance from Rye, New York to Brooklyn, at a time when people didn't travel much in England. Andrew thought it was an especially nice thing for anyone to do for a kid. Most people would have let him take the train or any other device he liked. But Jill was enterprising, to Andrew's mind, and 'a natural, true English rose', less burdened with a consciousness of class and tradition than some other people. And he observed her as 'a nicely educated sophisticate', who went off into the world with glamorous jobs, while he spent his adolescence beating up other boys on a rugby field in a British public school. His accomplishments seemed dull to him in comparison with Jill's panache.

Born in 1921, she was fourteen years older than Andrew's sister, Liz, and only three years younger than Joe Williams. Jillean's parents took her to sports events and plays, which she loved. She thought of her parents as reasonably protective and very generous about her education. She considered her childhood to have been very ordinary, with happy parents, who, though not very rich, never had to struggle for money. An only child as Joe had been, she made a lot of friends and kept them all her life.

'Liz Darcy, Joan Chaumeton', Joe could recall the names of the women who had been Jillean's room-mates in Chelsea in 1959, because they remained good friends. 'We still hang out together, on both continents, to this day.'

During World War II, Jillean served as a WAAF for four and a half years, then worked in various secretarial jobs for the British Broadcasting Corporation. And she went to sea with her most interesting job, with the 'P & O', the Peninsula Oriental Steam and Navigation Company. In 1947, it began sending women to sea as stenographers. Jillean went out with the second ship that carried women aboard, travelling from London to Australia twice. Aboard, she met an officer, Michael Hughes-D'Aeth.

The romance aboard a self-contained ship blinded her. So she married him and had a fine wedding party, with an arch of crossed swords, and an actress friend as a bridesmaid, at her family's house. Her husband was 'an absolutely charming person', Jillean thought, and she was sure 'he would always be, but he just was absolutely not right for her', she told people. The couple began drifting apart practically from the moment they got off the ship. 'So that was all a grave error,' she thought pretty quickly, never castigating the man, but, with her usual approach, looking for solutions, not more problems. And in this case, divorce was the only solution that occurred to her. She never mentioned any intimate details about her first marriage to anyone, not even to Joe, about why Hughes-D'Aeth was not right for her.

Following British law, the couple lived apart for three years and showed no interest in reconciling, to qualify for a divorce. Legally Jillean was married from 1948 to 1956, but separated after 1953. Shortly after her separation, her cousin Andrew recalled Jillean asking him at what age he thought a person began to grow old. Andrew answered, 'Thirty-three.' Then he guessed that she must have been about that age at the time. She said nothing, probably thought nothing, either, Andrew guessed. She tended to take people at their word, straightforwardly, 'and usually ended up to be correct about them', he noted, while he was growing up to have the more cynical turn of mind that would lead him to become a journalist. Not long after her divorce, she had been sent to the US for the first time.

When she returned to New York in June, 1959, she and Joe began seeing each other every day. 'We used to meet for lunch in the Waldorf,' Joe recalled. 'I'd have tuna salad, good tuna salad over there at the Waldorf. And it was too late then, I guess. And that was it.'

# 10 Time to Leave Home Again

The Alvin Hotel stood on the corner of 52nd Street and Broadway, shopworn but lively, with advertisements and fire escapes all over the façade. Inside, the hotel had a small lobby; each floor had several sets of fire doors. The Colony Record Store was housed on the ground floor. And some people recall that the lower floors had transient rooms to serve the purposes of hookers working in the area, while show-business people rented the upper floors. For them, the Alvin was *the* hotel with everything, because it stood a couple of paces from Tin Pan Alley, the building famous for its music publishing tenants. And the Alvin had a special, bustling ambience. Joe saw one teenage girl wearing long, Shirley Temple-style banana curls and her 'mama' who kept rushing to auditions. Songwriters plunked out their tunes on upright pianos or guitars in their rooms. Hornplayers practised, filling the corridors with pretty melodies. Joe watched several child-actors, dancers and singers growing up in the Alvin. Coaches rushed from their rooms to teach acting, speech, ballet, tap dancing, and music in offices and studios around the corner from the hotel.

On the street, too, Joe often heard music, when the studios had their windows open. He could walk across the street from the Alvin and down the steps into Birdland. If he walked two blocks uptown to 54th Street, eventually to become Manhattan's official Swing Street, he found the Palladium Ballroom. The neighbourhood was still swinging with jazz musicians even though the jazz clubs had closed. He could always find friends walking around. So the Alvin Hotel made a perfect headquarters for him when he came 'home' to New York City.

People constantly milled through his life, such a public life, and the more exposure to his fans and other musicians, the better for his career. He liked the movement and the people always around and did his share of milling, too, always climbing on and off the bus, the plane, the train, even though it meant leaving Jillean behind for a while. And privacy was a luxury that he could not afford and didn't want anyway, even though by 1959, he could afford some luxuries.

On a decent salary, with a share in Basie's music publishing company, Joe wasn't pinching pennies any more and would probably never have to again, because he did rely upon the advice of a 'wise, old man' in a childhood homily: 'The time to save your money is when you're earning it.' And he wondered if he could ever parlay his assets into genuine affluence, with monumental deductions. The whole aura of his life made him look as if he were fabulously rich. In 1959, the Basie band went back into Waldorf's Starlight Roof, where the crystal gleamed, catching the light, and the musicians and their brass glowed, as if ignited by some mystical sense that let them play such exciting music. Surely they must be handsomely paid, audiences might think simply from looking at the bills that the waiters gave them.

Joe, dressed in a perfectly tailored Basie band uniform, choreographed his own stage movements; he sat behind Basie's piano, close to the bassist and drummer, to develop good rapport with them. Previously with other bands, Joe had sat in front of the band, as 'boy' singers had traditionally done; showpieces, a little remote from the instrumentalists. Now Joe's technique was honed by his own instincts, so he could take his cues from the audience and the musicians simultaneously. And he shone with the vibrant power of his own talent, as if he had been designed to enhance the panache of his lavish surroundings, and vice versa. With his aura – his voice, his tall, rugged body and his big, bright-eyed face, he could dominate a room.

Ella Fitzgerald stepped in to play with the Basie band for the first two weeks of the Waldorf engagement and with Joe created a frothy scat tune, 'Party Blues'. She also sang 'Too Close for Comfort' and 'April in Paris', while Joe did his 'signature' blues, 'Every Day'. And afterwards, audiences sent for Joe to join them at their tables, or went backstage to get his autograph. Very beautiful women in stiletto-heeled, pointy-toed shoes, racy in their low-cut dresses and glittery nylon stockings, suggested to Joe that he could put his autograph any place on them that he liked. And at the tables, Joe sometimes saw the totals of the bills and recalled an anecdote he had heard about 'Prez', Lester Young, who had gone to the Lincoln Hotel in the forties to hear the Basie band. 'Prez, who had a whimsical sense of humour, was with his wife, whom he called his 'pound cake'. He picked up a bill from a table and said, 'Oh, baby, chandeliers.' And that's how it is at the Waldorf, Joe thought.

After two weeks, Ella Fitzgerald left the band; Sally Blair and the Hi-Los stepped in. And Joe felt excited, working with the Hi-Los, too, one of his favourite vocal jazz groups, popular at the time. All the money that he watched pass from the hands of the patrons to the Waldorf staff, Joe thought, had to do with the great music, the split-second timing of the practised and passionate musicians, who made glamour palpable in sound. It was his immersion in that music, he knew, that made audiences think he was glamour personified.

Jillean still thought he was much quieter and more dignified than most people she had met in his world. But she often found herself smiling gamely at the awesome number of people trooping through his life. So noticeably refined, and at ease with American informality, she was hardly the sort to try to outshout the stage-wise business people, musicians, actors, entertainers and noisesome fans. She also had trouble, when she went along to clubs, seeing women fling their arms around Joe's neck and kiss him. She didn't particularly like smoke-filled clubs anyway and could contentedly stay away from them to avoid looking at scenes she found distasteful. In effect, she decided to act like an ostrich and put her head in the ground. She expected problems. But whenever she took her head out of the ground, she didn't find any. Joe had no difficulty whatsoever peeling strange arms away from his neck. 'Joe keeps coming home,' she noted. And that was 'super'. She felt happy and secure with him, thankful she wasn't in her twenties; she doubted that she could have withstood the pressure, if she had been very young.

In clubs she saw that Joe concentrated on his music, his performance, his audience as an entity and didn't pay attention to her in his usual, low-key way. And she knew that she must neither resent his absorption in the music nor the adulation of the crowds. She was happiest when she stayed away from the limelight, leaving him at centrestage. And they put a great deal of energy into working out a good *modus vivendi* for their private life. Joe's career was his career – paramount. Without it, he knew he would be emotionally lost – and poor. But Jillean was the most pleasant companion in the world, he thought. And they agreed that she was always free to come back to him, and he to her, accepting each other as they were. And they had a deep, friendly concern for each other's welfare. The moral of the story, as Joe assessed their love-and-let-live arrangement, was 'You don't fuck with love.' Jillean and Joe played the relationship by ear, the way Joe had become expert at with his career. It turned out that Jillean had a great ear, too, in her own way.

She spent her days with a male co-worker in the Rockerfeller Center office of Mead Carney and her nights at various residences. She tried to get back into a no-frills, economical hostel, where she had stayed during her first visit to New York City. But she wasn't accepted in 1959, because she had just passed the age limit for residents. She felt very ancient and disappointed – and moved into the Barbizon Hotel for Women for a while, then a Y. None of those places satisfied her. But she pressed on, rewarded by the adventure of the rest of her life. Often she found herself on the Basie bus, going to Boston with the band, eating tuna fish out of a can and drinking champagne out of a paper cup. On her own, she returned to New York City at about four o'clock in the morning, slept for an hour, took a bath and rushed to the office. At lunchtime, she had a fine view of a statue of a golden Prometheus Unbound, who had stolen fire from the gods, presiding over the Rockerfeller Center skating rink. And she could stand the pace; she liked it. Joe Williams was very glad that she liked it. And life in New York City for a pretty, little Englishwoman, whom Joe Williams liked better than almost anybody else in the world, had its definite compensations.

Jillean sent her cousin Andrew Heath a present, an album of love songs, *Joe Williams Sings about You,* that Joe had made with Jimmy Jones, a pianist who played with Sarah's trio, as leader and arranger. Jillean also sent a note to Andrew: 'Joe said you wouldn't like this. He was sure it wasn't your cup of tea. However I insisted upon sending it, because I know you'll like the accompaniment. And Joe will have a devastating effect on your girlfriends!' She added that she had been in the studio, when Joe recorded the album, looking at her. Andrew actually loved the record, because it was filled with love songs to someone else and not serenades of self-love, as he found so odious in the rising tide of rock lyrics. Furthermore, Joe had a beautiful voice. Even though Andrew preferred jazz from an earlier era, he also thought *Joe Williams Sings, Count Basie Swings,* which Jill sent, too, was as good as jazz could get.

After Joe finished singing 'Here's to My Lady', looking at Jillean in the recording booth, the band took a break. And Jillean, who had been gazing at Joe, put on her coat. 'It's time to go, isn't it?' she said. 'No,' he said. 'Aren't you ready?' she said, 'I thought we could go home right now.' He smiled. 'Wait a bit,' he said. 'We'll be through soon.' Reluctantly, she took off her coat; reluctantly, he helped her.

Afterwards, they went directly back to his room at the Alvin, where she told him, 'Sound your "a", darling,' which made them laugh hilariously. And as they lay in each other's arms, she said coyly, 'I just needed some human warmth.'

When he went on the road, he noticed, she took some money out of her account, which she had built up with Mead Carney paychecks, and flew to meet him in other cities. She stayed with him in all kinds of hotels, taking the pretty along with the seedy. He was absolutely thrilled that Jillean kept showing up for some of his engagements at a considerable distance from New York. She had already come a long way from London to see him. And 'here's a woman who flies to anywhere I am with her own money', he thought, looking for her little blonde head in audiences.

And a makeshift routine endured as their lifestyle for the last half of 1959 and into 1960. They had separate hotel residences in New York City, with dim light, scanty furniture and no kitchens as the setting for their love affair. Once, when Joe was studying some sheet music, Jillean cleared her throat. Joe, absorbing the sound as a signal, suddenly looked up and decided it was a cue to make love to her. After that, happy with her secret signal, Jillean cleared her throat quite often. Joe told Jillean to keep clearing her throat. And Jillean was very happy with the musician who could, by turns, become remote, both by necessity going on the road and by temperament exercising a great need for *lebensraum;* he loved being out on the scene, working, partying, with friends, and then sought her embrace for passion, love and sharing. They loved touching each other and hurried to be together.

When she couldn't follow, Jillean found a great deal to do and people to see. In England, friends had told her to call Leslie Beresford, an Englishwoman working in New York City, too. Jillean and Leslie, a blue-eyed redhead, spent a lot of time together. Both had beautiful figures and pretty faces that drew looks in restaurants, where they went to eat and gossip about Joe Williams and the men that Leslie was meeting.

On the Basie bus without Jillean, Joe passed along the message to Benny Powell that a musician should never do everything that he knows right away in a performance. Always save something, a little bit, for the next song, set or encore, Joe told Benny. Don't give it all up, because then you won't have anything left to say. If you have a ninety-minute performance coming up, prepare enough to play for 180 minutes. Then you can select what you feel like doing from your bag of tricks. And if you're well-prepared, well-rehearsed and well-stocked with material, you can work with confidence and cockiness. Your audience will appreciate you enormously, sensing that you still have more to offer. Count Basie had taught him this lesson, Joe said.

Whenever he went back to New York City, Jillean was happy to see him, golden-haired, cuddly – and essentially, as he was, homeless – still living out of a suitcase. They needed a place to live. It was unfashionable for couples to live together at the time. But in May 1960, Joe was still legally married to Lemma. And there was nothing else to be done about that unsettled matter, he felt, because of financial discussions going on and the welfare of his two children, Joe Jr not quite five, and JoAnn, only seven. Jillean and Joe found an apartment at Central Park West and 106th Street and moved in for a while, becoming the Williamses to their friends.

Then Althea Gibson, the tennis champion, moved out of her corner apartment in the same building. Joe and Jillean moved in and had a broad view of Central Park. 'Super,' Jillean said. 'Yeah, super,' Joe said, beginning to pick up a few of her expressions; at the same time, when she thought of the future, it appeared to be shaping up as one gig after another.

Their living-room ceiling had big, black streaks across it, because Althea had practised her serve in that room, constantly scraping the overhead paint with her racket. Joe decided not to have the streaks painted over. He liked them. They fascinated guests, too, good for at least ten minutes of cocktail conversation, Bruce Cooper, a talent co-ordinator for the Johnny Carson show and a frequent guest at Joe's apartment, noticed. Joe loved the place, too, because it had two bedrooms and two bathrooms, one for each of them, and a lot of space for his 'a' to resound in. He thought it was absolutely essential for a husband and wife to have private bathrooms; they ensured a bit of privacy, the secret of success in any marriage.

And with perfect eyesight, he could see from any distance the alluring cleavage of the dainty Englishwoman, who was so perfectly shaped and ample in places and exactly where he wanted her to be – near him or waiting for him at home or hurrying back to be with him, if he were heading for home. It didn't get better than that, he thought.

Songwriter and publisher Marvin Fisher, one of the Williamses' friends, helped the couple settle in. Fisher took Joe to Sam Goody's store, outfitted him with stereo equipment, then hooked it up for Joe. And Jillean amused herself with the stereo and the apartment, turning it into a home when Joe was away with the band.

Staying in touch with old friends and easily attracting new ones, especially her confidante Leslie Beresford, Jillean made plans to meet them and wrote to them at holidays or whenever something came up that she thought would interest them. Even though she owned no pets in New York City, she joined several be-kind-to-animal groups. She had always rescued stray dogs, fed stray cats and put out seed for the birds. She rather missed owning animals and living in the sort of environment that they thrived in. Not having animals, she began toying with cameras. It might be nice to get into photography, she mused a little.

Every now and then she still dipped into her savings to fly to meet Joe at an out-of-town engagement. The rendezvous were romantic, recharging their love affair – 'just two only children, mother, father, sister, brother, lover and friend to each other', Joe said, telling Jillean how close he felt to her. And they made a pretty pair, the small blonde woman trailing after the strapping black man.

Sometimes, when he was away, Jillean drove across the country, occasionally alone or with Leslie Beresford, two lovely English girls with lilting voices and beautiful figures – and Leslie decidedly built 'like a brick shipyard', as Joe described Leslie to Jillean, approving of Jillean's taste in girlfriends.

One time Jillean drove through the South alone, where she discovered that her English accent was very popular and attracted a lot of attention. 'How lovely,' people said, trying to engage her in conversations. Southerners were, in short, welcoming, gracious and hospitable in hotels and restaurants. They said, 'Ya'll come back now, you hear.' At the same time she found it unbearable to see blacks and whites kept separate. She thought: 'How hypocritical, because if you knew that I lived in New York City and was married to Joe Williams, you wouldn't let me into the hotel in the first place probably. But you don't know. You don't take me for myself; you take me for my situation.' While she had never really thought about the race difference between Joe and herself, she knew very well that it could cause a great deal of trouble in some areas. She felt so terribly aggravated by some incidents that she decided never to visit places where she and Joe as a couple would face difficulties.

Her courage in facing bigotry came from her not thinking about it. surely not in terms of having courage to combat anybody else's feelings openly. She considered only whether she and Joe would make it together. He joked to himself, 'I married three coloured girls, and nobody ever said anything to me about marrying them. So why should anybody say anything about my marrying Jillean?' The only reason he could think of that a black man would hesitate to marry a white woman was fear of whether he could find acceptance with blacks as well as whites. Ultimately the decision was personal, and one had to realize that nobody cared what you did, really, except for yourself. And if you cared, you took it from there.

Neither told friends that they weren't legally married. Everybody assumed that they were married, Jillean assumed. And whether legally married or not, she remained perturbed: only about the many temptations Joe faced, as he travelled. No legality or lack of it came equipped to deal with that bothersome situation, she thought. But Joe kept coming home. And she was very happy for him that his career was going so well. Joe told a friend that Lemma, his legal wife, would be very surprised by his success. She had been sure that he would never amount to much, she had actually told him. Jillean would never dream of such a thing. At the same time Jillean stated proudly to a friend that she had always thought Joe was an exceptionally exciting performer and singer, totally deserving of all success. He could sing anything: jazz, blues, ballads, 'Palm Court songs', by which she meant unusual standards, such as 'Miss Otis Regrets', and even opera if he wanted to.

But with the Basie band Joe was constrained by the limitations of the Basie repertoire and by the closing days of 1960, if not exactly surfeited with all he had learned from Basie, Joe felt that he didn't want to give over all his gifts and ambitions and throw in his lot with the Basie band for ever.

One day, he was chatting with the Count's manager Alexander; he was annoyed with an artist who wasn't showing up for $2,500 engagements.

Joe said, 'Am I a bigger attraction?'

'Of course,' said Alexander.

'Well, I'd show up. And I'm only getting $50 a night,' Joe said.

Alexander nodded.

Joe thought instantly, 'I'm out. I think I just got out of the scratching and fighting, the morass. Ignition, control, orbit, and all the planning comes to fruition.'

So he thought that he would work hard, plan well, and make more money as a solo artist than he could ever earn as a bandsinger. He knew he could make any group swing, and the people would pay to hear him. He wanted to challenge himself musically, call all the shots, select all the music. 'When one grows up, it's time to leave home,' he thought. Jillean stood securely in his corner, wherever that was – at least for then; he knew. Joe took Count Basie aside to have a diplomatic chat about the future.

Basie didn't argue and actually sat down to help plan Joe's strategy, so that later, overridingly, Joe would recall in a musing tone, 'What a beautiful man, Count Basie, Count Basie.' First they called Willard Alexander and started to set up bookings. Trumpeter Harry 'Sweets' Edison, who had played with Basie's band, led his own quintet, with tenorman Jimmy Forrest, alternate bassists Ike Isaacs and Tommy Potter, and drummer Clarence Johnston, and varied pianists – Sir Charles Thompson among them, and Jimmy Jones to start out. Alexander put them on Joe's payroll, with a valet, to play as Joe's group. As 1960 came to a close, the list of bookings grew, six months and many miles long, covering a territory from Boston to Toronto to California.

On 12 January, after the last note on the last night of the Basie band's January 1961 engagement at the Apollo Theatre, Joe and the Count, who had never even shaken hands, embraced on the bandstand. Basie hugged slender trumpeter Joe Newman, too, who was leaving the band that night. The next day Joe was officially off Basie's personnel list, scheduled to go to the Bradford Hotel in Boston. He would open with his quintet at Storyville, the club owned by Newport Jazz Festival entrepreneur George Wein.

As Basie and Joe travelled together by train to Boston, eating and drinking, Basie told Joe what would happen to him: 'You'll suddenly become father-confessor to the people who work for you.' And they included complex, strong-willed men; for example, the hard-drinking, fun-loving Forrest, who wrote the hit 'Night Train'. A tall Midwesterner, he had once damaged a hand in a foundry accident and spent months exercising the hand back to normal operation, clenching and unclenching a pink rubber ball thousands of times a day. Doctors told him he wouldn't succeed, but he kept squeezing, because he wanted to play the tenor saxophone again. And he did. All the musicians in the quintet had wives and children with the attendant problems of families. 'When the rent's due, they look for you,' Basie said.

Arriving in Boston, Joe looked up and saw 'Count Basie Presents' in small letters and 'Joe Williams' in big letters on the club's marquee. Count Basie introduced Joe that night, then took a train back to New York City, leaving Joe on his own.

It was a hectic time; he was constantly moving, with all the responsibility of making sure that he got paid. Then he in turn paid 'the bills, the bills', he noted daily, as well as planned the peformances. He disliked all the ramifications of bookings, routings and payrolls.

His bookings stretched out longer than the original six months. Altogether he worked forty-six weeks that year – as much as he ever worked in one year in his life. The reviews were very good. His earnings went up tremendously.

He spent the end of his first year as a solo, he spent New Year's Eve singing at the Mocambo in Hollywood, then looked back and saw that he and his quintet had never made so much money before. And they had spent a very good time doing it. He looked back, too, on a welter of extremely complicated logistics and decided that he needed a top-drawer manager whom he could trust and who would give him personal attention.

John Levy, the bassist who had recommended Joe to Duke Ellington in 1942, had become a popular manager with entertainers, adept at taking care of bookings and dealing with clubowners. He represented some of the best musicians in jazz: singer Nancy Wilson, the Adderley brothers – saxophone player Julian 'Cannonball' and his little brother, trumpeter Nat, who had signed with Levy in the mid-fifties. And Wes Montgomery, too, and Ahmad Jamal, with his open piano sound that, with its innovation, leaving a lot of space for the bass and drums to play in, had wide appeal, and Ramsey Lewis, who had a hit with the record 'The In Crowd'.

When Joe called John for the 1961 schedule, John gladly

decided to concentrate on Joe's career. Joe had many fans and was easily booked into the chic supper clubs and hotel rooms. Levy had tough judgement and experience about overhead costs, underhanded paymasters. He liked to stop trouble before any started. The nuts and bolts of business details could aggravate Joe. John could make money move in Joe's direction. All Joe had to do was follow the itinerary. He had gotten all the proof he needed twenty years earlier that John liked his singing. So much so that whenever John went to hear Joe sing, with the intention of coming up with a helpful critique, John became so enamoured of Joe's work that he couldn't think of anything rational to say except for praise. Their talents complemented each other's. And they decided never to try to do each other's work and aimed to speak to each other every day at 5 p.m., if possible, or any hour they could. 'It's 5 p.m. someplace,' Joe said, calling into home base daily.

Joe handled his personal finances himself, with Jillean's increasing participation. She kept records for taxes and ran a tight ship with her secretarial skills, Godfrey Murrain, a New York City lawyer, discovered. Godfrey, with an undergraduate degree in accounting, had worked as an Internal Revenue Service investigator, looking for tax evaders for several years by day, attending law school at night. His friend, Al Gaines, an accountant also working for the IRS, did Joe's taxes every year. When Al got a promotion that precluded his doing Joe's taxes, he recommended Godfrey. And then Joe recommended Godfrey to Benny Powell, who had a little tax problem one year during Joe's Basie days. Godfrey lived in a two-family house in St Albans, Queens. Benny Powell moved into the house next door and gave a party, which Godfrey went to. He saw Joe Williams there, too; they talked and had a few drinks together – two low-keyed men who liked to laugh. And when Joe became his own boss, in the years AB (After Basie), Joe called Godfrey to do the year-round accounting and legal work. Look after the taxes. Keep receipts for the Edison quintet salaries. The valet, the trains, planes, dinners, breakfasts, the monumental miscellanies, dear Godfrey. And Joe was freed to take care of the book that held his repertoire and his harmonics and faith.

A slightly-built, mild-mannered man, Godfrey became the

sort of loyal fan who went to as many of Joe's performances in New York City as possible. Joe never demanded that Godfrey hang around or report all the time about his every move. 'He doesn't need me to hold his hand,' Godfrey noted with relief, as he had discovered so many other entertainers were prone to require. Joe turned out to be sweet, reserving the final decisions, which affected his life and career, for himself, listening to advice, then delegating responsibility gladly but never sloughing it off, and expecting Godfrey to take care of the technicalities and legalities with a minimum of fuss and games. Joe disliked having to repeat himself.

By 1961, the management team of John, Jillean and Joe's man Godfrey stood squarely behind the singer, ready to protect and defend him. 'I think it's going to work out,' Joe said to himself, satisfied – and liked what he had done. In every member of his team, he had detected something he could trust. And in him they detected something ever so slightly vulnerable and kind, something that really did prefer to elude opponents, bores, timewasters and thieves. They especially brought out an impatient streak in him; even friends sometimes tapped it, if they weren't quick to catch on to Joe's train of thought. He needed the pressure off him. With trustworthy management, he thought, he probably wouldn't get hurt behind. He could sing his heart out and not find himself yelping instead; no outsider would find an unprotected spot while he was busy programming a set, thinking about adding a tune to his repertoire. The home team – another kind of trio – of John, Jillean and Godfrey had patience to do the bookings and cash flow, the records and taxes, the *sine qua non* of life. The trio met occasionally, kept in touch by telephone and shared the sterling quality of getting things said affably and quickly. And they showed every sign of living together happily, prospering from the serenade.

Jillean, a Jack Paar fan, became involved in Joe's publicity inadvertently. She got tickets for the Paar show and coaxed Joe to go along. That night, Joey Bishop substituted for Paar and introduced Joe in the audience. The accidental exposure took his image into millions of homes.

And on and off from the time that Joe signed with John Levy, Joe worked with Cannonball and Nat Adderley, touring the

Apollo, the Howard in Washington, the Uptown in Philadelphia – the theatres known as the circuit. Cannonball and Nat wrote the shows, touring, too, with Roberta Flack, Les McCann, planning the transitions, with lights and backdrops and music, to get from one artist to another. Nat sang a blues, with Cannonball playing, in the styles of various blues singers. Nat imitated Muddy Waters, T-Bone Walker, and then did an chorus in Joe William's style. But Nat would only lipsynch 'Every Day'. As the people applauded, he walked offstage, while Joe walked onstage, singing. Joe also went to Japan and many US cities with Nancy Wilson, an entertainment-world pairing of his clients that John Levy loved to do.

On the road alone, Joe read the good news about himself. In the *Toronto Daily Star,* a critic wrote that Joe 'was dishing out a healthy portion of honest-to-goodness blues . . . cooking it up with the help of the Harry Edison quintet.' The reviewer wrote about an 'air of achievement' about Joe, who, 'wearing a tuxedo, went through a well-selected repertoire of blues and ballads such as "I Don't Know Why" to the uptempo "Thou Swell" and closed with a much-requested "Every Day" '.

Some reviewers still complained, as they had from time to time, that he sounded a bit stiff on ballads, compared with the outrageous abandon of his blues. But the redoubtable John S. Wilson of the *New York Times,* a canny jazz expert with catholic tastes and expertise, said otherwise in a review of Joe's album *A Swinging Night at Birdland* on the Roulette label in December, 1962:

> The new Joe Williams – the polished, skilled showman who has been on display for the last year – is finally caught on records in this set, picked up during one of his engagements at New York City's Birdland.
>
> With Edison's band backing him and given clean, close-up recording, Williams mixes ballads, blues and his own intriguing manner of talk-sing-shout projection. He uses this last method in a beautifully accented and shaded performance of 'Come Back'.
>
> Ballads, which Williams once seemed to take so seriously that they were stiff as rods, now come from him in a manner

> that is at once casual and strictly disciplined, so that they throb with a swinging feeling.
>
> He swings overtly, too, and much more effectively than he did with Basie. He seems to have come through a period of adjustment that he was caught in when he left the surroundings of a big band and had to create his own momentum. And he has emerged on this disc, as he is in person, as one of the more forcefully communicative singers to be heard today.

'It doesn't get better than that,' Joe thought.

He turned out quite a few recordings in his early days as a soloist. Not all the records were raved about. One critic said that Joe was an exceptional vocalist tottering between being a balladeer and a pop singer, though he was actually a blues singer doing a pleasant and relaxed date on an album called *Together.*

No matter what people told him to sing, he was ubiquitous, 'live', in person, sitting in at Max Gordon's Village Vanguard one night, making Art D'Lugoff happy by filling up the Village Gate another night, then taking off for a Midwest engagement the next night. He worked hard, and maintained perfect professional protocol, never missing a gig, never showing up late or drunk or recalcitrant.

Peter Long, the New York City jazz promoter, began to notice, as other people did, that he had never seen Joe give a bad or dull performance. Joe was almost an oddity. Long couldn't think of many other performers who always gave exciting shows. Godfrey Murrain observed the same thing. If Joe were particularly tired, he might exhibit an almost imperceptible difference, a slight dreaminess, in his manner for a second. But he was always exciting and in control.

By 1963, Junior Mance's trio, by definition more manageable and compact for travelling, replaced Edison's quintet. A blues-based, boogie-woogie pianist at the start of his career in Chicago, Mance had gained enormously in sophistication and experience through his stints on the personnel lists of Dinah Washington and Dizzy Gillispie, among others. Some critics thought that Mance provided an even more compatible backing for Joe than Edison had done. (Not musically pertinent,

Junior's mother and Joe's had attended Paine College in Augusta.) Joe himself was amazed by some of Junior's finger-dancing virtuosity on one recording in particular, *Joe Williams at Newport, 1963,* which Joe made with a group that included Mance, his drummer Mickey Roker and his bassist Bob Cranshaw.

Helen McNamara wrote in a Toronto newspaper, 'As an accompanist, Mance is ideal, playing with a dramatic flair that may be expressed in a delightfully rocking figure', communicating his deep blues feeling, 'behind Joe's voice'. Mance's playing could 'subside to a murmur or swell to a dynamic dimension, depending on the mood of the moment'. More consistently than any other pianist of his generation, Mance communicated the angst and joy of the blues.

Joe was travelling with the trio during one of those never-to-be-forgotten moments. Driving with Jillean to Idlewild Airport in New York City one afternoon, heading for a club in Detroit, Joe heard a radio news broadcast: President Kennedy had been shot. It was 22 November 1963, Jillean's birthday. Jillean said, 'We might as well turn back. Nobody's going to open a club now.' The President wasn't reported dead yet. Joe decided to meet the trio at the airport anyway. They telephoned Detroit to find out what the clubowner planned to do. He would stay open. Even after Kennedy had been pronounced dead, the clubowner kept the doors open. Joe played three sets on his opening night, with most of the audience crossing the border from Windsor, Canada. And the owner was planning to stay open another night, Joe told Jillean by telephone. 'Are they joking?' she said. No, it was true, the musicians were working, though almost the entire country had become muffled, in shock, from the assassination. In New York City, restaurants had locked their doors, Jillean said; the streets had a ghostly look; the stores had grates pulled down over their windows. But Joe kept working. The second night, the crowd came from Windsor again. On the third night, the Americans, finding the period of national mourning too onerous, really unbearable, went to the club in droves, seeking relief. Kennedy's assassination took the lustre off that day for Jillean and Joe for ever, since they had been particularly fond of

Kennedy, with 'his promise of tomorrow', as Joe had sensed it, and the spiritual lift given to the country by the Peace Corps and the lesser-heralded anti-nuclear proliferation pact with the Russians and the Alliance for Progress. And most of all Joe had thought that he had sensed a shift in the mood of the country about race, because of Kennedy's intelligence and social views.

Another important moment for Joe with Junior's trio happened in London, where Joe won rave reviews. Joe's group opened a concert; George Shearing played for the second half. Then Joe went onstage again to sing with Shearing. And Joe was thrilled that the English critics stopped viewing him as a mere replacement for little Jimmy Rushing.

Junior liked travelling with Joe. For one thing, Joe was so successful that Junior had no money worries. The management team made the cheques move smoothly. And the musicians lived the good life, ate gourmet foods, drank good wines and dressed very well. Joe was happy with a houndstooth coat with a bright red lining, which he had bought at a fashionable men's clothing store on Broadway at 49th Street. Jillean had disliked the coat at first and, when she saw the lining, actually cried. Tears rolled down her face, making Joe laugh raucously. To stop her from crying, he took her to the store and bought her a coat exactly like his. That cheered her up. The coat looked fine on her. And when they walked down the street in His and Her coats, she started smiling. Joe took his coat on the road and used it as a prop to establish intimacy with his audiences; he said that his wife disapproved of his 'Sportin' Life' lining. Walter Booker, a bassist new to New York City, who sometimes substituted for the exciting Bob Cranshaw, one of Joe's favourite, most powerful, supportive and creative bassists, thought Joe was delightful: 'The whole shit about Joe Williams is ineffable,' Booker thought.

At the time, Joe was already playing golf in the high seventies and low eighties; he enticed Junior Mance to go along to the public courses or the private clubs where fans invited them. Junior never broke 100. It was just as well that he never became attached to Joe as a golf partner. Junior wanted to go off and lead his own trio. And Joe, who still sang with Count Basie in reunion concerts, also kept listening to Basie's advice, one piece of which concerned the complexities of taking groups on the road: 'Get rid of them, kid. Just get your piano player and go anyplace in the world.' Dispensing with the bills for travelling with a group, Joe hired a man with a virile pianistic style – a powerfully-built and versatile musician, Harold Mabern, to travel around the US for a while. But Joe's personal attachment to his own groups for many years never became as deeply entrenched as his old tie to Count Basie and that band.

In July 1964, Joe did some work on Long Island with bassist Milt Hinton, then with Jillean took a ferry across a bay to Marvin Fisher's cottage on Fire Island. Many times Joe had made that trip to visit friends on the island, an idyllic resort on a sandbar sprinkled liberally with sparkling stone and whitewashed houses. Ocean Beach, FI had a miniature golf course. Fisher once took Junior Mance fishing. And Joe could also say 'hello' to other friends with Fire Island houses: to Sonny and Claire Meyrowitz, who had a jazz club in Seaford, LI, and Ben Rosner, an RCA executive, and his wife Julie, whose very New Yorkey lifestyle, with private schools, 'Nutcracker Suite' tickets, and coiffed dogs for their children, tickled Joe's fancy. In Fisher's living-room on that clear, hot sunny Sunday, Joe was sipping a cold drink, toying with an iron, as welcome and cosy as a family's beloved puppy, savouring the ease of life. It gave him a bright idea: 'Let's drop in and see Bill,' he said to Jillean. So they drove to St Albans, Queens, where Count Basie lived, and thought they might have a peaceful dinner with the Count and Catherine Basie. First Basie decided to call his club on 132rd Street and Seventh Avenue, just to see how things were going along. It was such an idyllic day, with soft, dry air, that even Harlem couldn't be as steamy, Joe thought, as it often was in summer. On the telephone, Basie heard popping noises in the background. He said, 'What's that?' 'Those are gunshots,' a musician in the club explained. 'There's a riot going on.' The first of many race riots in the US in the sixties, the Harlem riot had been triggered by the shooting of a fifteen-year-old boy, Jay Power, by a policeman. Basie told Joe, who said, 'You've got to be kidding, man.' He listened on the receiver for a second, shocked, Basie took it back and said, 'Get out of there.' But they decided it was safer to stay in the club, until the riot ebbed. That night, Joe looked around for signs of the riot in his own neighbourhood a few blocks below Harlem. But 106th Street and Central Park West stayed quiet.

Against the background of those riots, a more chaotic, simplistic music with an elemental beat swept the music world: rock. In the 1960s, hundreds of black jazz musicians, and white musicians, too, fled the US and settled in Europe, where they could find audiences. The bebop singing team of Lambert, Hendricks, and Ross with a fresh, zany approach to jazz, singing Hendricks' lyrics at breakneck speed set to elaborate instrumental solos, split up in the early sixties, about to be eclipsed in any case by rock. The Beatles ruled the world, tracing their musical lineage to bluesman Bill Broonzy, not jazzman Louis Armstrong. Replacements for Annie Ross in the bebop trio kept it lingering for a while. But Dave Lambert died in a road accident. Jon Hendricks, an eminent lyricist with a swinging, exciting vocal delivery, became discouraged by his prospects in the US. He went to London in the mid-60s for a brief engagement at Ronnie Scott's club in Soho and decided to stay five years, since the British enchanted him by voting him their favourite jazz singer. In the US his departure barely caused a ripple. Jazz singer Eddie Jefferson, who wrote the lyrics for 'Moody's Mood for Love', began driving a taxi in New York. But the US kept Joe Williams alive and well, working and affluent, performing in major hotels and clubs, on records and on television. He decided that he owed his continuing success most of all to his exposure on television.

A talent co-ordinator for the Johnny Carson Show, Bruce Cooper was particularly instrumental in bringing Joe on to the show. Cooper, an amateur musician himself, had first heard Joe in Birdland with Count Basie and fell purely in love with Joe's singing. Cooper was always looking for talented people to bring on to the Carson guest roster. So one day he included Joe's name in the lineup. The Carson staff met every day to work with the day's schedule and position the five or so guests slated for the taping. Bruce and Dick Carson, the director, were sitting around in producer Perry Cross's office, high up in the Rockerfeller Center headquarters of NBC, studying the Master

Booking Board hung on a wall. As usual, 100 stations would pick up the first fifteen minutes of the broadcast, then at least another 100 would join in. Johnny Carson came running into the meeting a little late, to hear the plan.

Fair-haired, with a pat, wide smile masking an intense concern about nearly everything, Bruce Cooper said, 'We've got Joe Williams scheduled for tonight, OK?'

Carson said, 'As far as I'm concerned, Joe's one of the greatest singers that ever lived.'

And when Joe showed up, with palms ever so slightly moist and shook Johnny Carson's hand, Carson said, 'Oh, you'll be fine.' That show went so well that Joe returned at least once a month.

'Exposure is what I'm dealing with,' Joe analysed his survival.

> I have something to expose, and the doing is up to me. I've been fortunate to be presented to the media, through the John Wilsons, the Leonard Feathers, Nat Hentoffs. They write about me. The rock thing doesn't affect us, because it's for youngsters, kids, teenagers, not for what we would call sophisticated people. And the public relations for the clubs where I work are excellent. And all the television shows beginning with the Basie days. So many people keep calling out to me in the streets.

Godfrey Murrain, who took walks around New York City with Joe, noticed that primarily blacks yelled 'hello' to him. None of the thirteen lawyers in Godfrey's Madison Avenue office knew who Joe was. But occasionally one showed up and said, 'Hey, I saw your client on TV last night.' And they liked him and watched for him to do a live performance in a club or a hotel. Joe added to his following that way and greeted anyone who wanted to go backstage to meet him. He could dress and drink, eat and hold a conversation with five people in a small dressing-room minutes before going on stage. And people were impressed with the big, friendly man with the regal bearing, the quiet, conversational tone and the quick laugh.

He did occasionally flee into the men's room, if strangers

babbled at him for a very long time. But ordinarily he was a gracious, quiet host, offering fruit and cognac and any drinks that the club management or fans had sent to his dressing rooms.

There was, therefore, no exit for Joe, even during the rock blitz. He had to stay in the US and work.

He reflected years later:

> Promotion and exposure are everything. Mike Douglas, Joey Bishop, Dick Cavett – their shows, too. The record companies went into the production business, spending money to get their artists on television for high visibility, as part of the promotion and the package. Because there is no substitute for taking whatever it is you do musically to the public in a visual way. Which is why an Ellington, Basie, Kenton or Woody Herman always travelled around the world and took the music directly to the people. The great bands' music was there in the hearts of the people. A combination of the live performance, the television appearance and the record – that is how it is done. And that's how I did it.

# 11 'You Finally Did It'

He showed Jillean his itineraries and let her choose the places that she wanted to go. If he went to Europe or most foreign places, she went with him. They were special treats for her – heady, glamorous and emotional times. She went with the Edison quintet to Las Vegas for Joe's first appearance at the Flamingo without the Basie band. She went out on the town in Los Angeles with Joe to see Nat King Cole at the Cocoanut Grove. They found Bruce Cooper, who lived only a short walk down Central Park West from them, sitting in the audience. And Chill Wills and the Hollywood set.

Afterwards Joe went backstage to say 'hello' to Cole, thinking, 'God, he's an elegant, master musician, master of his craft, a beautiful fellow.' Joe reminded Nat of the last time he had performed at the club in Cherry Hill, New Jersey, when Joe was able to catch the show. (Later Joe would play there with a big, swing band.) Cole's valet had told Cole: 'Joe Williams is sitting right down front.' Cole had said, 'Well, I don't want him sitting there, looking right up at my tonsils.' The singers laughed, had some drinks together, with Nat chain-smoking and Joe borrowing a cigarette – and never met again. In February 1965, Nat King Cole died of lung cancer.

And then Jillean found herself in Connecticut with Joe, at Jackie Robinson's house, in the wake of the killings of civil-rights workers Michael H. Schwerner, Andrew Goodman and James E. Chaney, who had disappeared the previous June and were discovered on 5 August 1964, in Mississippi. The Southern Christian Leadership Conference was appealing for funds. Reverend Martin Luther King went to Connecticut, to give a speech. And by the time he was through speaking, people were ready to rip the shirts off their backs, Jillean thought. The sun set. Since there was no stage, Joe used the lawn. Several people shone their cars' headlights to catch him with the beams. He stood alone in the dark, singing 'The Lord's Prayer' *a cappella*, his beautiful baritone pealing through the clear night air. Jillean started crying and noticed that other people were crying, too. Joe ended with high notes on 'for-aver'. (Not 'for ever', a more nasal sound that a perfectionistic singer knew would have a less profound effect.) Afterwards in the hush, she tried to say something and ended up tongue-tied, so touched that he could move people to tears or laughter and help in the civil-rights struggle, with which she had become passionately involved.

Jillean had been writing to her father once a week, from 461 Central Park West, beginning in May, 1960. After several years, it had surely become plain to him that she was settled. Though her cousins Liz and Andrew knew Jillean was living with Joe Williams, she never mentioned her arrangement to her father. He never mentioned it, either. She assumed that he knew and didn't mind, so long as she were healthy, not in trouble and not pregnant. Joe and Lemma still hadn't divorced.

Joe's children came to New York and stayed with him for about two weeks, usually in summers. 'Those children are having a hard time,' Jillean noticed during their visits. She knew that their mother had told them how terrible white people were and particularly Jillean, who had 'stolen Daddy away'. Jillean confided in a friend: 'Which really is not true, but they just don't know any better.' Jillean also knew that they adored their mother. They spent most of the year with her and only a bit of time with a total stranger. 'And I look funny to them, with funny hair, and I speak funny. They're in an environment with a man that they don't know that well. It isn't easy for them.' Her perceptions guided her during the very hard time she and the children had in living together. 'I break my neck, trying to give them a good time,' she confided in her friend, 'since often Joe is away or else working in New York City at night, and he sleeps in the daytime.'

She found herself always telling the children to be quiet, or she was taking them outside to everything she could think of. They went to the ballet, the zoo, the movies, the theatre; they went to Palisades Park across the Hudson River, because the children liked to swim. 'But they are not really content or happy, they don't care for me, that is true. And how much you can blame the kids for that, I don't know,' she told her friend.

Godfrey Murrain noticed how quiet, even sullen, he thought JoAnn was in the Williams menage. For it was the Williamses' menage by then. Joe had legally changed his name to Williams, while the children remained 'Goreed'. Godfrey's daughter, just getting ready to start school, was impressed by Jillean and called her 'the pen lady'; Jillean always used felt-tipped pens in all colours, one of the first people to adopt them, Godfrey thought. She had a distinctive, backhand script and put her feminine touch on letters and everything else – the well-equipped kitchen and the light and airy design of the apartment. She cooked everything from veal blanquette to chilli . . . 'and she makes sauces for days', Joe observed affectionately. In her own quiet way, she had an attention-getting personality, in part because she was so refreshing to look at and natural to talk with. The children were essentially quiet visitors, puzzled by both their own mother and Joe.

One night, Joe came back late from work, when everybody in the apartment was sleeping, and looked in to see JoAnn, who was visiting. She was more curled up than usual, sleeping in a foetal position, he thought; he said to himself, 'Shit, she's about to become a woman.' In the morning, he telephoned Lemma in Cincinnati and asked if she had ever spoken to JoAnn about getting her period.

'No,' Lemma said.

'What do you want her to do? Wake up one morning and think she's dying?' Joe said. He turned around and told Jillean: 'Take her someplace and get her a sanitary belt, get her straight and explain what's happening to her, oh, Jesus Christ.'

When JoAnn woke up, Jillean took her away quickly. Joe stayed behind alone to recall the times he had observed JoAnn closely, if not frequently, for signs of any trouble, any change, since she had been born. He looked at the big, empty bed in the guest room and recalled a neat crib, where he had checked her at dawn, when everyone else had been asleep, whenever he, Lemma and the kids were living under the same roof. He had assured himself that JoAnn was dry, comfortable, all right: not about to smother to death. In the beginning, he remembered, she was going 'goo goo' and 'ga ga', with people holding her all day. Then when he came back from work, she would lie in her crib and look up, and there he was, alone with her, for a peaceful moment.

Somehow those intimate times with JoAnn had culminated in her unresponsiveness, her estrangement, because of his troubles with Lemma. Even so, he could sense what was going on with his children. He loved them, though he couldn't change the situation for which they resented and blamed him. They might as well blame the wind. He had to be free to be himself – and not a subject. He wanted to give them anything reasonable that he could afford, any possible advantage. College, for one, if they wanted it. So he would watch and hope and see if things might go better. He would keep inviting them to become part of his new family with Jillean. Perhaps the kids could grow up and into it and have a calmer view one day. Godfrey Murrain was working quietly with a lawyer in the Midwest to help settle the financial agreements in the divorce action between Joe and Lemma.

On 10 September 1964, Lemma and Joe became legally divorced. Then he and Jillean planned their wedding, after spending five years together – 'as near as makes no difference', a legal marriage, Jillean thought. But she very much wanted to become Jillean Williams technically, too. Their friends still had no idea that the couple was unmarried. But Godfrey Murrain, who handled the legalities, knew. Joe called and asked him to go along to the Bronx County Courthouse for a civil ceremony scheduled for 7 January 1965.

Dapper little Godfrey had been to the Courthouse several times before. But that morning, he found the atmosphere unusual. A middle-aged woman of no particular beauty or homeliness hurried them through a ceremony. Godfrey thought that the woman looked like any ordinary civil-service clerk – and then some. He didn't see her smile once. It was as if she felt, 'Well, I've got to perform my duty. Let me get this over as soon as possible.' Little Jillean, nearly two heads shorter than Joe, sensed that the woman was thoroughly stiff, because the groom was black and the bride was white. 'She obviously spat out the words "till death do us part",' Jillean remarked after the ceremony. 'She doesn't expect us to last more than a few months.' Well, that was that, Jillean thought.

Their wedding day was a little unusual because Joe was awake to have lunch at midday with Jillean and Godfrey. After that, the Williamses continued as usual, celebrating their birthdays but not anniversaries, not really mindful of the exact date, since it had come so long after the commitment. Soon after the ceremony, they went to visit London. Joe had never met Jillean's father, because Jillean had worried about how an elderly man would react. She merely told him that she knew Joe. And it occurred to her that her father might expect Joe to arrive 'with a bone in his nose'. But she loved her father, thought he was 'a super man', and found it a pity that he didn't have a son who could carry on 'his marvellous ways and characteristics', which she often spoke about proudly. She decided to count on his good will.

She went to the house alone, leaving Joe in London, and told Andrew Milne right away that she had married Joe Williams.

Her father said, 'Well, you finally did it.'

Jillean said, 'Yes.'

He said, 'Well, great, I'd like to meet him.'

So Jillean brought Joe to the bungalow, where a spinster aunt acted as housekeeper, tended the plants and flowers, cleaned and cooked for her widowed brother-in-law. Jillean's father was cordial – and seemingly unexcited by the inter-racial aspect of the marriage. He immediately called the Savoy Hotel Grill and reserved his usual table for lunch, this time for three people, to entertain the newlyweds. Upstairs, in the bar, waiting for a table in the grill room downstairs, Andrew Milne introduced Joe, the only black man in sight, to all the publicity and advertising types that frequented the well-known place, as his son-in-law. In the crowded grill, the food was traditional British and French cuisine; there were small bouquets of flowers on the many tables. Jillean's father mentioned, during the lettuce course, with a spiced, oily dressing, that a friend of his had confided only recently that he was worried about his granddaughter in New Zealand. She had married a Chinese man. 'Wait till I tell him that I have a black son-in-law,' said Andrew Milne, and then laughed with a deep, resonant sound.

For dinner Joe and Jillean went to Wheeler's, their favourite seafood restaurant, on Old Compton Road, in Soho, where Joe could see the plate through the delicate slices of smoked salmon. He always ate at Wheeler's and told people that he and Jillean really went to London for that restaurant. They would have consoled themselves with Wheeler's, if Jillean's father hadn't been so sporting. Then Joe and Jillean moved into the bungalow for a visit.

Jillean guessed that as long as Joe would look after her and wouldn't be mean to her, her father would remain happy. He had reconfirmed her fine opinion of him, all the more remarkable in his reaction because, as far as Jillean knew, Joe was probably the first black person that Andrew Milne had ever associated with, she told Joe.

He replied, 'I think I'm the first one ever to sleep in the house with his daughter.'

'Yes, I suppose that has to be a bit of a shock for him, I don't know,' Jillean said. 'He doesn't show it.'

With her father setting the tone, Jillean's British friends accepted the marriage without any question and seemed 'thrilled to bits', Jillean thought – of course she was in that state of mind herself. Everyone except for the retired naval officer, now an admiral, who had introduced the couple in the Waldorf lobby. Joe noticed that ultimate hypocrisy of the admiral's snub.

'An admiral should never snub a former WRN,' Joe said.

'No, I was a WAAF during the war, darling,' Jillean said.

'Yes, and you've been giving me a lot of WAAFs ever since, lots of WAAFS, WAAF WAAF,' Joe said, and caressed Jillean, careful to mute his 'a' in Andrew Milne's house.

Back in New York City, Jillean discovered that a woman we'll call Mary Taylor Smith, who lived in Texas, was disgruntled about the marriage, too. When Jillean wrote and told Mrs Smith, at whose house Jillean had stayed during one of her personal Discover America tours, Mrs Smith replied that she had seen Joe on television. She tried very hard to accept the situation of the marriage, had even talked to her minister. But she really couldn't cope with it. Jillean years later would think that she should have kept the letter. 'It was quite a museum piece,' she could recall. Mrs Smith had enjoyed meeting Jillean and was quite sure that Joe was a charming person. But Mrs Smith was very sorry that the marriage would mean the end of her friendship with Jillean.

'I think the opinion is absurd,' Jillean remarked to Joe. 'But I can understand that. When you live there, and that's all you've heard and seen, it must be quite hard. I think it's very strange, but I can understand how some of these older people feel that way. I honestly and truly never think about it. I never really have thought about it.'

The Williamses counted very few negative reactions. They had thousands of easy relationships. Bruce Cooper and Joe had an increasingly affectionate friendship. One Christmas Day, Cooper and his wife invited about fifteen people to their apartment at 84th Street and Central Park West. Joe showed up with a gift for Wilhelmina Cooper, but whispered to Bruce: 'You can't tell her.' It was a vibrator. Joe and Bruce went into the bedroom to attach it to the bottom of a low-slung, king-sized bed. They wriggled under it painstakingly because the vibrator switch had to be attached to Bruce's side of the bed. Then Joe couldn't dislodge himself. He was stuck under the bed. Bruce and Joe began laughing hilariously. The other guests became curious and filed into the room. Richard Gautier, the actor, lifted the bed, while Bruce pulled Joe free by the feet. Even Wilhelmina laughed. That day, too, Joe joined William Walker from the Metropolitan Opera to sing 'Vesta La Giubba' from *Pagliacci.* And the Coopers had a really swinging party. Jillean liked it so well that when she and Joe went home, she asked him to sound his 'a' again; she had really liked that. He said that he was tired and would make it a b-flat. Then they laughed, went to bed and made love. Merry Christmas, Mrs Smith.

Whether it was because Joe and Jillean steered clear of negative people or because people were happy for them, Jillean didn't know. But the Williamses lived in peace with people. As attitudes changed in the South, with passing years, Joe tried to encourage her to go to New Orleans, for one place, with him. But she wasn't sure that she would want to go there – and decided not to. Though eventually told not to worry about Atlanta, Georgia anymore, where inter-racial couples walked down the street together without drawing comments, Jillean didn't go there, either.

Andrew Milne died in December, 1966, without ever having made a derogatory remark, Jillean noticed.

'He didn't show anything except to be happy that I have someone to take care of me. That he was really happy about, wasn't he?' she said to Joe.

'Yes, he knew that,' Joe said. 'He knew that you were secure, independent of him and all that, no matter what happened.'

# *12 Goodbye to Miss Anne, Goodbye to the Amen Corner*

Joe was on the road, where he usually was, when news of any sort reached him, and he could mark his trail around the world by historical events. This time his mother called him with the news that his Aunt Juanita, who had worked all her life as a clerk in Chicago, had liver cancer. Joe flew to Chicago to see her and found her very sick in a hospital bed. She didn't look ill, pale, thin or bloated. She was weakened, though.

'How are you doing?' Joe said,

'Oh, I'm doing OK,' she said softly. 'I'm getting out of here, though. Going back to stay with my uncle.' (Dr Joseph Gilbert in Royston, Georgia.)

'That's good,' Joe said. 'When are you going?'

'A few days more, when they finish taking their tests, that's all. I've got a feeling I might be able to get my strength back down there.'

But she didn't. Joe never saw her again. She died in Royston soon afterwards. Joe's mother insisted that he didn't have to visit her again just then. She was finding solace in church services and meetings and with her friends in the neighbourhood. But Joe made another quick trip to Chicago anyway to see her open the door for him and reassure himself.

John Levy's itineraries were long and held the promise of big fees, with down payments up front. John had the power to endorse the cheques and deposit them to Joe's account, taking ten per cent. John tucked many extras into Joe's itinieraries, aside from the club and hotel dates, and called Joe with special events that came up suddenly – political dinners in support of black candidates, fund-raising benefits for health organizations, hospital performances for veterans, jailhouse performances, March of Dimes, any health group running a benefit.

John Levy was also expanding his film, television and recording connections on the West Coast and by 1970 would move his office there completely. So Joe found himself doing a ballad, 'Somebody', for the soundtrack of a Jerry Lewis film, *Cinderfella.* But Joe didn't like the way he was singing the lyrics – 'Everybody needs to care for somebody'. Nobody criticized him but himself. He couldn't figure out what was bothering him. Using a ruse, Joe sneaked Rozelle Gayle past the security guards at the studio and sang for him. By that time Rozelle was living in California, acting on television, in films, and playing a little piano for private parties on the side. In the studio, Rozelle heard Joe make a vowel sound, sing an 'e' where he needed an 'a' sound to make a high note easier. And even though the 'a' sound distorted the word a little, people didn't notice because they knew the word. And that was it, that tiny touch.

By 1966, Thad Jones, Joe's old compatriot from the Basie band, had started the Thad Jones–Mel Lewis Big Band. It was packing crowds into the Village Vanguard in Manhattan on Monday nights, sometimes so many people that the musicians couldn't get in the front door. The band had more complex, bebop harmonies than Basie's, but the Jones–Lewis band was rooted in the same, hard-swinging, brass-loving tradition. John Levy worked out a deal for Joe to make a record of blues tunes with the new band; the record was nominated for a Grammy. Later Jones–Lewis and Joe made a record of ballads. And often, when Joe appeared in a festival and was asked what band he liked, he put in a word for Jones and Lewis. Joe's interpretation of an Ellington song, 'Come Sunday', on his first record with the band, sounded like a ballad done in a light vein, while the words were a prayer asking for the Lord's help to bring the black people through. And no one, except for an expert familiar with Ellington's sacred music, could tell it was written in a spiritual vein, so deftly did Joe mask it. He did a lot of recording sessions with Thad and drummer Mel Lewis after that, with and without their band. Lewis liked playing slow, blues tempos – a down, loose rhythm, so difficult for drummers, behind Joe, and liked Joe personally, thinking he was what he had always striven to be – a fine gentleman and a great singer. Lewis had the typical view of many musicians who knew Joe primarily on bandstands, with a hail-fellow – well-met hug and embrace, and an exchange of gossip. Then musicians went about their separate jobs and lives, passing the word about each other along the musicians' grapevine, one of the world's most effective communication systems. It could quickly spread the word about clubs closing, owners defaulting on payments, exceptionally gifted new musicians appearing on the scene somewhere.

Joe kept circulating in the music world, playing with scores of different musicians in a single month. He was likely to show up anywhere. If he heard that a friend was playing in a club, Joe would show up for a set, have a drink, maybe sit in for a song, always aware of what was going on, political but not ostentatiously so, having a great time listening to the music and making it.

One moment he was in Schenectady, NY, where he kept a weekend engagement in Roth's Restaurant and Delicatessen. It had a downstairs jazz club that attracted famous-named jazz artists. A young, struggling freelance photographer, Joe Alper, who had taken a splendid closeup picture of Joe with Jimmy Rushing at a Newport Jazz Festival a few years earlier, escorted his wife, Jackie, to see Joe perform at Roth's. The next day, the Alpers, whose finances were such that Jackie rationed the orange juice, invited the Williamses to have dinner in their modest house. It was a memorable meal, despite scanty food portions, because, as everyone sat in the living-room digesting their rations, talking and listening to music, Joe got up and danced a few steps with Jaye, the Alpers fifteen-year-old daughter. She talked about the dance for a long time afterwards.

And then Joe found himself in a Bellevue Avenue mansion in Newport, Rhode Island. One night, after a jazz festival performance, he and Jillean went to a socialite's party. As they walked up the circular driveway and through the massive front door, they saw a centrepiece fit for a palace – the biggest crystal chandelier they had ever seen in their lives dominating the foyer. Trying to find a bathroom, Jillean wandered into pantries leading to pantries, before she found her way. One small room with a buffet supper and a bar had a huge vat of pre-mixed greenish grasshoppers, which seemed to be a popular drink at that party. Everywhere Joe looked, he saw sun-bleached hair, watery blue eyes and the myriad glasses of the creamy greenish drink. The hostess cooked scrambled eggs and bacon and served him his plate. He nudged Jillean and whispered, 'I never thought I'd see the day when somebody like that would be fixing my eggs and bacon for me.' And afterwards, walking down the driveway, he sang to Jillean, 'That's old, old, old money,' descending to the nether reaches of his bass register.

Then things went on as normal, which is to say that Joe flew away to the next gig, while Jillean returned to the apartment in New York. Still mindful of all the crises and temptations that can beset even a couple who settle down together in one indivisible niche, Jillean occasionally kept expecting Dorothy Dandridge or Kim Novak or even some anonymous beauty to start popping her fingers and then start snapping them and – poof! But then Jillean looked up from that sort of vestigial, dreadful reverie and saw Joe, who liked the sound of popping fingers only on bandstands, coming in the apartment door. She did once keep a nutty letter from a woman to Joe. It said that she remembered a night that they had been together, making love. The next morning, he had bought the woman perfume and a purse. She still had the purse, she wrote, and closed the letter with: 'I'm in this hospital now. I need someone to sign me out. Tell them you know me, please.' Joe and Jillean laughed hysterically at that oddity together. Joe didn't find it as funny when some man called the house and harassed Jillean with an obscene phone call; Joe changed the phone number and had it unlisted. And Jillean felt secure and happy with him – and confident – 'though one should never feel too confident, I suppose, should one?' she ruminated. 'But . . .'

She shrugged, not knowing that a short while before one of his reappearances at home, Joe had told a friend that Jillean was his 'baby', his 'best friend', absolutely civil and sharing. He was incredulous that it had taken him two years to renew his original acquaintance with her and admit that he was in love.

'Can you believe that?' he said. And as it had been in the beginning, it still was. 'When I know I'm going home, I'm at the airport early. And when I'm leaving home, they've almost shut the door of the plane before I get in. And it could just go on for ever and ever . . .'

But where it would go on for ever and ever became a question by 1967. Jillean, well versed in stories of crimes and muggings in New York City, liked to write letters. 'Her' mailbox stood across the street from their apartment house, facing Central Park. At night, despite the canopies, the doormen and the oblongs of light at the front doors and windows, Central Park West became a dark, deserted neighbourhood. Jillean could look from her window into the infamous black void of Central Park. She armed herself with a can of mace to spray at any possible attacker on her night trips to the mailbox. Joe had brought her several mace cans from Philadelphia. Finally one night she asked herself: 'What am I doing, with a can of mace? I wonder if it works?' She pushed the lever and squirted mace in her own face.

Joe, who had returned from the road that day, was sitting in the living-room, watching television, dandling a golf club over his knees. Jillean came back through the door, crying, holding the mace. 'It works,' she said.

He laughed, helped her clean her face, and then took her to the window. 'Look at this,' he said and ran his finger along an edge of the window. His finger came up stained with soot. 'We're breathing that every day,' he said. 'Where do you want the house?'

'I don't want a house,' Jillean said.

'But you're going to have it. I can't stand to breathe that soot.'

So they thought about Mallorca, where Jillean had friends, and about Big Sur, filled with scenic vistas and bobcats but so remote, without convenient plane connections and no golf course, two hours from San Francisco. Seattle, which they liked, had a good climate, a restful, neighbourly ambience, and some cultural life. As they were visiting the possible settings, Jillean remembered: 'Darling, I love the desert. Let's live in Las Vegas.'

So that was settled. They went back to New York City, where Joe opened the Rheingold Central Park Music Festival with Stan Getz on 27 June, getting a mixed review, as he very rarely did. Most critics had got over the shock of his singing too few blues to be typified as a blues singer. But some critics thought he should be more inspired on every tune every time he opened his mouth. By then he had become as unflappable, he thought, about reading reviews, as he was about performing. He usually skipped reading reviews and didn't know until years later that John Wilson had written: Joe had become a master of the expected, except on 'Hurry On Down (To My House)', on which he showed 'an engaging sense of humour' and 'really reached the audience'. Stan Getz was panned, and that festival was over. *'I was a sensation in that park,'* Joe said, when he found out. 'I played that festival every year.'

Instead of reading reviews at that time, Joe and Jillean busied themselves with choosing a plan from a brochure for houses being built in New Orleans. Hearing about a new housing development on the Las Vegas Country Club they called the International Country Club, in Las Vegas, Joe flew out to look at the land. He arrived late in the day, checked into the Towers of the Sands at the invitation of Jack Entratter, and found himself reading a newspaper peacefully alone at 10.30 at night. 'Hmmmm, there's a whole glamorous city out there. What am I doing up here, with all that life going on out there? Looking at TV and reading. I guess I'm home,' he thought. The next morning, he went to look at the land on the country club and saw that he could have a house that overlooked the thirteenth green and the fourteenth tee. The sight gave him a special surge. 'Yeah, oh, yeah, here's where I want to be, looking through a green tree at a blue sky.'

He asked the architect if he could outfit the house with three large bedrooms instead of four smaller ones in the plan and three bathrooms, one for Jillean, one for Joe, one for guests. Joe expected his children to visit sometimes. The architect said 'yes'. So Joe decided to buy the land. In July 1967, he asked Godfrey Murrain to fly to Las Vegas and settle the purchase.

By December, Joe thought that he ought to go and see the house under construction. It was a convenient time for him, when he usually stopped working for a while, telling everybody, 'See you when the snow melts.' He didn't like flying around the country in the rugged weather, getting delayed for nerve-wracking hours on planes, in airports, in snowdrifts on strange, impassable streets. Furthermore, he knew, he could kill himself by trying to do it all. Once his motor started going, it was the hardest thing in the world for him to turn it off.

The season encompassed Jillean's birthday, then his, Christmas and New Year, and then their anniversary, even if they had relegated it to obscurity. Joe loved to take the time to rest, watch his favourite soap operas, listen to music and practise his golf swing, while planning the coming year's itinerary with John Levy. But as Joe was packing to go to Las Vegas, he got a telephone call to sing in the Rainbow Grill, an art-deco room with floor-to-ceiling mirrors, hard by the burnished brass rails supported by lead-crystal ballusters and crystal chandeliers of the Rainbow Room on the sixty-fifth floor of the RCA building. He accepted the engagement, as he had done in the year before, when John Wilson had taken note of Joe's growing *élan* in a subdued performance appropriate for that setting. So he delayed a view of the house and gave John Wilson a chance to rave again about his 'rich, dark voice' and 'superb showmanship'. And by the time Joe finished singing, a movers' strike had started. The Williamses didn't know if they would have to postpone their official moving date set for April.

Anyway it was time for Joe to leave town with his new itinerary. Jillean waited out the strike in New York City, packing and cleaning. She didn't mind that Joe wasn't present. By then she knew that he was never present to pack up or move or leave or put away, she told a friend. That was not Joe. He was like a bump on a log, if he had to do things like that, so she would rather he wasn't there anyway. If he had been there, she would want him to do something, but if he wasn't there, she really couldn't. So that was all right, so please go, Joe.

He headed for Chicago to see his mother, as he had been doing very often lately, because she had been admitted to a hospital for heart trouble, complicated by a stroke and diabetes. Joe kept in touch with Jim Mason, her husband. Seeing him in the unfamiliar hospital corridor now regularly instead of in his mother's living-room, Joe noticed more sharply that Jim was a tall man with a smaller, more delicate face than either Joe or his mother had. Jim had massive, capable hands with thick fingers; for a long time he had worked as a cobbler, 'a good cobbler', Joe mused, and then a porter, cleaning up in a nightclub after hours. Joe made sure that Jim always had his phone number, as Miss Anne had always had when she was well.

Joe was upset that his mother was so ill, but he was not surprised. Though she was only in her sixties, she had spent too many years enjoying the rich foods that she liked to cook. He could not recall her ever having been slender; maybe she had been as a girl. He never saw her get particularly overweight, either. But 'she eats, eats, eats, she's eating herself to death', he summed up for himself with a dead-on, unflinching manner. And there was nothing he could do about it. He couldn't help her; all he could do was go to the hospital, call – and wait. The waiting to hear if things would get better or worse was unbearable. Her hospital bed, high and white, underlay all his thoughts. Sometimes he forgot the lyrics of a song he was singing and scatted more than usual. And when he scatted, the audiences thought that he was having fun, so they had fun listening.

Jim Mason had the phone number, that early spring, of the Hilton Hotel in Dallas, Texas, where Joe was working. He was planning to meet Jillean afterwards in the Imperial 400 on the Strip in Las Vegas. The movers' strike had just ended, so she was able to oversee the loading of their possessions. She was about to start a marathon drive across the country, carrying some boxes in the car, with a stopover in Chicago to see Joe's mother.

Not disconnected yet, the phone rang in the Williamses' apartment. Joe, lying in his Dallas hotel bed, listening to the drawl of the newscasters on the television set, had just got the call from Jim Mason. Joe's mother had died in her sleep that day, 3 April, 1968. The service and burial were planned for April 7, from St Paul's CME Church on Dearborn. Joe would finish his job, go to Chicago, and meet Jillean there.

Depressed and shocked, Joe dressed and went onstage that

night, working with pianist Freddie Crane and bassist Ed Soaf, unable to imagine what else to do. There was nothing. The waiting was over. Going onstage seemed to be the only thing he could rationally do, stuck in Texas. Still, it was unimaginable, sick as she had been, that his mother was dead. He performed by rote, reflexively. During the performance, he forgot his shock a little, hearing the music behind him and listening to his own voice. Dazed, he got through the set, with the music holding him upright, standing on his feet. The pianist played more fills than usual. Soaf, the bassist, helped out, too. Joe could hear that reliable walking bass going along behind him surely, not laying out for a minute, taking solos. The audience didn't notice the imperceptible difference.

Between shows, instead of lingering in the club, Joe hurried to his bedroom and spoke to Jillean again to find out how she was, what she was doing. She told him how things looked in the apartment; she would go out the door first thing in the morning, Friday, to get to Chicago by Sunday and meet him. 'I love you,' she said. 'I love you, too,' he said.

After the second show, he had a couple of drinks with the backup musicians and, extremely quiet, went to his room, lay down on the bed, with the television set off and no noise anywhere except the whisper of the air conditioner. He sank into a dreamless void. In the morning, the first thought that occurred to him was that his mother had died. Stunned, he didn't move, didn't turn on the television set, and began waiting for the night's performance and the next night's, and then he would get the hell out of there to go to Chicago. He called the airline to reserve a seat on the plane for Sunday and lay back down again, crying, helpless. The phone rang.

'Joe?' Jillean said with her musical voice lifting his name. 'Oh, my poor darling. I'm on the road, It's horrible. Just horrible news. Everything all at once. I had to speak to you. Are you all right?'

'Are you all right?' Joe said, sitting up.

'Me? I'm fine. It's King. You do know, don't you?'

'No,' Joe said, his voice rising slightly to a soft falsetto note; his voice often touched that register lightly when he wasn't sure of what was going on. 'What is it?'

'Reverend Martin Luther King, darling. He's been shot in Memphis. The news just came over the car radio. They've shot him. I'm sorry to tell you – he's dead.'

'Oh, God,' Joe said. Holding the phone with one hand, he leaned across the bed, switched on the television set as he had normally done every other morning, when he first woke up, and watched news film of the crowd scene in Memphis. People milled around the building where King had been shot. Then the film switched to the Atlanta church, where King had been the minister. Joe recalled sitting in that Baptist church by the vestry one time. Another time he had sat in the Amen corner, on the right hand side of the church, with the deacons and officers of the church and with King's father. King had included Joe in an Easter Sunday service. And there on television was the Reverend King, Sr, grim-faced, walking down the church steps, not looking at the cameras that followed him.

Joe went downstairs to the club, where the white audience was depending on the black musicians. After work, Freddie Crane and his wife, Lucy, Ed Soaf and the drummer, too, went to Joe's room with him and sat there eating and drinking all night. Joe kept the television set tuned to the turmoil in Memphis and Atlanta and saw films from the ghettos, too, with some rioting and looting. Mostly blurred images and people moving fast.

On Saturday morning, Dick Hitt, a newspaper writer, a fan and a friend, driving a shiny Jaguar, picked Joe up at the hotel's front door and headed towards a golf club, trying to divert him from his mourning and help him through the hard time. Hitt, a tall man who always had a twinkle in his eye and not much of a drawl that Joe could discern, drove past Dealey Plaza and, in the brilliant sunlight, pointed to a building. Lee Harvey Oswald had fired from there and killed President Kennedy. And Hitt reached over and patted Joe on the shoulder.

The country was killing off its best men, Joe thought. Now King, too, the public leader whom Joe had revered – absolutely adored and respected, an even younger man than Kennedy, was gone. And Miss Anne, too, his first and most important private mentor, who had loved him and truly, deeply wished him well, when others had not cared or barely noticed. Two profoundly sad losses coming at once. He stayed outwardly calm in public in Texas, while he felt that the African, the Indian, the essential man in him were dealing with the spirits of those whom he had loved and what they had wanted and meant – and how they had taken a part of him.

Hitt steered Joe by the arm into the club. The white members looked at Joe coolly – the only black man playing golf among them. But they didn't say anything to Hitt, who was taller than Joe, with a far sharper manner of speaking. The game seemed endless to Joe. He kept score but sometimes forgot what tee he was on.

Getting dressed for work that night, he watched the television peripherally and heard that there were quite a few riots going on around the country. Not everywhere, but in Chicago, yes. His pulse raced at the news. King would have stood up to talk against the violence. Joe was thoroughly impatient and wanted to say something to the rioters, but he had to finish dressing, go on stage, and get the night over with. He was making it through the ordeal in Texas, somehow, until the last song of the night: 'Goin' to Chicago'. He sang, oh yes, he was going to Chicago, and he wasn't going to take anyone with him, and he wasn't going to find Miss Anne living there, so it would be an empty, desolate town. He began to cry on stage: 'Here I am, singing with tears in my eyes, I can't even hear the music', he thought. Afterwards the musicians sat with him again all night.

He arrived at the Executive House Hotel on Wacker Drive before Jillean the next day and called the Metropolitan Funeral Home right away. At the funeral home, he saw a dozen roses that Sammy Davis, Jr had sent, took a rose and put it in his mother's hands as she lay in the coffin.

The next morning, he went to a florist shop that he knew and tried to buy roses, too, but the florist gave him a rose instead, saying: 'All the flowers you bought for her? You take this.' Pianist Jimmy Jones, in town, went to the funeral home and told Joe to keep his head up during the church service.

While the minister was talking at the St Paul's CME church at 46–44 Dearborn, Joe's head kept going up – and up – until he was nearly looking at the ceiling. He started crying when the minister started talking about all the social services and organizations his mother had worked for. Joe was incredulous that the minister didn't mention that she was a musician, too. She could play the organ. But the minister didn't say so. Why not? Joe, Jim Mason and Jillean drove to the Lincoln Cemetery and buried Joe's mother next to her mother's grave.

He and Jillean agreed that they would still meet at the Imperial 400 on the Strip the following Sunday. She would continue driving alone, taking the car and the crates. He would stay behind and help Jim with his mother's business, then fly to meet her. As Jillean left, Joe was watching King's funeral on television, along with films of the riots in the black neighbourhoods. Immediately after the funeral, Joe rushed to the ABC television studio and found many other celebrities and well-known black Chicagoans, some of whom had preceded him on the air; others would follow, trying to convince people to stop rioting.

Joe broadcast: 'I can't remember any of you rioting, burning or looting after President Kennedy was killed. I see no reason why you should honour the Reverend Martin Luther King any less.'

# *13 Love and* Lebensraum *in Las Vegas*

Late on Sunday night, he flew to meet Jillean, who had already arrived, seen the house and loved it. She was waiting in the hotel room they had reserved. They spent the night browsing for a while in one of the Strip casinos, where neither had ever gambled for more than a few minutes, and having dinner. Joe decided to wait until the morning to look at the house. And they spent the night holding each other. Early they saw the sun rise over the Sierra Nevada, with a roseate-coloured splash spreading into the blue sky over Sunrise Mountain and the other snow-capped mountains ringing the flat desert town entirely. In the distance, the pastel-coloured mountains didn't look very tall, rather like a toy range, but in the aggregate, they made a magisterial impression. The moving parts of the neon signs on the Strip kept revolving in some places but they didn't capture the Williamses' attention so much as the mountains and the warm wind blowing on a bright, desert winter morning. And Joe and Jillean had a sense of having an horizon in the midst of their losses. The moving vans were at their house, when they arrived.

Fairly soon Joe was on the road again, as he usually was thirty to forty weeks a year, because he could not sit tight for long and stay in his income bracket. Jillean loved Las Vegas, still a small place, with mostly one-storey houses in those days. It wouldn't sprawl and acquire a quarter of a million population for another decade. While Joe was away, she explored neighbouring Henderson, a little town built for workers on Boulder Dam renamed Hoover. Henderson nearly ran into Boulder City. Such lore appealed to Jillean. She liked the stucco walls and the wood-shingled roofs with such a pretty Spanish feeling that typified the town's architecture, even though she thought it was stupid to have such easily flammable roofs. She and Joe had a roof like that. One early morning, as she was putting the dogs out, she sat watching a picturesque roof two fairways away catch fire. It happened far enough away from her house so that she didn't have to worry. But the roof burned rapidly and made her want another type.

Joe thought more about plane connections. He could get back and forth easily, so long as he got to Los Angeles first. Then he found good connections to Las Vegas. Plane services became better, as time passed. The airport grew; more airlines scheduled direct flights. And Joe found that Las Vegas was a ball. He could go into any casino he liked and watch the rehearsals. He always enjoyed them and often found that they were better than the shows.

One afternoon he wandered into a rehearsal of a Frank Sinatra show about to open at Caesar's Palace and listened to Frank sing. Then he listened to Frank yell bloody murder at somebody for quite a few minutes. Joe cringed. When he and Frank sat down to have lunch, Joe said, 'Frank, we do not yell, unless there are many thousands of dollars involved.'

Sooner or later, Joe found, all his friends arrived in Las Vegas. Bruce Cooper made special trips to Vegas when he visited Los Angeles on business and even co-ordinated his schedule to coincide with Joe's. Jillean's travelling friends flew in for the day from Los Angeles, too. Rozelle Gayle and his wife who lived in LA visited Joe and Jillean without Rozelle having to pack his own tennis or golf shoes. So Rozelle's suitcase was lighter and easier to carry than if he hadn't shared Joe's shoe size. Joe sometimes had a surprise gift of patent-leather shoes for Rozelle, because Joe usually bought several pairs whenever he found something he liked in the right size.

From the vantage point of his house, Joe could take photos of Frank Sinatra and Jack Nicklaus, the famed golfer. And when Joe Louis visited Las Vegas, he stopped his game and went to the Williamses' house for a glass of orange juice every day. The house was separated from the course by a short hedge with a hole in it. Louis could have conversations through the hole;

once he told Jillean that he was wearing Joe Williams's green and white golf shoes, size 13½, loaned to him by the country club's valet. Perry Como stopped his game at the Williamses' house, and Pat Boone and his daughter took a break from their games, too.

Las Vegas temperatures usually rose to about 102 in July and August, though sometimes to 110. But Jillean didn't mind, since she didn't run around a lot at noon. She played golf very early in the morning or late in the afternoon. Soon after arriving, she discovered a humane society for animals and took in a stray dog. So before and after golf, she took the dog for a walk. When she couldn't find a home for it, she kept it. That began her collection of cats and dogs. She volunteered a lot of time for humane-society work and walked several dogs at once. Some people thought that she might be substituting the animals for children, but she told Joe that was nonsense. If she had wanted children, she would have had them. She said she was 'lousy' with babies, 'great' with children – and 'great' with animals.

After a while she owned the legal limit for the neighbourhood, cleaning them, making them as fit and cuddly-looking as possible, fluffing white hair, healing a lump on a collie's neck that made him look like a yak for a while. Among the strays that she couldn't find homes for and couldn't bear to part with anyway was a canny, blind, part-poodle called Radar; it learned where every stick of furniture stood in the house.

Joe was glad that Jillean was happy, not sitting around the house, not twiddling her thumbs or getting fat, waiting for him to arrive. A happy person made for a pleasant companion in life's journey. He wished that everyone could find as happy a companion as he had done, for we were all in the same boat, on the same planet, he was afraid, *'Isn't that nice?'*, he ruminated with a trace of ferocious irony, thinking about the crowd scene on the planet.

To have a happy marriage with a musician, you had to have your own thing going, Jillean had known from the start – and had always wanted. Having it was not as difficult for her as switching it off, when Joe came home, she discovered. She sometimes scheduled meetings for humane societies and then found out that Joe was arriving at the same time. She cooked his dinners and ran out of the door – not a popular arrangement with Joe, she thought, but he never stopped her or said that he objected. Still, she felt guilty about going out on the first night that he came home. Then she went and came home clearing her throat.

He liked that part. Anyway, when he arrived, he didn't want to whoop it up and take her out, because whooping it up was part of his job. It was important for him to rest for the next trip. So if she wanted to go to restaurants, theatres and clubs, she could go with him on the road anytime she chose, as long as she could get one of her two sitters to stay with the animals.

In Las Vegas, they lived modestly, without flash, never going to the casinos. When they first arrived, Joe worked for fifteen weeks at the Tropicana and the MGM on the Strip, and he once substituted for Lainie Kazan at the Sahara. Otherwise he never worked in the casinos except to do benefits. Jillean wanted him to work there, because she thought it would be nice to save the expensive plane fares and have him work and live at home part of the year. But John Levy didn't book Joe into casinos. Jillean thought that Las Vegas was afraid of so-called jazz singers and only wanted big-name 'pop' and country-and-western singers. You had to become a politician with the influential people, if you wanted to perform regularly in Las Vegas. You had to drink, gamble and generally lobby with the entertainment directors. Joe didn't like to do that. After singing, he liked to have a quiet drink in his dressing-room with fans who came to see him and give him their news or eat and drink at their tables, where he was invited. He wasn't the type to push himself.

A few times his children visited. There were ten pools on the country club and one pool for every few houses. The children loved the pool three doors away. But aside from the pool, they didn't like Las Vegas and insisted that Cincinnati was the best place they could think of. They visited less and less frequently, calling occasionally to tell Joe what they were doing.

JoAnn started college, which Joe sent her tuition money for. But she dropped out and worked for a while as a civil servant, he thought. Then, having met a man with whom she became involved, she had a son, Dante LeShawn. And Joe started carrying a photograph of his grandson in his wallet, along with a shot of Jillean in a ravishingly beautiful pose, and a picture of JoAnn, too. By phone, Joe asked JoAnn if she were thinking of marrying the young man. But she said, 'Oh, no, no, Daddy, he's not much.' But she had another son with him, too. Joe Jr began working in Cincinnati and had a daughter with his girlfriend. Joe Sr made a trip to Cincinnati and found his son driving around in a 'hog' – a Cadillac. While his father admired the car, Joe Jr complained that it was guzzling gas – and he was thinking of switching to a fuel-conserving BMW, which Joe thought was very impressive, he later told audiences, talking about his kids sometimes in clubs. He was happy his son had a Cadillac and delighted that he knew enough about cars to see the advantages of the BMW. And the whole idea of his son being able to afford either car amused Joe Sr very much. But out of touch with his son for a while after that, Senior didn't learn if the BMW ever came to pass.

And mostly he found it difficult to talk about his children; they had never taken advantage of the things that he had wanted to give them and rejected his world altogether. He had never been able to communicate the aspirations and vision, which his mother had imparted to him. And the kids had their own mother to be loyal to. So if he talked about his children at all, he said that he was proud that Joe Jr could afford a BMW and glad that JoAnn could confide in him that she absolutely wouldn't have any more children; 'She knows that she can tell Daddy anything,' he told a friend – and then fell silent. Between Lemma and himself an unquiet truce was administered by a bank.

After Joe and Jillean had been living in the Las Vegas Country Club Estates for seven years, another, larger house with a garden site at the back appealed to them. They moved in 1975 to the corner of K— and H— Drive. To Joe the house in the spare, unfrilly neighbourhood symbolized a place that he had bought at the best possible interest rate. And the house was important so that he could rest, be loved and love someone. By 1977, he was already getting a thrill out of the good interest rate he had managed to buy at.

'Talk about lucky, ha ha. We got in about two years before

interest rates went up,' Joe told Eddie 'Lockjaw' Davis, who had moved to Las Vegas, too, by that time. 'I had no idea that would happen. So we put in at eight something. The first place had been a seven.'

And he and 'Jaws' sat around, having a holiday at home in a sunny resort. And there was an ease in life.

# 14 Intimations of a Renaissance

Bespectacled, with a pianissimo speaking voice and a 'Minute Waltz' speed of conversation, Ellis Larkins completed all his courses in the Juilliard School of Music between 1940 and 1943, then went to work as a jazz pianist. He enjoyed critical success in jazz, despite a short stint, one of his less glorious undertakings, as a whorehouse pianist in *Pousse: Cafe,* a Broadway show that lasted six days in 1966. The show was based on *The Blue Angel* and had Duke Ellington's music. But something was wrong with it. Larkins went back to being a jazz pianist.

In 1968, through a mutual friend, John Levy called Ellis and said, 'Would you mind helping Joe for a while?'

'I don't mind,' Ellis said.

So he was flown to California and introduced to Joe, who was singing with Thad Jones and Mel Lewis quite often. In keeping with his temperament, Larkins had probably the softest touch in jazz piano. His approach blended well with Joe's intimate style. The itinerary was settled. In February, 1969, Joe and Ellis set off for an eighteen-day tour of the NCO camps in Germany. From there they flew back to the Hong Kong Bar in the Century Plaza in LA, where they would play together a couple of times a year from then on. And the Tropicana in Las Vegas. And they made rounds of clubs in San Mateo, Chicago, St Louis, hiring bassists and drummers in each town.

Not only did Larkins love Joe's voice and regard him as the greatest living male singer, but lyrics especially attracted the pianist. He had always played with them in mind; anyone who didn't, he thought, was just playing a block of notes.

Sometimes Joe and Ellis worked without a bassist or

drummer, asking them to 'lay out'. Then Joe displayed the whole range of his voice, riveting an audience's attention upon him; he could dominate that way. Ellis thought that Joe could sing anything effectively, even the Billie Holiday tune 'You ain't Going to Bother Me No More'. Quickly Ellis began to sense Joe's moods and habits; Joe would scat if he were having fun with the group. He rarely rehearsed and simply told Ellis the lineup on opening night. They knew thousands of tunes and could choose from them easily or stay with Joe's book. If Ellis played something new once, Joe could concentrate totally and know it right away. So Ellis admired how retentive Joe's ear was. Furthermore Ellis had good times with Joe, who had a sense of fun, while Ellis was simply an 'innocent bystander', he claimed, practising the traditional jazz musician's code of *omerta.**

For Joe could go out on the town with pretty girls swirling around him, drinking a little, though he couldn't take more than a couple of drinks before he started to get a vague look. But he could still sit in and sing on a friend's gig and not look at all woozy. And he could simply go out on the town with the boys, most of whom could drink him under the table in the first half hour of a night of club crawling, and have a great time and in the morning look as neat and clean-cut as a gym teacher.

There was nothing new in Joe's lifestyle repertoire; he lived pretty much the way he had always done, flirting, working hard, eating fruits, vegetables, hearty soups. For a while he took some pills for slightly elevated blood pressure. And he knew how to pace himself to stay healthy. He didn't bother to worry about his voice; he never got into the habit of nose and throat sprays. He didn't think about being tired, and he wasn't usually.

Once Ellis and Joe travelled to Boston, Mass. to perform, taking Joe Jr on the road with them. Senior, not one to condone free rides, told Joe Jr to take care of the music – 'Never leave the book behind!' Ellis, watching Junior sit in for a few minutes with a drumset, got the idea that he might like to play. But his father didn't think so; he thought Junior was more impressed with his father's female fans. One took him to a Red Sox

*'Silence' in Italian

baseball game during an afternoon. Another took him to her summer house in Marblehead, Mass. 'Altogether the ladies are being very nice to him,' Senior observed, chuckling.

And Joe Sr was having a good time, not necessarily expecting things to get very much better, not expecting anything cataclysmic, either. But life was like golf, he knew. Sometimes it went better than he could ever imagine, if he just kept swinging. He did notice that the reviewers began treating him with greater deference by the early seventies. In 1972, John Wilson wrote: 'In the twelve years since Joe Williams left Count Basie's orchestra to follow his own path as a singer, he has grown slowly but steadily from the powerful blues singer he was . . . to an extremely perceptive and convincing singer of ballads and unusual pop songs and eventually to a relaxed, witty and debonair monologist or on-stage conversationalist.' 'Thank you very much,' Joe said to himself, reading.

> At the Half Note . . . where he is making one of his infrequent New York appearances . . . Mr Williams is putting all his attributes together as casual, low-keyed, compleat entertainer. He has a personal warmth that communicates particularly well in a small room such as the Half Note. It is this close rapport with his listeners that is an important factor in making the varied aspects of his performances come off so well.
>
> The blues he sang with Basie are still the strong backbone of his repertory, but he has become so skilful at making something provocative even of songs that, on the surface, seem relatively routine that one is left with the conviction that he could bring a sparkle to any bit of musical dross.
>
> Mr Williams is sharing the bandstand with the Charles McPherson quintet, a group given to bop-influenced themes and long solos.

Basically John Levy kept the organization running as usual. He even found Joe a film role as a moonshiner in the hills. Joe dressed as a hayseed in *Moonshine War,* starring Alan Alda. Later, when he saw himself in a publicity still, sitting in a rocking chair on a ramshackle front porch, in clothes that would also have been suitable for a workday in Cordele and heavy shoes that could massacre a golf green, Joe cracked: 'Things ain't been going too great lately.' As an actor he was fine, though he had not found the role he had been dreaming of all his life. No, the film was not the highlight of his career, nor Alan Alda's either. But it was interesting to do a film; Joe thought it might have been nicer if the picture had been entitled *From Here to Eternity*. That kind of vehicle, in which another baritone he knew had fared very well.

More to the point, Joe signed up to do a record with Cannonball Adderley, the saxophone player and leader, and his little trumpet-playing brother, Nat. They were two educated musicians, and Cannonball was extremely influential in jazz circles. Joe had sung with them so much on the road anyway and sat in with them whenever their paths crossed. Pittsburgh had been just one of the lucky rendezvous spots. And they had starred in a tribute to black music in New York City. The Adderleys had a contract to make a series of records for Fantasy. With Joe along, the record, *Joe Williams Live*, turned out so well that the Adderleys decided to keep his magnificent voice in mind for something else important they were working on. *Playboy's* review said the album title should have read *Joe Williams Lives*. Joe had thrived on all his experience. He liked his own work on that record, too. 'We're all Sagittarians,' he mused, 'so sure enough there would be fire.'

He particularly liked Ellington's 'Heritage', which he sang slowly, thoughtfully, with the effect of an elegy. And Joe did a tune unusual musically on that record because bassist Walter Booker, who had become a regular in the Adderley group, switched to guitar to accompany 'Sad Song' – 'Here's a sad song that has no purpose except to excite the mind,' Joe began in a deep, dolorous voice.

And in 1974, when a critic wrote that Joe was 'singing the ruggedest blues with great polish', it was in effect the essence of his whole style: what everyone was writing about him. He could take a ballad or a pop, jump tune and imbue it with blues feeling. He could give a blues the feeling of *lieder*.

In the mid-70s, something happened in jazz generally. Not

the only good example but as good as any, Count Basie's band in the Newport Jazz Festival concert on 8 July 1974 in NYC seemed to come to life gradually, as the old soloists returned to their chairs. Al Grey's music teemed with joy from his first trombone note; he loosened up the newer Basie personnel with his earthy sounds. Basie's new bandsinger, because of his overtones of Jimmy Rushing and Joe Williams (the new singer wasn't allowed simply to be himself, either) stirred up some excitement for a while. Veteran saxophonist Jimmy Forrest let go, too. And then John Wilson wrote:

> The most powerful catalyst of the evening was Joe Williams . . . Reunited with the Basie band, singing some of the blues he had once sung with along with other things that have become part of his repertoire since he has been working as a single, Mr Williams built up a long, utterly triumphant performance that was a masterpiece of pacing, projection and a fascinatingly winning personality.

First intimations of a renaissance, as critics told the public that the music from the old days – the thirties, forties and fifties – had really been great. And you had to hear it now, vital and stylish to realize what a priceless American family jewel that old jazz had really been. There was nothing like it. If America had loved it once because it was fresh, different, novel, America would rekindle its passion now, because the music sounded even fresher, cheekier, more rambunctious and absolutely musical. Rock would never ever be that good. So let's hear more of that great old jazz, critics implied.

Exactly what made people pay newly enraptured attention to jazz again, nobody knew for sure. The hippie movement was waning. Skirts were getting longer, attitudes more conservative; money was tighter. Jazz musicians began trickling back from Europe, with the notion that they could find more jobs in the US than in Europe. Rock music didn't have as much cachet anymore. Some of Rock's fans were defecting, many looking for diversions in the even more chaotic, elemental punk rock. And other people knew not what they wanted.

The harmonies of progressive, bebop jazz, which had been

too sophisticated and convoluted for audiences in the forties and fifties, now sounded mellow. People heard more of that and even older jazz on radios and juke boxes. And the swing bands, which had never stopped touring, began commanding more attention. Shortly after Joe went out as a solo, Basie's band played for President Kennedy's inaugural in Washington. Then the band became the darling of the rich, playing at private parties on estates – the Mellons, for one. But now the band began attracting larger audiences to concerts and one-night stands. Critics wrote with greater zest and got more space in the papers, it seemed, about the vitality of those swinging bands: Basie's, Ellington's, and other bands of the famous old-time white leaders, now led by newcomers, who retained the old band names and played the old music; and smaller, black groups led by famous leaders, too. Fine singers, retired by rock joined the big 'ghost' bands and toured again.

Stopping to listen, people were refreshed, reminded of how exciting that music had been. The bands had seemed larger than life because they had played great music. And everyone knew at least a little dab of something about the bands, about jazz, about standard tunes written in the twenties, thirties and forties.

An ageing Duke Ellington seemed to have taken on the patina of an icon during his television performances with his band and on his road tours. Once denied a Pulitzer for composition when he was in his sixties, he had gallantly remarked that fate was being kind to him. It was preventing him from becoming too successful too young. A decade later, his fate changed, as audiences became enthralled at the familiar sight of his slightly roguish face, with his ironic smile, his elegant posture, his swept-back hairdo, and his elegant, subtle gestures. He had acquired – mystique. And the music was stirring. Even younger, avant-garde jazz musicians, who toned down their wails, were able to find a little work in a few clubs, catching on to the coat-tails of the sweeter, less intense, more seasoned jazz sounds that had graduated in public perception from infectious tunes to popular classics.

Possibly the racial situation in the US, improved since the 1960s equal-opportunity acts, passed in part to quell the riots of the Black demi-revolution, had paved the way for some blacks to find their way into the Establishment. By the late sixties, the National Endowment of the Arts gave the nod to jazz. Black jazz pianist Bobby Timmons was one of the first to receive an NEA grant for jazz. And powered by its own energy, jazz relaunched itself, this time into a more lofty orbit.

With two bars of music, Count Basie's brass section could decapitate a rock group, or so it seemed for the prodigal audiences above twenty-one, who were returning to jazz and paying high prices for concert tickets. Among the younger leaders in jazz, Dizzy Gillespie, a bebop innovator, began to get more television exposure and attention for his ersatz loony, charming public personality, as well as for his music. And a TV vignette of him dressed as a swami on 'The Muppets', singing 'Swing Low Sweet Cadillac' started to be broadcast and rebroadcast. With Count Basie attracting wider attention, Joe Williams, as part of the Basie band's history, began dominating stages on which he appeared in Basie reunion concerts. Joe was singing with a slightly deeper voice and wider experience, in many ways better than ever. He thought to himself; he was putting everything he knew into every performance – 'Now's the time to do it, I'm not a kid any more.' Younger and healthier than Basie, Joe had invigorating dash. And both he and Basie were, most of all, still swinging, the secret of their original success.

Essentially not much more than a decade after he became venerated, Duke Ellington found his health failing. He kept travelling somehow. In May 1974 he died. And not long afterwards, so did many of the veteran musicians in his band. Joe, who had always loved singing Ellington songs, including at least one in nearly every performance, went to sing in a memorial concert at the Hollywood Bowl. Benny Powell, who after a dozen years had also left Basie's band, played in the orchestra of Mercer Ellington, Duke's son, behind Joe. Benny lived on the West Coast and played in the Hollywood Bowl, about half a mile or six blocks long, quite often. Suddenly he heard a powerful voice fill up that enormous space, as Joe began singing *a cappella* from Ellington's 'First Sacred Concert' – 'In the beginning, God.'

For Powell, Joe transformed that afternoon's performance into a divine service. It no longer seemed to be Hollywood or the Hollywood Bowl but an extraterrestrial sphere where a heavenly power had come through Joe and lifted Powell's spirit. Powell was quite startled, when he realized how magnificent Joe's voice had become – or was. When Joe had sung 'Every Day' with Basie, Benny had always noticed the richness of Joe's voice. But when Joe began singing with neither orchestra nor riffs nor chords behind him, he was plainly a different Joe Williams from the bandsinger, who used to sit across the aisle from Benny on the bus, he thought.

There was a grandeur to many of the jazz concerts by the mid-70s. Occasionally there was more pomp than swing. But it was a time for some people to reminisce with old sounds, and it was also a time for others to try more ambitious projects. A writer named Diane Lampert was looking for a score for lyrics she had written based upon the legend of John Henry, whose livelihood was destroyed by the machine. She called her libretto *Big Man* and spent thirteen years in search of the right music. She approached all kinds of musicians, even Duke Ellington. Nothing had satisfied her.

By the early seventies, she got in touch with Cannonball Adderley. And he and Nat wrote a little music, which Diane and her production team liked; she liked Nat Adderley's composition, 'Work Song', in particular. And Cannonball and Nat spent four years writing the entire score for *Big Man,* as they travelled on the road. It was a new kind of project for them; they had never scored a whole show before. They liked what they were composing and decided to record it as an original cast album, even though there hadn't been any production of the show as yet. That might come later or might not. Neither of the Adderleys knew or cared much about production. But they knew music. And by contract they still owed a record to Fantasy.

One day, when the music was written, Cannonball looked at Nat and said, 'Joe Williams.'

Nat said, 'That's right.'

After getting Joe to agree to sing the role of John Henry, the Adderleys hired the rest of the cast: Randy Crawford, with an earthy yet youthful soprano, played Carolina, Joe's love interest. In 1975, the cast went into the studio. Musically the record came off so well, with Joe an authoritative hero doing an enlivening score, that the team got the idea to produce it on stage.

George Wein's Newport Jazz Festival in July 1976 in New York seemed to be a convenient forum. Randy Crawford was replaced by Denise Delapenha. Joe stayed in the cast. Cannonball Adderley had died suddenly the previous fall. So Nat Adderley led the Basie Black and Blues Band on stage. Then the sound system failed the singers, who also held scripts and, concentrating on the papers, occasionally tripped over wires and underfoot. The performance became a case of fine melodies and lyrics in search of a producer. Joe won good notices for his intepretation of John Henry, however. Once in a while, after that, Joe thought about how *Big Man* could be a very good show, as long as he didn't have to sing the role every night. He didn't see himself that way and talked about how Hal Frazier, with his massive head and shoulders and a glorious baritone voice, would be fine as John Henry. But Joe preferred to have the blues every day rather than work every night.

The Basie band reunion concerts held no surprises for Joe; they were tantamount to Thanksgiving Day dinners several times a year. Less known to the public but special thrills for jazz musicians were the State Department jazz tours. In 1979, a State Department official approached trumpeter Clark Terry and asked him which singer he would like to take along on his tours of Asia and Africa. Terry said, 'Joe Williams.'

And so Joe and Clark and his quintet went to their doctors to learn when to take the Aralen, an anti-malaria drug. Terry's quintet consisted of the alto saxophonist Chris Woods, who later toured with Basie's band; pianist Charles Fox; bassist Victor Sproles, and Dave Adams, a young, white, blond drummer. Joe was tremendously excited at the prospect of the tours, first the Asian, then the African tour later in the year. Since Clark Terry was the leader, he got an assignment to write some of a semi-official diary of the African trip, which was published in *Jazz Spotlite News* late in 1979:

> Our first concert in Freetown (Sierra Leone) . . . attended by 200 jazz-starved people was a smashing hit. We . . . did our bit, and Joe Williams wowed them with his recorded hits, such as 'Every Day' and 'Goin' to Chicago'. It was quite refreshing after the concert to attend the reception given in our honour and hobnob with all the African and US Embassy dignitaries and to indulge in the palatable hors d'oeuvres and small talk.

Before Joe ate anything, he always had a moment's pause about the effect the food might have on him. He avoided fresh fruits, unless he peeled them himself; he never ate raw vegetables. Just for good measure before every meal, he began drinking a shot of vodka with a beer chaser, no ice thanks: you can get dysentery, even amoebic dysentery from ice. Mmmmm, but no vodka or beer before breakfast; he would take his chances on breakfast. And every day, he noticed, he still hadn't got sick. Clark Terry again:

> Sunday we were given a brunch at the home of US Ambassador Jack Linehan . . . The residence was a palatial home equipped with servants, great food and a fantastic view from atop the highest peak of Freetown . . . Sunday night was soul-food night at the home of the US Public Affairs Officer Clathan McClain Ross . . . Mrs Ross . . . did her own cooking . . . Theirs, too, was a cool pad, up in the hills of Freetown . . .

And from there to Ghana, where Joe was supposed to be interviewed by the country's equivalent of Johnny Carson. But he didn't show up and instead the American Embassy staff took the musicians for a tour of Accra – Jamestown, the beach, the Black Star Monument, the old Portuguese castle where Nkruma had his offices and the new monument to Peace and Freedom. Joe loved it. Next came Lagos: ' . . . a big, thriving city and a busy one. You can feel the pace of people doin' things the minute you step into the airport', Terry recorded.

Nigeria is the most populous nation in Africa, the richest in

Black Africa . . . In some countries of Africa, they experience an occasional power failure or water cut-off. When you walk into your hotel room, even though the room is beautiful, clean, air-conditioned, attuned to room service, etc, you still find a few candles in the drawer – just in case. It was customary for us to be alert enough to leave the taps on and sleep lightly, because the minute we heard the water running, regardless of the hour, we'd jump out of bed immediately to 'shit, shave and shower' and do our laundry and then plop back into bed with smiles on our faces.

The first of two scheduled concerts was held at the University of Lagos where there were approximately 2,000 in the audience. They had Art Allade and the Preachers with guest star Zeal Onyea appearing before us and of course the ultimate finale was the combined session with all performers doing 'When the Saints Go Marchin' In' . . . Then, in anticipation of things to come, I couldn't help but think of the lyrics of one of Joe Williams's songs ['Goin' to Chicago']: 'Hurry, down, sunshine, let's see what tomorrow brings'.

Tomorrow brought continental breakfast. Continental breakfast doesn't mean the same thing in Africa as it does in Europe, at least at the Eko Hotel. I had a thimble of weird-tasting tomato juice, a pot of jailhouse coffee and two puckered rolls with butter. The price was 3 Niara, 10 Koboc, the equivalent of $7 . . .

The lowest point for everyone in our entourage occurred as the result of a decision that we should really see Africa by surface – two vans and one air-conditioned car, from Ibadan to Kaduna. They told us that it would take ten hours, which was not a pleasant thought to begin with but it turned out that it took fifteen and a half hours. While the ride was bad enough, that was not the worst part of the trip. This two-lane highway, A-125, was literally lined on both sides with vehicles that didn't make it! Most of them trailer-type oil tankers plus lorries and practically every type of vehicle that you can imagine. They had all overturned and burned to a crisp! . . . The vehicles suddenly ran into unwarned areas with potholes a foot and a half deep. And that's putting it mildly! Imagine encountering this condition for a least twelve

> of the fifteen odd hours . . . We figured out that on the average, every 100 yards there was a grim reminder. I'll never again complain about the potholes in Bayside, my home town, nor about the kamikazi taxi drivers in Tokyo after that experience on 'The Road to Kaduna'. I hope that the first 'must' on the agenda of the new regime is to cool out the Road to Kaduna . . . As the song goes, 'Everything Must Change'.

'And furthermore,' Joe Williams noted, 'there's no such place as Kaduna!' as the musicians searched for it in vain, never arriving there.

Terry continued: 'My heart stood still, as we passed the gravesite of Kenyatta' (in Nairobi, Kenya) 'where the eternal flame burns, just like the ones at the tomb of JFK in Washington . . . '

In Madagascar:

> the concert was held at the home of Acting Ambassador and Mrs Robert South Barrett IV. A select group of sixty to seventy special invitees was there – mostly diplomats and dignitaries with their spouses. It was a very special privilege to play for this audience, even though I'm sure all of them were not jazz fans . . . A lady diplomat from Peking was noticed sleeping while Joe was belting out 'Every Day I Have the Blues'.

'She was *sound asleep*,' Joe saw. Afterwards, when she woke up, she told him that his singing was marvellous.

Terry continued:

> Just as we knew it would be, the soul-food dinner at Mr and Mrs McGaffie's home was out of sight. Madagascar red beans and rice, collard greens, cornbread and fried yardbird. I think we all OD'd on the musical fruit. I know I did, as I suffered for a few days thereafter. Although the cooking was done by their Malagache staff, you could tell that Nell [Mrs McGaffie] was into each one of those pots . . . Unfortunately for me, through some quirk of fate, I encountered a case of the 'African Quickstep', which kept me moving rapidly to the

> john for about a week. Thanks to the Embassy doctor in Abidjan [Ivory Coast, the group's next stop] for introducing me to paregoric. For about a week I was busier than a one-legged midget in an ass-kicking contest . . . '

And since the water wasn't running in the hotels all the time, Terry's misery was compounded. A black American diplomat in one of the African countries had been telling Joe about some of the hardships of Africa. The diplomat had finished by saying he was sure that all Americans, black and white, were glad that their people had made the boat. To cheer Terry up, when he was sick, Joe passed the message along in a more droll way. 'Ain't you glad you made the boat?'

All along the way, Joe managed to ferret out golf courses. That was the good news. He also had to watch Victor Sproles's dismay when his $7,000 Italian bass got a foot-long crack from a jolt in a pothole on another marathon trip by land from one city to another. Joe knew it would not be what he would become best known for, singing his way through Africa, riding elephants, visiting the Pyramids with their bazaar for the tourists at ground level and the camel dung all around. Joe could endure it as long as he was atop a camel and out of harm's way. And he backed out of trying to squeeze his big frame through an entrance to a pyramid. But he was endlessly fascinated by the spectacle. No plumbing, no electricity for the people; when the fire went out, then everybody went to bed.

In Lagos he looked out the window from his posh hotel at 6 a.m. and saw people leaving their huts, going to the public toilets; people urinating in the streets as a matter of course, as he had seen them do in Asia earlier in the year. While he survived several difficult rides through the countryside, he saw the mud huts that Africans had built for themselves. In the cities, the meat hung on pegs, covered with flies in the market stalls.

He marvelled at the stamina of the Peace Corps workers, black and white, who left their villages and made long trips to the cities to see the jazz musicians, thrilled to hear them and have a personal contact with the US. One worker had spent six months trying to get the ear of the elders and women in a village, he told Joe, asking them to boil water, so parasites wouldn't eat the guts of their children.

Joe found mixed reactions to jazz, depending upon whether the musicians played in an embassy or a university or a village, and whether they played for Africans who spoke European languages or native tongues. He sang mostly blues, thinking that everyone could appreciate the music.

There was a phenomenal reaction to Clark Terry and Chris Woods, who sang their invention called 'Mumbles', a double-talk routine in scat language that could sound like a political speech. And Joe Williams added his own scat tongue to the babble, a candidate for the opposition party, and the audience elected them.

Another day Joe watched with amusement when Dave Adams, the white drummer, whom Joe thought it was daring and novel for Terry to invite along, sat in with an African group. Adams could play the Africans' rhythms, but the Africans couldn't loosen up and play his very well. On the other hand, it wasn't so funny when Dave Adams got served first in restaurants and in lines at hotel desks, as all the musicians waited to dine or pay. Obviously residual colonialism, deference to the white man. So in restaurants, the group gave Dave their orders; he passed them along to waiters and commanded quick service.

By the end of the tour, back in the US, almost as a barometer of the renaissance of jazz and the belated respect for the music, Joe found out that he was going to win another *Down Beat* poll as the best male singer, as he had been doing nearly every year since 1974.

He had spent only six years with Basie – almost a peripheral amount of time out of a long, active life. But many people still thought of him as Basie's former bandsinger, a blues singer. For he had had his greatest hits during the Basie years, and proved that a very important part of life can take place in a very short period of time. So he had put a lot of energy into acquiring an image as a singer, not a blues or ballad or jazz singer. He wasn't even sure that he had actually acquired the image that he wanted. But he knew that he was simply singing, in every possible style, every possible type of music. And the polls noticed.

He liked lyrics that had meaning, that he could feel were full of sensibility – whimsy – even if they were only spoken. A song in which he asked a woman how it could possibly matter in one hundred years if she passed her kisses around now. That kind of thought: Jillean's definition of a Palm Court song, a genteel song, derived from the British expression, for which the elegant, decorous snack area of the Plaza Hotel in New York City was named. Joe liked to juxtapose tunes with antithetical sentiments, both of which made sense. So he sang 'Everything Must Change' and followed it with 'It's the Same Old Story'. And by singing one right after the other, he could communicate his idea of how complex and delicate people's relationships were. He tried to stay fresh, demanding some improvisation from his backup musicians, each time he sang his standard blues repertoire in clubs and hotels. And the critics did write that he was 'a tremendously vital performer who can find constantly fresh sources in his oldest material'. He sang 'with a forceful appeal that virtually lifts his listeners out of their seats'.

Eventually Ellis Larkins, still Joe's primary accompanist at the end of the seventies, decided to get off the road and settle down into a regular gig offered him at the Carnegie Tavern, a dark, fashionable little boite near Carnegie Hall. And Ellis could come from his New York City apartment, where he lived with his wife, Crystal, dressed in a fresh, ruffled formal shirt and tuxedo every night without having to pack and unpack. So Joe needed the right replacement, a pianist with whom he could develop intense rapport.

He worked with Sir Roland Hanna at Buddy's Place in New York City and with John Young in Chicago. Young had played piano with Andy Kirk's orchestra when Joe worked with Kirk. And Young had worked with Jay Burkhardt's orchestra. Sy Johnson played for Joe in New York City, Boston and Pittsburgh and did some particularly good arrangements for Joe – 'Just the Way You Are' in bossa nova rhythms. That was a crowd-pleaser. Joe could turn out his usual performance with any musician, even one whom he saw rarely or had never met before. The practice had been in Joe's earliest singing days. And he felt totally at ease playing on a special album, *Joe and*

*Prez*, part of a tribute to Lester Young. As Joe prepared to do the tunes, arranged by Bill Holman, whose swinging work Joe loved, he conjured up the whimsical tales he had heard about Prez, rather than the darker side of the man's life, which had ended in alcoholism in the Alvin Hotel. But Joe recalled the imaginative intensity of Prez's soft-toned horn playing and, inspired by the memory, sang one of the most exciting , all too brief scat versions of 'Lady be Good'.

Once Bruce Cooper heard Joe sing right through the work of a guitarist playing counterproductive nonsense. When Cooper asked him later how he did it, Joe said, 'You learn.' Joe didn't lean on the groups, but he needed a musician to work with regularly.

Pianist Norman Simmons first got a call from Levy to play with Joe in 1965 and found Joe's book very difficult. After that, occasionally Levy called Simmons to sit in for Ellis Larkins, but Norman wasn't at the top of the list. By 1979, however, he felt that his musicianship had improved. He had become familiar with Joe's repertoire. Called again, he played superbly for Joe.

In the music, Norman felt, he and Joe were having a love affair. Ten years younger than Joe, smaller and rounder, with a charming smile, Norman was constantly trying to organize his teaching, composing and playing careers. But life with Joe went smoothly. Norman felt happier with Joe than he had, in some ways, with his former employer, Carmen McRae. With Carmen, Norman had been learning the art of accompaniment: when to fill in for the singer, what to fill in, when to leave space for the voice; he learned to always lead and never 'lay out' and let a drummer take over. With Joe, Norman simply enjoyed himself, having learned all the lessons he needed from Carmen and then later, varied experiences.

Furthermore Norman had a fine, stable trio: Lisle Atkinson, the bassist, a Manhattan School of Music graduate, who learned the names of the tunes for the convenience of knowing what he was supposed to be playing, when a tune was called. Lisle, like Joe, had a special love for the harmonics. New Orleans-born Vernel Fournier, from the Ahmad Jamal trio in the 1950s, could play the loose rhythms for Joe's repertoire. And Norman held everything together.

Pretty quickly Joe and John Levy developed a strategy to save Joe's voice. Joe began delegating work to Norman, grooming him as a musical director. If they travelled on the road together without the trio and picked up bassists and drummers along the way, Joe told Norman what he wanted. Norman passed the word to the new musicians.

Joe would always say: 'Play it in any key you want, and we'll make the adjustment,' referring to himself as 'we', as he had always done, not quite sure why. But it was the team's 'we', the musical group's 'we', and even, he knew, the royal 'we'.

Norman appreciated Joe's generosity. Joe could sing in any key, as he had learned to do in Chicago, when no one adjusted for the singer. The singer had had to adjust or perish. Joe never gave all the responsibility to Norman and never blamed him if anything went wrong. Joe rehearsed Norman with a new piece of music until he knew it. On stage Joe could put a tempo right where it was supposed to be.

And Joe could keep his musicians fresh and entertained by coming out on stage and telling a raunchy joke about an African executioner's weapon, involving death by 'poonda', an overdose of sodomy. When his musicians heard any of his new jokes, they laughed along with the audience and felt reanimated. So Joe didn't rely upon their support totally but kept replenishing them, too.

Norman also noticed that Joe would start out with a piece of paper, such as the music for 'Changes', which he loved very much. At first Joe told Norman, 'Play this little hook' (lick or musical phrase). Then after a few performances, Joe said, 'I don't want to hear that all the time. We're playing jazz.' And after Norman improvised, Joe said, 'You see what you played there? That's what the cat would have written, if he could have thought of it.'

Norman saw that Joe could open and close shows with ballads, sometimes two or three in a row, in the mood of 'The Very Thought of You'. Most singers needed a bombastic entrance or exit. And Norman told a friend that he thought Joe was one of the strongest performers he had ever seen: 'Maybe it's only the strong, the big, that can give. The midgets are fighting for their lives every minute.' So Norman settled in to the job, watching audiences come to hear Joe because he had made them his friends by playing golf with them, doing benefits they had attended and talking with them, instead of trying to save his voice. Some other singers usually did back away. But fans and critics could find Joe, between shows, tucked away in odd corners of hotels, practising his golf swing, ready to chat. He liked talking. Everywhere he went, he found pressure on him to talk, backstage, on the telephone, on radio and TV, in addition to the night-time performances. He accepted many dates and, by never taking advantage of his opportunities to insult people, he consciously established his image as a debonair, friendly man.

So in addition to sharing in the Basie legend, he set his own example. And he thought about it consciously and hoped he would get the credit for it or persuade people to live up to his standards and be as civilized and respectful towards him as he acted towards them. Masters of ceremonies introduced him as 'Mr Jazz'. Musicians and behind-the-scenes people in the music business came to hear him, shake his hand and hear a pleasant word.

Norman, for one, felt that Joe cared about him. They didn't hang out together. Even on the road they gave each other space. Joe didn't ever talk to men the way he did to women and didn't think that men usually knew each other as candidly as men and women did. If a man had an overwhelming personal problem, he could talk to Joe about it. But normally musicians interacted on stage all the time. And that was the powerful connection. From that, Norman had the sense that he and Joe had implied to each other: 'Whatever you need, you get it.' So Norman regarded Joe as more than an employer, and he thought that many people felt that if there were anything they could do for Joe, they would do it.

'Most people have a few friends who feel that way. Joe has bunches,' Norman told his friend, 'because Joe becomes involved in things that affect other people. He's here to be with you. That's his message.' And Norman thought that the music and the camaraderie came first in his relationship with Joe, with money as a side benefit, and looked forward to the nights of work with Joe.

# *15 In Performance*

Before opening in a club at night, Joe and Norman discussed the performance. After that they let each other rest. Joe whiled away the afternoons lying on a couch, beside a TV set tuned to 'Days of Our Lives' or, if he were lucky, a sports event. In the evening, he put on work clothes – sometimes a canary-yellow jacket or a pale pink-coloured one. One jaunty ensemble, a dark jacket with a bow tie, made him look as youthful as a gym teacher dressed for assembly. And patent-leather shoes, some in pale pastel colours, others dark with buckles. He ate dinners at his favourite restaurants in all the cities. In New York, La Scala and from there, in October 1983, he went down to the Blue Note club in Greenwich Village.

He greeted everyone he knew inside the club. Michele Hendricks, Jon's daughter, a slender young singer with closely-cropped hair, a heart-shaped face and a torchy interpretation of 'Angel Eyes', walked by one night. Joe said, 'Yes, you do have angel eyes,' so offhandedly that it seemed diffident. Then to the bandstand, where he opened with a ballad: 'September in the Rain' came first; he scatted it, making his improvisation seem like his own bright idea born that moment – 'Swinging in the rain, we're swinging in the rain, September – in the rain.' The second tune was a ballad, too. He unified the music with the lyric so effectively that the audience thought it was hearing an electrifying jump tune. And then he alerted the audience with 'When Sunny Gets Blue' – 'and ho-old her nee-eer – when Sunny gets blue-ooo-ooo,' rising to a blue note and a major note. He introduced Lisle Atkinson and went smoothly into 'Everything Must Change' – 'a wounded heart must heal but never too soon.'

He told people about going to Sao Paulo, Brazil for a club engagement and eating marvellous breakfasts. And rice and beans – 'oooo—beans—oooo—beans'; he had worried about what to sing for a Portuguese-speaking people. But they asked for a tune he had even forgotten recording with Thad Jones – 'Imagination'; a plaintive ballad in Joe's interpretation, and done *rubato*, out of tempo. Even so he had had the full attention of a people enamoured mostly of the samba rhythm.

Then he shifted to his 'blues department' and prowled around the stage the way he liked to do when there was enough room. 'Crazy about you baby, but I just can't stand your price.' So he was going back to a woman whose plainer tastes he could rely on – 'kidney stew, kidney stew is fine'. And from there, 'You don't love me, and I don't even care – it's a mean old world to live in by yourself.'

A haunting lick from 'Kinda Blue' in a higher register lifted the performance to another level: 'The sea, the sky and you and I.' But that tune wasn't pursued and instead led into the raucous, get-your-frustrations out: 'EVERY DAY! Every day I have the blues.'

'My repertoire is varied like life is,' he once told an interviewer.

> The repertoire had grown, and there's a turnover and there are the things that people want to hear all the time. And then you can throw in some newer things. I do a lot of things I've never recorded. It's all stuff I like. I learned stagecraft as an MC in Chicago. And my consideration for each detail I learned by doing radio broadcasts every night from a club, El Grotto that became the Beige Club, for two years with Jimmie Noone. On radio you must be succinct and clear and treat everything as if it were not visual.
>
> The excitement I can generate is stage presence as well as a knowledge of dynamics, tension and release. It's done by interacting with the people on stage. Each song is like a play. The play goes onstage and yet, if the audience is watching you, the people feel as though you're really involved with them. But while you're facing the audience, your entire fibre,

your intensity of concentration, is on interacting with what is happening onstage. It's as if the audience is a camera. And the people you're dealing with are here, behind you, the musicians. And you do the whole thing with your back to the people you're dealing with. That's the trick. I'm dealing with the music. That's the secret.

The second set began with a Milton Nascimento tune, 'Bridges'. He sang with his full, rapturous voice, envisioning a woman across a bridge and hoping to meet her halfway, his voice soaring and impassioned.

From 'Bridges', he began to scat horn sounds, jolting the audience, making it look up fast to search for the saxophone. That simulated horn sound kept up the pitch of tension begun with 'Bridges', and led to another ballad, on which that beautiful baritone let out all the stops. He sang at first, then suddenly shifted and talked a few words, having a persuasive conversation with the audience.

'Singing is nothing more than good conversation,' he once said, laughing. 'Perhaps that's why it's not more popular.'

And from the ballads back to the blues department: 'Who She Do'. This one was unadulterated fun about a woman who isn't; she comes to see him so often that, even though she belongs to someone else, Joe's beginning to think she's his. He played with the song, starting it with, 'I told her oo bop shebop daddy got to go now,' and explained to the audience: ' "Oooooooo" is very important in your life. You can take that anywhere, to the bank, baby. You haven't lived until you get your "oooooo" together.'

He ended the song with: 'She calls "come back come back come back come back daddy love me one more time",' a mesmerizing chant. And then he explained the importance of 'ooooo' another way, singing:

'It was early one morning, I was on my way to school. Baby, that was the morning I saw you and broke my mother's rule. I was in love with you, baby, and couldn't even call your name. You're in love with someone else, and I know that's going to drive me insane. Ooooooooooeeeeeeebaby, sure look good to me, ooooeeeeee baby, double o double e — I'll spell it so you know . . . . '

Then he called out to a waitress to bring him a glass of white whisky because 'You can't sing the blues on pina colada.' And arrived at the quintessential sophistication of 'Lush Life', which he always told audiences Duke Ellington called a perfect marriage of lyric, melody and harmony. (Joe sometimes mentions that Billy Eckstine claims that Billy Strayhorn wrote the song while still in high school in Pittsburgh.) After that tune, 'Don't Get Around Much Anymore' ended with his voice dropping way down symbolically, wittily, to the bass register: 'It's a drag without you. Don't get around much anymore.' Spontaneously he began ruminating with some old blues lines, 'Sometimes I think I will, sometimes I think I won't, sometimes I think I do, sometimes I think I don't,' leading, as a seemingly aimless but restful stroll through a park, to 'In the Evening'. He began, 'I feel as low as a snake in a wagon track . . . I've got rocks in my bed, rocks in my bed, rocks in my bed, My girl's gone, and instead I've got rocks in my bed,' with a soft, morbid repetitiveness, rather like the sound of the wheels of a slowly moving freight train through a still countryside.

Someone asked him to sing, 'My Kind of Town, Chicago is', to which he replied, 'Does anyone sing that except for Sinatra? I'll sing that as soon as he sings "Every Day".' Instead he did 'Goin' to Chicago', careful to say that Jon Hendricks wrote the lyrics. Then 'Roll 'em Pete' came equipped with outrageous scat virtuosity. 'Hydromatic kiddie cars' are infinite fun, when your baby buys them for you. Joe sang the lyrics so fast that they sounded like pure scat and melded into that anyway.

Then he sang a ballad by Tommy Deering, a writer and singer whom he met and hung out with in Las Vegas: 'It's about "Changes",' Joe told the audience. 'Either we're going through them or looking for them,' and sang: 'I'll stop being the person that I think you want me to be, You'll stop being the person that you think I want to see, You'll be you, and I'll be me, and we might see some changes . . . ' The audience loved that straightforward melody with the acutely intelligent lyrics and listened carefully.

Then Joe mentioned another Deering tune: 'It's Not Easy Being White'. 'I know, I know,' Joe commented. 'I've tried.

Maybe if I speak properly, dress properly, and act like I don't like white women – I said *act!* You know, if I do all the right things, they'll say, yes, we don't like them either.' The audience laughed, but there were a few holdouts, including one black woman, who later went to his dressing-room and said she had thought that she would have liked his autograph on one of his albums. But now that he had said what he did, she didn't know. It was the first time he had ever done that commentary in public. He didn't regret it. Many people found it hysterically funny, but he recognized that it could be controversial. 'She wasn't even on the same page with me,' he surmised to a friend after the woman left his dressing-room. He didn't plan to backtrack, though, liking it at the barricades or anyway standing fast there.

In his third set of the night, he included one of his newer tunes. Ordinarily no tune went without the considered introduction of its history, composer, first interpreter, best interpreter. And the audience discovered that Damita Jo sang 'I Had Someone Else Before I Had You', and 'I'll bet Bessie Smith sang this. I can just see her with her hands on her hips.' Joe was already singing professionally in Chicago when he first heard Bessie Smith. 'And I'll have someone else after you've gone. Public transport and sweethearts don't worry me, there's always another one coming along, I'll have someone after you've gone.' He commented further: 'I keep doing these things in schools. I forget that the kids change partners quicker than they change underwear. But they get up and shout.' And he made sure that the last note of the tune, 'gone', came out with operatic force.

Joe moved the audience along at his own pace, not too fast to leave anything undelineated. Neither did he linger too long on any tune or tale. He kept shifting from the blues written by the country's poorest people to the sophisticated popular standards of the country's eminent performers, composers and lyricists, cutting across cultural and racial barriers with an easy charm, comedic patter, a vast vocal range, and boundless, impeccable craft.

There was no alteration in his suave manner, when he said that he had learned a Cliff Norton tune in pianist George

Shearing's house one day. The tune started as a ballad, 'I love you, I swear by every star above you, and this is no shit. I pray that when you hold my hand that you will understand what is on my mind. But if I'm to be denied, then you can step aside and kiss my behind.' The audience tittered at 'this is no shit', but it laughed raucously by the time he got to his behind. 'Take me, never to forsake me,' he sang, full blast, 'If this is a dream, don't wake me . . . ' The corny lyric acquired a very dramatic, heavily operatic delivery . . . 'And I know at last this – IS – NO – SHIT.'

Sometimes his performances ended that way. Other times he was serious: 'Let's remember that some people would like to be like us. Let's try not to disappoint them.'

Norman received his itinerary and money directly from John Levy. Joe never discussed money; occasionally he did a performance for free but otherwise gave John carte blanche to sign the contracts. And Joe took the initiative for his music and his performances, doing whatever he pleased on the bandstands.

In the spirit of Give-the-Young-a-Chance, which Basie had shown him, Joe invited a latterday Basie bandsinger to sit in on a gig at Sweet Basil in New York. Dennis Rowland, who could shout the blues for the Basie repertoire, actually had a predilection for a Broadway style of singing *á la* Ethel Merman. And he made a big hit on Joe's gig, calling, 'I want to be here on the street where you live,' repeatedly, 'I want to be here, I want to be here.' Afterwards Joe came back on stage and cracked, 'I want to be here! I want to be here,' mimicking in a falsetto. 'Don't you never come on my come on my job and do that again!' He followed with a nicely contrasting, intricately improvised blues.

Another time Rowland's more strident voice suffered by comparison with Joe's in Basie's eightieth-birthday concert. But that type of contrast happened to many young singers. A much-touted singing starlet in a Broadway show stepped to a bandstand one night to sing a duet with Joe and howled a blues off key. After one tune, Joe said he wasn't going to sing with her any more, and the audience could take his remark any way it pleased. He spoke affably enough. (He recalled how Peggy Lee had met him as he came off a bandstand once from a Basie gig in Las Vegas and said to him, 'Sing sing sing baby just sing.' He liked to pass her message along to people who told him that they wanted to sing. 'Just let it come out,' he told them. Then, hearing them, he thought better of what he had said. There were many young musicians as well as singers, whom he got up on bandstands with and told: 'One, two, you know what to do,' and they didn't. Even older, experienced musicians and singers had difficulty holding their own in duets with Joe – and most of them sounded coarse and flat in comparison.)

While Joe doffed his hat to Basie with the invitation to Dennis Rowland, Joe picked talented musicians, whom few had heard of yet, to boost sometimes. And so he surprised a young guitarist one night in Eddie Condon's, by then a mecca for traditional jazz fans, located next to La Scala on West 54th Street; Condon's was one of Joe's regular stops to say hello to old friends.

Howard Alden, a slight, sandy-haired young man, had wended his way across the country to New York City. He had begun playing for pennies in pizza parlours when he was prepubescent in southern California. Deciding that New York City would be the best place to find work in jazz, he settled into a Spartan lifestyle, sitting in wherever he could, whether he were paid to play his guitar or not.

One evening, after sitting in during the regular Wednesday cocktail-hour gig with George Simon's group at Eddie Condon's, Howard was approached by bassist George Duvivier. Duvivier said: 'Do you want to say hello to Joe Williams?'

Alden saw Joe sitting at the bar and said 'Sure', but didn't move.

'Well, go ahead,' Duvivier encouraged him.

So Alden went up to Joe, who asked: 'What are you doing tomorrow night?'

Alden wasn't doing anything.

Joe asked him if he would like to play at Marty's, an elegant Upper East Side supper club, where Joe was starring for the next two weeks. Howard said, 'Sure'. Joe added that he wanted

Alden to play for the whole job, if he were free. Oh, Alden was free.

After that, whenever Joe sang in New York, he worked with Norman Simmon's trio plus Howard Alden, as Joe added to the Who Will Be Who in Jazz category of his résumé. If he could inspire a youngster, that was great, he thought, remember how inspirational he had found it simply to listen to trumpeter Roy Eldridge in the forties in Chicago.

# 16 *Saying What's Watt*

During a 1978 performance with pianist and arranger Sy Johnson, shortly before Norman became an integral part of Joe's retinue, Joe met Jillean's cousin Andrew Heath again. Andrew, who had not seen Joe since Newcastle-on-Tyne, moved to the US that year to become an editor at *Business Week* for a while. But he couldn't stand the pay and moved to the Pfizer pharmaceutical company as a writer. Jillean met him in New York and took him to Hopper's, a Greenwich Village club bedecked with mirrors and a very long bar popular with noisy singles. Behind it, on the bandstand, stood Joe, singing with Paul West* on bass, Johnson, and a drummer who played too loudly, Andrew Heath thought. The drummer never showed up in one of Joe's groups again. If there was one type of musician that Joe couldn't stand, it was a drummer whom Joe had to subdue with his voice, which wasn't as hard as a drum.

The next day Joe insisted that Andrew, fresh from eight years of working in Italy, join him and Jillean for lunch at La Scala. 'This place has wonderful food,' Joe bragged. Knowing that Joe adopted restaurants where he felt comfortable, in familiar surroundings, Andrew went along and thought the scampi was edible. He started telling Joe that he wasn't sufficiently well-represented on records and should sing with some old-time musicians, people from the heyday of the Kansas City era, for example. They were some of Andrew's favourites. Joe listened quietly and, Andrew thought, vacantly. Andrew felt rather awkward and wondered if Joe liked him at all. Perhaps Joe was bored.

*Paul West is a frequent player in Joe William's trios.

So Andrew went to his new house: in Rye, New York, taped some music from his sizeable collection of early jazz: 'Sawmill Man Blues' – 'I didn't make this world, but I sure can tear it down' – and 'Dimples', a John Lee Hooker tune, and gave them to Joe. Shortly afterwards Andrew discovered that Joe had added them to his repertoire; he even had a new arrangement done for 'Dimples'. After that, Joe, impressed with Andrew's knowledge and affection for the music, had much more to say to Andrew and made a point of introducing him, if he were in the audience, as 'my English cousin'. Or even if Andrew wasn't in the audience, he got credit for his knowledge and influence on Joe's repertoire.

Joe was working in New York City at Marty's, a long, elegant club with a glass wall overlooking a stone courtyard. Andrew stopped in for a performance, as he usually did, to hear Joe, and brought along a guest – the great but irascible drummer, Papa Jo Jones, who had played with Basie's first band in Kansas City. Jones, who was already frail in the aftermath of a bout with cancer, plus a persistent alcoholism, got up and walked with the aid of a silver-headed cane to the tiny, glowing bandstand, uninvited. Vernel Fournier left his place and handed his sticks to Jones. He played with fire and plainly didn't want to quit. Finally he was persuaded to give Vernel the sticks back.

Afterwards Papa Jo sent a message in extremely questionable taste, reflecting upon one of the main industries in Williams' birthplace, to Joe's dressing-room. Joe sent back a very small sum of money to Jones, advising him to invest in that industry. The drummer became increasingly drunk. Finally unnerved by Jones's incoherent patter, which usually revolved around his eminence and everyone else's lesser value, Andrew asked another friend to give Jones a ride home. But Jones said that he was going off to Eddie Condon's. Impressed by Andrew's incomprehensible patience with the old curmudgeon on top of Andrew's deep love and wide knowledge of early jazz, Joe became comfortable with Andrew and felt truly related.

Then Andrew's sister, Liz, married at the time to an American, arrived from Switzerland and went to live in Vermont. It was convenient for her to go to hear Joe perform in

Toronto, where he had a big following and starred repeatedly in the clubs. One of his recorded tunes, 'Poor You', which didn't cause a stir in the US, became a hit in Toronto. Lumberjacks went to his dates, asked him to sing it and practically cried, he noticed with amusement. Sometimes Liz travelled to New York to see Joe perform. And her arrival in the US made the family, decimated by the loss of Joe's and Jill's parents, a little larger and happier. He and Jillean told Liz that the Heaths were their only real family.

Joe knew few of his mother's relatives, though he remained in touch with the daughters of his grandfather's brother, Joseph. Gilbert's daughter Josephine married a dentist named Kimbers in Baltimore. Their son went to study dentistry, so he could go into practice with his father in the 1980s. Joe had met the Kimberses' son in Washington and knew where Louise Gilbert, Josephine's sister, lived, too. But he usually dashed in and out of Washington too quickly to spend time with distant relatives, though he felt proud of them. Except for Jillean, Joe had no family except for those brothers he had adopted and who had also graduated from 'his' era of the Basie band. And it had not escaped the attention of the former only child that he had to keep an eye on his brothers occasionally.

In 1980, he went 'home' for a visit, signing on to do a Basie band alumni tour of Europe with Benny Powell, Joe Newman, Harry 'Sweets' Edison, Marshall Royal, Buddy Tate, Billy Mitchell, Nat Pierce, Eddie Jones and Gus Johnson. Willard Alexander always sent for Pierce, who had emulated Basie's spare, economical style, to sit in for Basie on the rare occasions when he missed performances. And Pierce went to Europe with the nine-piece group, with the approval of Basie, who always kept a close watch on the alumni tours.

Each time Benny Powell got the chance to work with Joe again, Benny was impressed with Joe's increased stagecraft and ripened voice – and aware of the growing list of kudos that Joe had been winning by the late seventies. But Benny suspected that some of the older instrumentalists wished they could still treat Joe as 'old Joe, the bandsinger'. In a dressing-room backstage a few minutes before a show in Amsterdam, one of the alumni said, 'We don't really need no singer. People come to hear the instrumentalists.' Benny looked at Joe, who seemed to shrug the remark off; he didn't even turn around. Benny assumed that Joe was thinking: 'Oh, well, if that's the way you feel, fine.' It was somebody else's insecurity, Benny thought, that made him snipe at Joe. And Benny felt that, as hard as Joe worked and tried to get along with everybody, he surely didn't need to hear a demeaning remark. Actually Joe was concentrating on the upcoming performance and didn't even hear the remark. He went onstage and sang as if nothing had happened, because he didn't know that it had.

And none the wiser, the next year, he went on another Basie alumni tour of Europe and then played the Newport Jazz Festival in New York, the Playboy Festival in Hollywood at the Bowl; he toured Japan, tacked again and went home to the Chicago Jazz Festival. A usual calendar. The following year, at the Newport Jazz Festival, renamed Kool, he sang and went on to jazz festivals in Monterey, Chicago, Stockholm and the American Song Festival at the Hollywood Bowl, then the Empire State Jazz Festival in Albany, New York. And he sang in countless smaller festivals, too.

His path crossed Junior Mance's at the Harbor Lights Festival in Baltimore for a night; they had dinner and talked together in their soft-voiced ways. Junior had become sartorially Fancy Mance about twenty years after their original alliance. It was a pleasant time. 'One, two, you know what to do,' Joe could say to Junior, and Junior would. Afterwards they went their separate ways, Junior back to New York City, where he led a duo with a bass – the latest trend in jazz groups in New York City, which had zoning laws in some places that were killing off the drummers. And Joe continued with the lineup on the itinerary, including the usual Basie band concerts.

There was no question in Willard Alexander's mind that he had a legend on his hands in Basie. Even though his health was failing, Basie moved on and off stages in a small golfcart, sometimes ringing a little bell to make a joke of his disability and dominating audiences as usual; Basie didn't dream of quitting. John Levy also had the idea that it was legend-building time for Joe Williams, both with Basie and in his own performances and activities.

In June 1983, Joe made a quick trip to Los Angeles, stood up on a raised, temporary platform and listened to a lot of speeches about himself. The ceremony, paid for by Playboy, celebrated the implantation of his star next to Count Basie's in the Walk of the Stars on Hollywood Boulevard. About a hundred people stood in the audience: David Chertok, the jazz film collector, and Red Callender, the bassist, and many officials of the musicians' union and the National Academy of Recording Arts and Sciences. Joe talked about his gratitude to other people, particularly John Levy, who had helped put the star next to Basie's for as long as Los Angeles would last.

Some people thought that Joe had never got the credit that his great talent should have earned for him, blaming race for anything Joe may have missed out on. Others rued the absence of a pretty face. Joe listened particularly to the latter idea, because he still hadn't got used to himself photogenically. But his only gripe was against the record companies. They didn't make sure his records went into store windows. They didn't even make sure his records were distributed to stores. Yet Joe could sell his music personally in clubs where people paid high prices to hear him do the same songs that the record companies claimed they couldn't sell on records.

Still he had to listen to the official line of record companies that his records weren't getting a first-rate push because they didn't sell as well as those of rock groups. Through a grapevine, Joe heard that some of the young rock musicians, who couldn't find either their drums or their behinds with both hands, actually went into the studios and defecated on the floors. Of such little rumours are legends made, he knew, and he didn't give that tale much credence. Anyway he had to think about the problem of getting money up front to make a record and of getting money for records sold back from distributors, to the record companies, to himself. And there was always a question of how much he had really earned and whether there was a discrepancy between that amount and what he received. Even John Levy couldn't put the record finances right, for all his skills at finagling with papers and cheques, despite his adroitness in taking hard-nosed positions, let the chips fall where they may, dealing in a soft, cool voice. The whole situation prompted Joe to say one night in an aside to an audience: 'Don't talk to me about record companies.'

But the reviews were priceless. And in the lobbies of concert halls and at coat-check counters in clubs, the records did sell quickly, for cash. If it were true that he had been caught in a seemingly immutable racial vice as a young man, that time had passed. The old days made fodder for pointed comedy in shows. 'In the last fifteen years, we've had to deal with people who got black all of a sudden. We used to fight with someone who called you black. I remember when we were all coloured. And "Po–po" is a derivative of the word poor . . . We had a white bass player in Selma, Alabama. We were waiting for a coloured taxi, and the bass player said, "reminds me of a snake was so po' he didn't have a pit to hiss in". That broke the tension. The white musicians said, "It's OK. The coloured guys are laughing . . ." ' Joe didn't cling to any bitter thoughts about those days but was more concerned with current signs of racial bias.

One morning, awaking in a hotel after finishing a long, gruelling club date – twenty-two hours of singing in a week and a half, he put on a bright red caftan and matching red Japanese rubber-thong sandals – a colour scheme that set off the grey hair at his temples nicely, giving him the aura of a cross between Caesar Romero and Simba, and watched a broadcast of columnist Art Buchwald. Buchwald was asked: Why is everyone jumping on James Watt? Watt, a Reagan cabinet member, had said that he had a black, two Jews and a cripple on his staff – a lineup that proved he was fair-minded. It was no more than passed as ordinary chitchat everyday in cloakrooms. As a few friends visited his hotel room to watch Joe relax, he decided to explain why he was disturbed by Watt's kind of thinking: the subtle depreciation had permeated the entire society to the degree that even people who were concerned found themselves mimicking that kind of thinking, perpetuating the inegalities. One thing Joe had taken away from his time in analysis was a little understanding about why things are the way they are, he said. He could free his own mind from Wattism; he wanted everyone to get his mind free, now that the body was free.

And then he dressed to hurry downtown to Times Square to do a broadcast about his recording career for a syndicated radio show. He explained how he had got involved in golf: 'Better to spend four hours on the golf course rather than broad-jumping,' he said, then giggled at his own gaffe and stuck a cigarette in his mouth to shut it fast.

# 17 A Distinguished Situation

A few curious, classical musicians on the Broadway scene wandered into Carnegie Hall to hear a rehearsal for the July 1983 concert to be hosted by Joe during the Kool Jazz Festival and came out with the advance word that Joe sounded wonderful.

Backed by Woody Herman's latest Herd, Joe brought out chubby Jay McShann, a great stride-boogie-woogie-blues-jazz pianist, who had started a Kansas City band in the 1930s. And then Joe introduced Big Joe Turner, reduced to under 300 pounds, who walked on crutches in the dark to his spot on stage, unseen by the audience, and was illuminated during his songs. Joe thanked Jillean in the audience for her judgement about something in the concert plan. And the evening came to its last moments, when Joe began singing the Ellington song, 'Come Sunday'. 'Lord, oh, Lord above, God Almighty, God of Love . . . Please look down and see my people through.' This time, unlike his earlier interpretation in a light vein, Joe sang *a cappella*, treating the song as if it were an aria, with his magnificent voice. He raised the song as if it were a flag over a battlefield. The moment could not have been less arresting than the second before Samson pushed over the pillars of the temple.

Afterwards in a hushed and plainly furnished dressing-room upstairs in Carnegie Hall, with rugs muffling the sound of the feet of the fans tramping upstairs to congratulate him, Joe Williams sat with John Levy, both men cross legged in dark suits. A crowd converged upon the room. Joe jumped up and introduced Jillean to many people. John Levy wandered around, shaking hands, too, telling someone: 'I don't ordinarily get excited about anything. Nothing ever excites me. But this night I got excited! I never heard anything like that in my life! He outdid himself! He was splendid. The best I ever heard him or anyone else.'

John had arranged for Joe to go to Chicago for a gig at Rick's Café Américaine anyway. And Joe was glad, because he wanted to visit the family of Buddy Young. Buddy had played football so well at Wendell Phillips High School that he had gone on to the University of Illinois and become All-American. And from that to playing pro ball for New York and Baltimore. Then prominence as an assistant to Football Commissioner Pete Rozelle. Young, driving alone at night down South, where he had gone to handle some official business for the National Football League, had crashed his car and died.

'He should never had been driving alone! A man over fifty! In his position! A billion-dollar business! That's sheer negligence! He should have had a driver!' Joe announced to John Levy.

Although Buddy's family no longer lived in the same old neighbourhood, Joe, who knew his way around Chicago very well, found everybody. By chance, on the way to visit old friends, he passed through the streets where he had lived and saw some houses burned down and theatres and the South Center complex torn down, become a vacant lot, as it had been when he first moved there. After visiting Buddy's family at the funeral home where the body lay on view, Joe walked a little way to 7155 Wabash Avenue and knocked on the door. Diminuitive Marietta Simmons, with a soft voice, recognized him and went to wake up her husband, Lonnie. He used to photograph Marietta, as she looked out a misty window; there had been a feminine mistiness to Marietta's appearance, Joe used to think. He could still see it. Lonnie still had a cherubic face. At age seventy he played organ as a regular gig in an Italian restaurant in town. Lonnie had always had money in his pockets, even in the DeLisa days, Joe remembered, so he wasn't surprised to find Lonnie working and living in comfort, in a single-family stone house with a yard big enough to build another house in – a property, including a garage thirty yards away, about half the size of a New York City block. But it was still Chicago. Trucks still picked up the garbage in back alleys wide enough for them to drive in two abreast.

Joe cajoled Lonnie to put on his clothes and go down the street to a barbecue feast at a neighbour's house – someone else that Joe hadn't seen in years. Joe reminded Lonnie about a morning when the older man had taken him to Chili Mac's for breakfast and offered to loan him money, if he needed it. Joe hadn't taken any. But he remembered the offer. Lonnie reminded Joe of the photographs of his daughter, JoAnn, of Joe's name on the DeLisa marquee, of Joe in bermuda shorts on the DeLisa stage. Afterwards Joe got into a car and left behind the South Side and the embers of a landscape of his childhood and went back to the bright lights of the clubs, where he had become totally at ease and safe during the thirty years after he left Chicago to star with Count Basie's band.

Then on to summer jazz festivals and back to New York City for a club date and from there to a one-night stand in the Midwest and another one in Seattle. Stopping in Las Vegas to swoop Jillean up, he headed for a festive weekend in Florida, where a friend was getting married. And there would be a lot of golf.

Then Jillean went home and Joe to another reunion, this time in Denver, with the Basie band. Benny Powell, playing with Joe for the first time in a couple of years, learned something again. Benny was supposed to play an encore at the end of the evening. But he didn't like the way he played 'Mood Indigo': the audience didn't agree and started applauding wildly.

Benny went into the wings, where Joe was waiting, poised to return to the stage. The band was supposed to play one more time in an ensemble. Benny was used to Joe's singsonging, which he often lapsed into on stage, when he wasn't singing, simply concentrating. And in that tone, Joe told Benny, 'Go back on stage, and I'll follow you.' But Benny wasn't really listening; he still was thinking about his own displeasure about his solo. He forgot that Joe could sound as if he were making a suggestion, when he was actually telling you what to do pretty damn quick. Benny hesitated. In that split second, Joe heard the applause start to die down. He couldn't let it happen, so he dashed ahead of Benny. Suddenly Benny was roused to attention and learned about taking cues from the audience as well as the music. You had to stay alert or in the fraction of a beat you could lose an audience. On the solo circuit for only a handful of years by then, Benny realized that a seasoned, stage-wise person knew what to do exactly when. A second's hesitation made the difference between a real professional and someone working towards becoming one.

Benny didn't know if Joe had learned that sense of stagecraft in the Basie years or before, when he had observed and worked with great performers in Chicago's heyday as an entertainment centre of the country. Basie was a great editor, Benny knew, able to get rid of anything extraneous. In any case, Benny thought that Joe had become so stage-wise that he couldn't make a false move. He could even twiddle his thumbs as fast as a windmill in a gale onstage and look perfectly natural and exciting doing it.

Joe didn't mention the incident and after a little chat walked off beside Basie in his cart. Onstage, as he always did by then, Basie had called Joe 'Number One Son'. And Benny went away feeling that he had learned a deft touch to use, as he watched Basie and the big man leaving the theatre.

Joe finished the year making forays in and out of Disney World and Los Angeles to make records and back to Las Vegas to plan the next year with Levy. They lined up a benefit performance at Madison Square Garden, where the tinsel decorations would shimmy as Joe and other famous performers would sing – Margaret Whiting, Tony Bennett, Mel Torme, filling the huge forum with the glamour of their music, and after that a celebration at the Hilton. At those places, the hosts would pick up the tabs. That would be nice, for at the Hilton, where Joe would stay during the Madison Square Benefit engagement, small breakfasts – a tureen of soup and a bowl of fresh bananas with milk and a pot of coffee – would cost $19. And the hosts would pay all the expenses for the privilege of having Joe come out on stage and sing two ballads with more artful improvisations than almost any other singer could begin to dream of. And there would be a film, too.

An interviewer along the way asked Joe if the travelling put a strain on him and especially on his wife. Long separations had obviously taxed and broken up marriages of other musicians and their families. But Joe said, 'Oddly enough' he didn't think his being away handicapped the marriage. He enumerated twelve weeks that Jillean had spent with him on the road that year, including a trip to Brazil. They had single days together, meetings on the road for special events or simply for dates. They met each other in New York City for a night to go to the theatre. 'So how can this be a hardship when you have home with you?' Joe said. 'And we're very comfortable, together on the road. I'm still not a nester.'

Furthermore, there was a streak of independence in Jillean. Once she flew to London, picked up her friend Leslie Beresford Wright, who had settled in England, and went off to India for a long, exotic vacation. Other times the women visited Africa for weeks without Joe or Leslie's husband.

'That's the way we live and like it,' Joe told interviewers.

And he could afford the overhead of the plane fares. The house in Las Vegas had plants and swinging perches for the cats and a cosy, round, wooden breakfast table in the centre of the downstairs level. The living-room had pale-coloured furniture; there was an airy feeling, with light blue and white decorations throughout the house. The Williamses could afford to do anything they wanted. But they didn't do anything outrageous.

The walls of Joe's private music room became studded gradually with excellent photographs from his career; his shelves filled up with records and cameras. And there was the *de rigueur* upright piano, which so many musicians did not dream of living without. And the nicest thing about money was not having to think about it, Joe said.

Occasionally Joe and Jillean found themselves invited away from their routine in Las Vegas to some very exciting events. In 1981, the Kennedy Center in Washington had honoured Cary Grant, Count Basie, Helen Hayes, Rudolf Serkin and Jerome Robbins. Jillean found herself seated at the same table with Cary Grant and her place card set next to Walter Cronkite's, while Joe sat next to Betsy Cronkite on his left and to his right Lew Wasserman and Senator Abraham Ribicoff of Connecticut and his wife.

'That was the most distinguished possible situation,' Jillean said to Joe, when the photographs had been taken in an outside reception room, and dinner had ended. 'That was the highlight of my life to sit next to Walter Cronkite.'

The next year, without Jillean, Joe had gotten a kick out of a Kennedy Center event honouring Eubie Blake, then 'ninety-nine percent one hundred'. Blake, riding in a wheelchair, saw Joe standing with the beautiful singer, sleek and fiery Lola Falana, and tipped his hat to Miss Falana. Joe had loved the gesture. And when Blake heard the band playing a tune he had written, 'I'd Give a Dollar for a Dime', Blake said to Joe, 'Did I write that? It's a pretty tune.' Joe loved life at the top – it meant that he had done a lot of singing and earned a lot of money – for it gave him the chance to stand beside extraordinarily talented gentlemen, the kind of people he admired. He was thrilled when black people earned and got their due, mortified when they did anything to detract from their possibilities for success, outraged when he felt they were being cheated out of their success. He supposed that some people might call him a snob, but he simply liked to be where the best things were happening, especially to blacks, and only wanted more of those things to happen. His sensitivity on that subject was boundless, and the concern usually on his mind.

In 1983, at the honours dinner at the Kennedy Center, Jillean, in a long white satin gown, sat next to Gene Kelly, which wasn't bad either, she thought, in a crowd scene of *la crême de la crême* of celebrities of the world. Joe liked having Jimmy Stewart sitting at the piano, playing 'Happy Birthday' for Carol Burnett's daughter with the Basie band, while Joe sang. And Sid Caesar, Hal Lyndon and Carol Burnett danced. Now, that was Joe's idea of a really great time any place, and especially at the Kennedy Center, where those talented people could dance – because he could sing, oh, he could sing, and have more fun than anyone could imagine.

A few days later, Joe, hearing that Basie had gone home to Freeport to rest for a few days after a band concert, got the notion that Basie might like a visit from the Williamses, even though Joe had just seen Basie in Denver. Anyway Joe would call him; if their schedules jibed, he might visit. Benny Powell might still feel awestruck in Basie's presence. After saying, 'How are you, chief?', Benny didn't know what else to say, unable to banter easily with a legend. But Joe could say to Jillean: 'Let's fly to Freeport, Bill needs us around him now.' And Joe felt that he and Basie were so affectionate with each other by then that Joe could understand him, and his pain at the unexpected loss of his wife, Catherine. Basie, who had had a stroke, had been the sick one for several years; not Catherine. But she had died suddenly that year. Joe thought that he and Basie would hug and embrace each other as usual. 'So guess we haven't shaken hands yet,' Joe thought. He was recalling that they had never shaken hands on Joe's agreement to go along with the band, and didn't shake hands when Joe left. They had taken to hugging each other by that time, jazzmusician fashion.

Joe was performing in a Fairmont Hotel in Dallas, Texas, when the news reached him. Count Basie was dead, on 26 April, 1984, in a Hollywood, Florida hospital. Basie's body was taken to lie 'in state', as it were, in Benta's Funeral Home at 630 St Nicholas Avenue at 141st Street in Harlem, not very far from the club he had once owned. Joe kept singing, backed by Norman Simmons at the piano and a regional bassist and drummer, in the Texas hotel. But when he went offstage, except for a television interview, Joe was incommunicado, barely able to concentrate; his room telephone went unanswered, as he made plans to fly to New York City for the funeral. On Sunday night, he flew to Kennedy Airport and, in the limousine that picked him up, he changed clothes for the religious service. By the time that the limousine arrived at the most famous church in Harlem, the Abyssinian Baptist Church, once the ministry of the late Reverend Adam Clayton Powell Jr and the seat of the greatest black political power in the US for many years, Joe was dressed in sombre, formal clothes. The limousine stayed in the curb outside the church, in the sunshine.

Joe greeted the producer, Quincy Jones, then often photographed with rock superstar Michael Jackson, and the legendary alto saxophonist, composer and arranger, Benny Carter.

Hundreds of musicians went to the funeral, all of whom Joe knew and recognized, thinking to himself how well one looked, how aged and frail another appeared, as he took his place to sing 'Come Sunday'. The unsinkable drummer Jo Jones, one of the few survivors of the first Basie band, was aided as he walked haltingly into the church. John Hammond, who had been in his twenties when he met Basie in Kansas City in the 1930s, arrived at the church. And something that had not happened to Joe since the death of his mother took place: his voice trembled, as he sang the Ellington song. Trumpeter Buck Clayton, also from the Kansas City band, looked slender and still handsome. In his early seventies, Buck seemed outwardly sanguine, accompanied by Nancy Elliott, a perennially youthful, pretty, long-haired photographer, one of his best friends for years. But Clayton was so hard-pressed to keep his usual aplomb that he objected when he saw Nancy start to cry.

Frank Sinatra sent flowers and a note saying: 'You will always be with me. I love you.' Outside, hundreds of mourners from the neighbourhood, who couldn't fit into the crowded church, milled around the limousines and private, shiny cars, while journalists collected comments. 'I used to play hooky and go to see Count Basie at the Apollo Theatre,' said one mourner. And without any glamour for the cameras to catch, the neighbourhood people, dressed in whatever their meagre budgets allowed, staged their own pageant at the end of the funeral service.

As Joe Williams got back into his limousine to return to the airport, Dallas and a show that night, the people began swarming around the car. They didn't shake it or rock it, but they surrounded it, not letting go yet. For a while, the car was simply stranded by the adulatory crowd. 'This is scary,' Joe thought. Hundreds of strange faces peered at him through the front windows. He hadn't noticed a crowd encircling anyone leaving before him. But then the sea of people began to part; he was able to ride to the airport in peace.

Later he heard that Quincy Jones's car had been waylaid for a while, too. But Buck Clayton's friend, Nancy, who was crying, noticed only the astounding sight of Joe Williams getting into a limousine and becoming engulfed by a gigantic crowd.

A few months later, Jillean Williams had her dream fulfilled: that Joe would work in Las Vegas and 'save overhead'. Someone – probably the entertainment director – at the Golden Nugget in Las Vegas called John Levy and asked if Joe would sing there. So, after doing a concert with the Basie band for the Count Basie Scholarship Fund in Las Vegas, Joe sang at the Golden Nugget, beginning 26 July, in a room he fell in love with, 'a gorgeous room not to be missed', he thought, standing on a sliver of a stage, a half moon – a stage that was shaped like a slice of pie. On three sides he was surrounded by an audience in plush chairs, chairs 'too comfortable for the people to get up from to give standing ovations', Joe had heard one performer complain. But Joe noted that he got standing ovations, and the lights and sound system were superb, too. Norman Simmons played piano with him, so Joe was working with a musician who knew exactly how he was going to perform. And Joe worked for six nights there. And on the seventh night he rested – and saw that it was good.

# *Discography*

## Section One: Joe Williams
## Section Two: Joe Williams and Count Basie

By Leslie Gourse, assisted by Dan Morgenstern, director, Institute of Jazz Studies, Rutgers University, Bradley Hall, Newark, NJ.

### Sources

*Bruynencks, Walter, Sixty Years of Recorded Jazz,* privately published in Mechelen, Belgium, by the author.
*Archives of the Institute of Jazz Studies,* Rutgers University.
King Kolax, Musicians Union, Chicago, Illinois.
*Jazz Records,* by Jorge Grunnet Jepson, 1942–1962, published by Emil Knudsen, Holte, Denmark, Vol. 8 © 1964 Karl Emil Knudsen; Vol. 1 © 1965 Karl Emil Knudsen.
Archives of Joe Williams.

### Abbreviations

| | |
|---|---|
| arr | arranger |
| as | alto saxophone |
| b | string bass |
| bar | baritone saxophone |
| bngo | bongo |
| bs-tb | bass trombone |
| c | circa |
| cel | cello |
| clt | clarinet |
| cnga | conga |
| cnt | cornet |
| cond | conductor |
| d | drums |
| el-p | electric piano |
| emcee | master of ceremonies |
| fl-h | flugelhorn |
| fr-h | french horn |
| g | guitar |
| ldr | leader |
| org | organ |

| | | | |
|---|---|---|---|
| p | piano | tpt | trumpet |
| saxes | saxophone section | va | viola |
| tb | trombone | vcl | vocalist |
| tb | valve trombone | vib | vibraphone |
| ten | tenor saxophone | vn | violin |

The following discography is a listing of all known Joe Williams recordings (commercial issues and generally, original LP release only). Singles are listed when they are the only issue and have not appeared on LP. Reissues and Japanese issues are not listed, with the exception of the album *The Heart and Soul of Joe Williams*.

N.B. Where two names and numbers follow the song title, the first indicates the single release, the latter the LP release.

## Section One

The first two recordings are officially listed in reliable sources as released in 1954. However, according to Joe Williams, the first was actually made in approximately 1950. King Kolax places the other as produced for a Chicago label in 1951.

Accompanied by Red Saunders Orchestra: Sonny Cohn (tpt), Riley Hampton (as), Leon Washington (ten), McKinley Easton (bar), Earl Washington (p), Walt Champion (b), Red Saunders (d), Ike Perkins (g)
*Chicago, circa 1950*

| | | |
|---|---|---|
| 54–103 | **In the Evening** | Blue Lake 102 Regent MG6002 |
| 54–104 | **Time for Moving** | Blue Lake 102 Regent MG6002 |
| | **Blow Mr Low** | Blue Lake 102 Regent MG6002 |
| | **It's Raining Again** | Blue Lake 102 Regent MG6002 |
| | **Detour Ahead** | Blue Lake 102 Regent MG6002 |
| | **Always on the Blue Side** | Blue Lake 102 Regent MG6002 |

*Accompanied by King Kolax (ldr, tpt), and according to King Kolax, the group included Dick Davis (ten), Benny Green (tb), Prentice McCarey (p), Cowboy Martin (b), Kansas Fields (d), Ike Perkins (g), Chicago circa 1951. According to official discographies, Kolax with Ike Perkins (g) plus unknown (tb) plus rhythm; and vocal choir

| | | |
|---|---|---|
| | **They Didn't Believe Me** (tb and g out) | Regent MG6002 |

| | | |
|---|---|---|
| | **Every Day I Have the Blues** (g out) | Regent MG6002 |
| | **Kansas City Blues** | Regent MG6002 |
| | **Safe Sane and Single** (with vocal choir) | Regent MG6002 |

*From a conversation between King Kolax and Leslie Gourse, March, 1984

*A Man Ain't Supposed to Cry,* accompanied by Jimmy Mundy's Orchestra
*New York, October 11, 12, 21, 1957*

| | | |
|---|---|---|
| 12446 | **What's New?** | Roulette R52005, (S7R52057) |
| 12449 | **Can't We Talk It Over?** | Roulette R52005, (S7R52057) |
| 12465 | **Say It Isn't So** | Roulette R52005, (S7R52057) |
| | **Talk of the Town** | Roulette R52005, (S7R52057) |
| | **I'll Never Smile Again** | Roulette R52005, (S7R52057) |
| | **I'm Through with Love** | Roulette R52005, (S7R52057) |
| | **A Man Ain't Supposed to Cry** | Roulette R52005, (S7R52027) |
| | **Where are You?** | Roulette R52005, (S7R52057) |
| | **I've Only Myself to Blame** | Roulette R52005, (S7R52057) |
| | **What Will I Tell My Heart?** | Roulette R52005, (S7R52057) |
| | **You've Got Me Crying Again** | Roulette R52005, (S7R52057) |
| | **I Laugh to Keep from Crying** | Roulette R52005, (S7R52057) |

*Joe Williams Sings About You,* accompanied by Jimmy Jones's Orchestra, personnel including Harry Edison (tpt), Ben Webster (ten), Hank Jones (p), Milt Hinton (b), Don Lamond (d), Freddie Green (g), plus strings and woodwinds
*New York, July, 14, 16 1959*

| | | |
|---|---|---|
| 14209 | **I was Telling Her about You** (Ben Webster out) | Roulette B52030 |
| | **Poor You** (Ben Webster Out) | Roulette B52030 |
| | **The Very Thought of You** (Ben Webster, Harry Edison out) | Roulette B52030 |
| | **If I Should Lose You** | Roulette B52030 |
| | **You Are Too Beautiful** | Roulette B52030 |
| | **The Girl in My Dreams tries to Look Like You** | Roulette B52030 |
| | **I Can't Resist You** | Roulette B52030 |
| | **You're a Sweetheart** | Roulette B52030 |
| | **When Did You Leave Heaven?** | Roulette B52030 |
| | **I Only Have Eyes for You** | Roulette B52030 |
| | **With Every Breath I Take** (strings, woodwinds out) | Roulette B52030 |

*That Kind of Woman,* accompanied by Jimmy Jones's Orchestra including strings
*New York City, 1959*

| | | |
|---|---|---|
| 14673 | **That Kind of Woman** | (S)R52039, (S)R52062 |
| | **Here's to My Lady** | (S)R52053 |
| | **Stella by Starlight** | (S)R52105 |
| | **I Only Want to Love You** | (S)R52105 |
| | **When a Woman Loves a Man** | (S)R52105 |
| | **Cherry** | (S)R52102 |
| | **Candy** | (S)R52102 |
| | **You Think of Everything** | (S)R52102 |
| | **Louise** | (S)R52102 |
| | **It's Easy to Remember** | (S)R52102 |
| | **Why Can't You Behave?** | (S)R52102 |
| | **Have You Met Miss Jones?** | (S)R52102 |

Similar
*New York City, 1960*

| | |
|---|---|
| **Day by Day** | Roulette (S)R52066, (S)R52105 |
| **Just as Though You were Here** | Roulette (S)R52066, (S)R52105 |
| **Darn That Dream** | Roulette (S)R52066, (S)R52105 |
| **Just Plain Lonesome** | Roulette (S)R52066, (S)R52105 |
| **For All We Know** | Roulette (S)R52066, (S)R52105 |
| **Ev'ry Time We Say Goodbye** | Roulette (S)R52066, (S)R52105 |
| **You Leave Me Breathless** | Roulette (S)R52066, (S)R52105 |
| **Did I Remember?** | Roulette (S)R52066, (S)R52105 |
| **Stay as Sweet as You Are** | Roulette (S)R52066, (S)R52105 |
| **How Deep is the Ocean?** | Roulette (S)R52066, (S)R52105 |

*Together,* accompanied by Harry Edison (tpt), Jimmy Forrest (ts), Sir Charles Thompson (p), Tommy Potter (b), Clarence Johnston (d)
*The Cloister, Los Angeles, February 1961*

| | |
|---|---|
| **By the River St Marie** | Roulette R52069 |
| **Winter Weather** | Roulette R52069 |
| **I Don't Know Why, (I Just Do)** | Roulette R52069 |
| **There's a Small Hotel** | Roulette R52069 |
| **Out of Nowhere** | Roulette R52069 |
| **Aren't You Glad You're You?** | Roulette R52069 |
| **Remember?** | Roulette R52069 |
| **Together** | Roulette R52069 |
| **Deep Purple** | Roulette R52069 |
| **Always** | Roulette R52069 |

| | |
|---|---|
| **Lover, Come Back to Me** | Roulette R52069 |
| **Alone Together** | Roulette R52069 |

*Have a Good Time,* accompanied by Harry Edison's Orchestra, Harry Edison (tpt), Jimmy Jones (p), Joe Benjamin (b), Charlie Persip (d), Ernie Wilkins (arr) and others
*New York, July 1961*

| | |
|---|---|
| **Have a Good Time** | Roulette R52071 |
| **Sometimes I'm Happy** | Roulette R52071 |
| **Old Folks** | Roulette R52071 |
| **Until I Met You** | Roulette R52071 |
| **I Won't Cry Anymore** | Roulette R52071 |
| **'Sposin'** | Roulette R52071 |
| **A Blues Serenade** | Roulette R52071 |
| **September in the Rain** | Roulette R52071 |
| **Summertime** | Roulette R52071 |
| **Moonlight in Vermont** | Roulette R52071 |
| **Falling in Love with Love** | Roulette R52071 |

*A Swinging Night at Birdland–Joe Williams Live,* accompanied by Harry Edison (tpt), Jimmy Forest (ten), Sir Charles Thompson (p), Joe Benjamin (b), Charlie Persip (d), Pee Wee Marquette (emcee)
*Birdland, New York, June 1962*

| | |
|---|---|
| **September in the Rain** | Roulette R52085 |
| **Come Back, Baby** | Roulette R52085 |
| **Five O'Clock in the Morning** | Roulette R52085 |
| **By the River St Marie** | Roulette R52085 |
| **This Can't be Love** | Roulette R52085 |
| **Teach Me Tonight** | Roulette R52085 |
| **Well Alright, Okay, You Win** | Roulette R52085 |
| **I was Telling Her about You** | Roulette R52085 |
| **Have You Met Miss Jones?** | Roulette R52085 |
| **Well, oh Well** | Roulette R52085 |

*One is a Lonesome Number,* accompanied by orchestra arranged and directed by Jack Pleis
*1962*

| | |
|---|---|
| **Somebody** | Roulette R52102 |
| **One is a Lonesome Number** | Roulette R52102 |
| **I'm Just Taking My Time** | Roulette R52102 |
| **I've Got the Cryin'st Shoulder in Town** | Roulette R52102 |
| **The Real Thing** | Roulette R52102 |
| **Autumn Leaves** | Roulette R52102 |

| | | |
|---|---|---|
| | **When She Makes Music** | Roulette R52102 |
| | **Warmer than a Whisper** | Roulette R52102 |
| | **All My Life** | Roulette R52102 |

No details; from Roulette session.

| | | |
|---|---|---|
| | **Ain't No Use** | Emus ES12015 |
| | **Just a Dream** | Emus ES12015 |

Accompanied by Oliver Nelson's Orchestra; personnel includes Joe Newman (tpt), Jimmy Cleveland (tb), Phil Woods (as), Bob Ashton (ten), Danny Bank (bar), Junior Mance (p), Bob Cranshaw (b), Granville W Hogan (d)

*New York City, October 25 1962*

| | | |
|---|---|---|
| N2PW5383 | **She's Warm, She's Willing, She's Wonderful** | Vic 47–8117 |
| N2PW5384 | **Some 'a Dis 'n Some 'a Dat** | Vic 47–8117 |
| N2PW5385 | **Come on Blues** (unissued) | |

Accompanied by Jimmy Jones Orchestra, personnel including Clark Terry (tpt), Urbie Green (tb), Phil Woods (as), Jerome Richardson, Phil Bodner (fl, ten), Bernie Leighton (p), Kenny Burrell (g), Milt Hinton (b), Sol Gubin (d)

*New York City, February 1 1963*

| | | |
|---|---|---|
| PPA1–3131 | **The Great City** | Vic LPM2713 |
| PPA1–3132 | **Work Song** | Vic LPM2879 |
| PPA1–3133 | **Just a Sittin' and a Rockin'** | Vic LPM2713 |
| PPA1–3134 | **I Went out of My Way** | Vic LPM2713 |

*February 1963*

| | | |
|---|---|---|
| PPA1–3135 | **You Perfect Stranger** | Vic LPM2713 |
| PPA1–3136 | **Wrap Your Troubles in Dreams** | Vic LPM2713 |
| PPA1–3137 | **A Good Thing** | Vic LPM2713 |
| PPA1–3138 | **My Last Affair** | Vic LPM2713 |

Similar personnel

*February 6 1963*

| | | |
|---|---|---|
| PPA1–3139 | **More than Likely** | Vic LPM2713 |
| PPA1–3140 | **She Doesn't Know (I Love Her)** | Vic LPM2713 |
| PPA1–3141 | **Soothe Me** | Vic LPM2879 |
| PPA1–3142 | **Jump for Joy** | Vic LPM2713 |

Similar personnel

*February 13 1963*

| | | |
|---|---|---|
| PPA1–3879 | **Sounds of the Night** | Vic LPM2713 |
| PPA1–3880 | **It's a Wonderful World** | Vic LPM2713 |

*Me and the Blues,* accompanied by Jimmy Jones's Orchestra; personnel includes Clark Terry (tpt), Phil Woods (as), Phil Bodner (ten, fl), Jerome Richardson, Jimmy Cleveland (tb), Junior Mance (p), Bob Cranshaw (b), Osie Johnson (d), Kenny Burrell (g)
*New York, April 10 1963*

| | | |
|---|---|---|
| PPA1–3881 | **A Woman** (remake) | Victor LPM2879 |
| PPA1–3882 | **Come on Blues** (remake) | Victor LPM2879 |
| PPA1–3996 | **Hobo Flats** (unissued) | Victor LPM2879 |
| PPA1–3997 | **April in Paris** | Victor LPM2879 |

Personnel includes Clark Terry (tpt), Urbie Green (tb), Phil Woods (as), Seldon Powell (ten), Danny Bank (bar) Hank Jones (p), Milt Hinton (b), Osie Johnson (d), Barry Galbraith (g)
*New York, November 18 1963*

| | | |
|---|---|---|
| PPA1–3996 | **Hobo Flats** | Victor LPM(s)2879 |
| PPA1–6701 | **Every Night** | Victor LPM(s)2879 |
| PPA1–6702 | **Good Morning Heartache** | Victor LPM(s)2879 |

Thad Jones (tpt) and Ben Webster (ten) replace Terry, Powell. Omit Woods, Bank and Green
*New York, November 20 1963*

| | | |
|---|---|---|
| PPA1–6703 | **Rocks in My Bed** | Victor LPM2879 |
| PPA1–6704 | **Nice Work if You Can Get it** | Victor LPM2879 |
| PPA1–6705 | **After All I've been to You** | Victor LPM2879 |

*December 5 1963*
Seldon Power (ten), replaces Webster. Add Richardson (as), Danny Bank (bar), Urbie Green (tb)

| | | |
|---|---|---|
| PPA1–6706 | **Early in the Morning** | Victor LPM2879 |
| PPA1–6707 | **I'm Sticking to You Baby** | Victor LPM2879 |
| PPA1–6708 | **Me and the Blues** | Victor LPM2879 |
| PPA1–6709 | **Kansas City** | Victor LPM2879 |

*Joe Williams at Newport '63,* acompanied by Clark Terry, Howard McGhee (tpt), Coleman Hawkins, Zoot Sims (ten), Junior Mance (p), Bob Cranshaw (b), Mickey Roker (d)
*Newport Jazz Festival, July 5 1963*

| | | |
|---|---|---|
| PPA5–5380 | **She's Warm, She's Willing . . .(1)** | Victor LPM(S)2762 |
| PPA5–5381 | **Without a Song** (Joe Williams and rhythm section only) | Victor LPM(S)2762 |
| PPA5–5382 | **Come Back, Baby (1)** | Victor LPM(S)2762 |
| PPA5–5383 | **Wayfaring Stranger** | Victor LPM(S)2762 |
| PPA5–5384 | **Every Day** | Victor LPM(S)2762 |
| PPA5–5385 | **Anytime, Anyday, Anywhere** | Victor LPM(S)2762 |

PPA5–5386 **April in Paris (2)** Victor LPM(S)2762
PPA5–5387 **In the Evening (2)** Victor LPM(S)2762
(1) Omit McGhee, Sims (2) Omit Terry, Hawkins
Same
*New York City, July 17 1963*
PPPA5–5377 **Gravy Waltz** Victor LPM(S)2762
PPA5–5378 **All God's Chillun/ Do You Wanna Jump** Victor LPM(S)2762
PPA5–5389 **Some 'a 'Dis 'n Some 'a Dat** Victor LPM(S)2762

*The Song is You,* accompanied by Frank Hunter's Orchestra, personnel including Urbie Green (tb) 1964

**Yours is My Heart Alone** Vic LPM3343, 7292
**I'll Follow You** Vic LPM3343, 7292
**Sleepy Time Gal** Vic LPM3343, 7292
**The Song is You** Vic LPM3343, 7292
**Prelude to a Kiss** Vic LPM3343, 7292
**Then I'll be Happy** Vic LPM3343, 7292
**People** Vic LPM3343, 7292
**I'm a Fool to Want You** Vic LPM3343, 7292
**That Face** Vic LPM3343, 7292
**My Darling** Vic LPM3343, 7292
**My Romance** Vic LPM3343, 7292
**You Stepped out of a Dream** Vic LPM3343, 7292
**I Really Don't Want to Know** 7292
No details, probably similar
**Feeling Good** RCA Vic 8501 (single)
**Nothing to Laugh About** RCA Vic 8501 (single)

*Mr Excitment,* accompanied by Bernie Glow, Jimmy Nottingham, Ernie Royal, Joe Ferrante (tpt), Urbie Green, Mickey Gravine, Muni Morrow, J.J. Johnson (tb), Alan Raph (b-tb), Leon Cohen, George Dorsey, Jerome Richardson, Bob Tricarico, Danny Bank, Sol Schlinger (saxes), Hank Jones (p), Sandy Block (b), Sol Gubin (d), Specs Powell (bngo), Mundell Lowe (g), Frank Hunter (cond, arr)
*New York, March 31 1965*
SPA1–4901 **Gypsy in My Soul** Vic LPM/LSP 3461
SPA1–4902 **Ol' Man River** Vic LPM/LSP 3461
SPA1–4903 **The Right Kind of Woman** Vic LPM/LSP 3461
SPA1–4904 **I Wonder Who's Kissing Her Now** Vic LPM/LSP 3461

Accompanied by Jerome Richardson (cl, fl, ten), Ray Alonge (fl-h), plus seventeen strings, Hank Jones (p), Sandy Block (b), Sonny Igos (d), Al

Caiola (g), Frank Hunter (cond, arr)
*New York, June 21 1965*

| | | |
|---|---|---|
| SPA1–4909 | **This is the Life** | RCA LPM/LSP3461 |
| SPA1–4910 | **Come in out of the Rain** | RCA LPM/LSP3461 |
| SPA1–4911 | **You Can't Get away from the Blues** | RCA LPM/LSP3461 |
| SPA1–4912 | **Last Love, Last Kiss, Goodbye** | RCA LPM/LSP3461 |

Accompanied by Thad Jones, Snooky Young, Jimmy Nottingham, Bill Berry, Richard Williams (tpt), Garnett Brown (tp, flh), Bob Brookmeyer (v-tb), Tom McIntosh, Cliff Heather (tb), Jerome Richardson, Jerry Dodgion, Eddie Daniels, Joe Farrell, Pepper Adams (saxes), Roland Hanna, Hank Jones, Billy Taylor* (p), Richard Davis (b) Mel Lewis (d), Sam Herman (g)
*New York, September 30 1966*

| | | |
|---|---|---|
| | **Get out of My Life** | Solid State SS18008 |
| | **Woman's Got Soul** | Solid State SS18008 |
| | **Nobody Knows the Way I Feel This Morning** | Solid State SS18008 |
| | **Gee Baby, ain't I Good to You** | Solid State SS18008 |
| | **How Sweet It is (to be Loved by You)** | Solid State SS18008 |
| | **Keep Your Hand on Your Heart** | Solid State SS18008 |
| | **Evil Man Blues** | Solid State SS18008 |
| | **Come Sunday** | Solid State SS18008 |
| | **Smack Dab in the Middle** | Solid State SS18008 |
| | **It Don't Mean a Thing (if It ain't Got That Swing)** | Solid State SS18008 |
| | **Hallelujah! I Love Her So** | Solid State SS18008 |
| | **Night Time is the Right Time (to be with the One You Love)** | Solid State SS18008 |

*Mel Lewis includes Billy Taylor on this record; Taylor sat in on 'Woman's Got Soul'.

*Something Old, New and Blue,* accompanied by the Thad Jones–Mel Lewis Jazz Orchestra. Similar or same personnel as preceeding session
*Los Angeles, April 22–27 1968*

| | | |
|---|---|---|
| | **Young Man on the Way up** | Solid State SM17015, Un. Artists ULP1188 |

| | |
|---|---|
| **Hurry on Down** | Solid State SM17015, Un. Artists ULP1188 |
| **Everybody Loves My Baby** | Solid State SM17015, Un. Artists ULP1188 |
| **When I Take My Sugar to Tea** | Solid State SM17015, Un. Artists ULP1188 |
| **Did I Really Live?** | Solid State SM17015, Un. Artists ULP1188 |
| **Honeysuckle Rose** | Solid State SM17015, Un. Artists ULP1188 |
| **Imagination** | Solid State SM17015, Un. Artists ULP1188 |
| **If I were a Bell** | Solid State SM17015, Un. Artists ULP1188 |
| **Everybody Wants to be Loved** | Solid State SM17015, Un. Artists ULP1188 |
| **Loneliness, Sorrow and Grief** | Solid State SM17015, Un. Artists ULP1188 |
| **One for My Baby** | Solid State SM17015, Un. Artists ULP1188 |

Accompanied by orchestra with Horace Ott (cond, arr)
*Los Angeles, 1970*

| | |
|---|---|
| **Something** | Blue Note BST84355 |
| **Can't Take My Eyes off You** | Blue Note BST4355 |
| **Bridges** | Blue Note BST84355 |
| **You Send Me** | Blue Note BST84355 |
| **I'd be a Fool Right Now** | Blue Note BST84355 |
| **Didn't We?** | Blue Note BST84355 |
| **Baby** | Blue Note BST84355 |
| **I Hold No Grudge** | Blue Note BST84355 |
| **Lush Life** | Blue Note BST84355 |
| **Oh, Darling** | Blue Note BST84355 |
| **Little Girl** | Blue Note BST84355 |
| **Here's That Rainy Day** | Blue Note BST84355 |

*The Heart and Soul of Joe Williams,* accompanied by George Shearing, (p)
*Hollywood, California, March 1–2 1971*

| | |
|---|---|
| **Heart and Soul** | Sheba Records |
| **Nobody's Heart** | |
| **Body and Soul** | |
| **Humpty Dumpty Heart** | |
| **My Heart Stood Still** | |

**My Heart and I**
**Blues in My Heart**
**Sleep My Heart**
**My Foolish Heart**
**My Heart Tells Me**
**Young at Heart**
**I Let a Song Go out of My Heart**

*Joe Williams with Love,* arranged and conducted by Benny Carter with large orchestra and chorus. Personnel: Al Aarons, 'Cat' Anderson, Johnny Audino, Buddy Childers, Gene Coe, Harry Edison, Chuck Findley, Ray Triscart, (tpt); George Bohanon, Nick DiMaio, Gil Falco, Dick Nash, Benny Powell, George Roberts, Frank Rossolini, Tommy Shepard, Bill Tole, Jr., (tb); Buddy Collette, Bob Cooper, Bill Green, Bill Hood, Plas Johnson, Jerome Richardson, Herman Riley, Marshall Royal, Bud Shank, (saxes); Jimmy Jones, Jimmy Rowles, (p); Ray Brown (bs), Louis Bellson, Shelly Manne, Earl Palmer Sr., (d); Vince DeRosa, Gale H. Robinson, Henry Sigismonto, Robert Watt, (fr-h); Jack Arnold, Vic Feldman, (vib); Barney Kessel, Ulysses Livingston, Alfred Viola (g); Rollice Dale, Joseph DiFiore, Myra S. Kestenbaum, Milton Thomas (va); Ron Cooper, Justin DiTullio, Marie Fera, Edgar Lustgarten, (cel); Samuel Albert, Joachim Chassman, Janice A. Gower, Bill Henderson, George Kast, Alex Koltun, Bob Konrad, William Kurasch, Marvin Limonick, Lou Raderman, Nathan Ross, Marshall Sosson, (vn); and chorus.
*Hollywood, California, November 1971–March 1972*

| | |
|---|---|
| All compositions by Bob Friedman with the exception of those tunes with lyrics by Sammy Cahn | Temponic (TB)29561 |
| **Love is a Feeling** (Bob Friedman) | Temponic (TB)29561 |
| **When You're Young** (Sammy Cahn, Bob Friedman) | Temponic (TB)29561 |
| **Satin Latin** (Bob Friedman) | Temponic (TB)29561 |
| **Got That Feeling** (Bob Friedman) | Temponic (TB)29561 |
| **Always on Sunday** (Bob Friedman) | Temponic (TB)29561 |
| **Care** (Bob Friedman) | Temponic (TB)29561 |
| **I'm a Lucky Guy** (Bob Friedman) | Temponic (TB)29561 |

| | |
|---|---|
| **Once upon a Happy Time** (Bob Friedman) | Temponic (TB)29561 |
| **Right Here in My Heart** (Bob Friedman) | Temponic (TB)29561 |
| **God Bless You** (Bob Friedman) | Temponic (TB)29561 |

*Joe Williams Live,* accompanied by Nat Adderley (cnt), Julian Cannonball Adderley (as), George Duke (p, el-p), Walter Booker (b, g-l), Carol Kaye (el-p), Roy McGurdy (d), King Errisson (conga)
*Berkley, California, August 7 1973*

| | |
|---|---|
| **Who She Do** | Fantasy F9441 |
| **Green Dolphin Street** | |
| **Heritage** | |
| **Sad Song (1)** | |
| **Goin' to Chicago** | |
| **A Beautiful Friendship** | |
| **Yesterday, Today and Tomorrow** | |
| **Tell Me Where to Scratch** | |
| (1) Unaccompanied or with Booker only | |

*Big Man, The Legend of John Henry,* an original folk musical, by Cannonball Adderley, with orchestra and chorus including Cannonball Adderley (as), Joe Williams, Randy Crawford, Robert Guillaume (vcl)
*Los Angeles*

| | |
|---|---|
| **A Folk Musical in Four Acts** | Fantasy (f.)79006 |

*In Concert, The University of Miami Concert Jazz Band and Singers,* featuring Flip Phillips (ten) and Joe Williams (vcl)
*February 16 and 23 1975*

*Jazz Gala '79,* accompanied by a big band conducted by Claude Bolling (p)
*Cannes, France, January 22 1979*

| | |
|---|---|
| **Work Song** | Personal Choice 51001 |
| **Blues in My Heart** | |
| **Just the Way You are** | |
| **It Don't Mean a Thing** | |

Add Carmen McRae (vcl), with Claude Bolling (p), and rhythm section.

**Them There Eyes**

*Prez and Joe,* featuring Joe Williams, accompanied by Dave Pell's Prez Conference, Dave Pell, Bob Cooper, Bob Hardaway (ten), Bob Efford (bar), Frank Capp (d), Monty Budwig (b), Nat Pierce (p), Al Hendrickson (g)
*Los Angeles, California, 1979*

| | |
|---|---|
| **Lady, be Good** | GNPS/Crescendo 2124 |
| **Getting Some Fun out of Life** | |
| **You Can Depend on Me** | |
| **Fooling Myself** | |
| **Boogie Woogie (I May be Wrong)** | |
| **How High the Moon** | |
| **If I Could be with You** | |
| **If Dreams Come True** | |
| **Easy Living** | |
| **When You're Smiling** | |

*Then and Now,* with Pete Christlieb (ten), Mike Melvoin (p), Jim Hughart (b), Nick Ceroli (d)
*Los Angeles, January 3 1984*

| | |
|---|---|
| **Falling in Love with Love** | Bosco |
| **I'll Follow You** | Bosco |
| **Alright, Okay, You Win** | Bosco |
| **I Want to Go Where You Go** | Bosco |
| **People** | Bosco |
| **That Face** | Bosco |
| **Singing in the Rain** | Bosco |
| **You'd be So Nice to Come Home to** | Bosco |
| **Close Enough for Love** | Bosco |
| **I Had Someone Else before I Had You** | Bosco |
| **I'd Give a Dollar for a Dime** | Bosco |
| **You and the Night and the Music** | Bosco |

## Section Two

Wendell Culley, Reunald Jones, Thad Jones, Joe Newman (tpt), Henry Coker, Bill Hughes, Benny Powell (tb), Marshall Royal, Bill Graham (as), Frank Wess (ten, fl), Frank Foster (ten), Charlie Fowlkes (bar), Count Basie (p), Eddie Jones (b), Sonny Payne (dr), Freddie Green (g), Joe Williams (vcl)

*New York, July 26–27 1955*

| | | |
|---|---|---|
| 2347 | **Every Day I Have the Blues** | Clef 89149 |
| 2348 | **The Comeback** | Clef 89149 |
| 2349 | **Alright, Okay, You Win** | Clef 89152 |
| 2350 | **In the Evenin'** | Clef 89152 |
| 2354 | **Teach Me Tonight** | Clef 89167 |
| 2355 | **Send Me Someone to Love** | Clef MGC678 |
| 2356 | **My Baby Upsets Me** | Clef MGC678 |
| 2358 | **Roll 'Em Pete** | Clef MGC678 |

Same personnel

*New York, January 4 1956*

| | | |
|---|---|---|
| 2620 | **Smack Dab in the Middle** | Verve 89169 |
| 2625 | **Amazing Love** | Verve 89171, MGV8288, ARS G402, CO9E, LB10040, Kar AFF1120 |
| 2626 | **Only, Forever** | Verve 89177, MGV8288 |

Add Harold Baker or Quincy Jones (tpt)

*New York, January 5 1956*

| | | |
|---|---|---|
| 2627 | **Stop Pretty Baby** | Verve MCV8288 |

Baker or Jones out

*Apollo Theatre, New York, January 16 1956*

| | | |
|---|---|---|
| | **I May be Wrong** | Vanguard VRS9006, Vng(E) PPL11044 |

Same

*Los Angeles, April 28 1956*

| | | |
|---|---|---|
| 20137 | **As I Love** | Verve 2004 |
| 20138 | **Stop, Don't!** | |
| 20139 | **I'm Beginning to See the Light** | |
| 20140 | **Our Love is Here to Stay** | |
| 20141 | **A Fine Romance** | |
| 20142 | **Nevertheless** | Verve 2004 |
| 20143 | **Singin' in the Rain** | Verve 2004 |
| 20144 | **There will Never be Another You** | Verve 2004 |

Same

*Los Angeles, May 1 1956*

| | | |
|---|---|---|
| 20145 | **My Baby Just Cares for Me** | Verve MGV2016 |
| 20146 | **'S Wonderful** | Verve MGV2016 |
| 20148 | **Come Rain or Come Shine** | Verve MGV2016 |

20149 **I Can't Believe That You're..** Verve MGV2016
20150 **Thou Swell** Verve MGV2016
Add Ella Fitzgerald (vcl)
*New York, June 26–27 1956*
2901 **Too Close for Comfort** Verve MGV8288
2902 **Salt Lips** Unissued
2903 **Every Day** Clef MGC743, KEP329
2904 **Party Blues** Clef 89172
2906 **Don't Worry 'Bout Me** Verve MGV8288
Same
*Gothenburg, Sweden, September 7 1956*
**Alright, Okay, You Win** MGV8407
**Roll 'Em Pete** MGV8407
**The Comeback** MGV8407
Same
*Newport Jazz Festival, July 7 1957*
**Alright, Okay, You Win** Verve MGV8244
**The Comeback** Verve MGV8244
**Roll 'Em Pete** Verve MGV8244
**Smack Dab in the Middle** Verve MGV8244
Same
*Los Angeles, August 1957*
21448 **I Don't Like You No More** Verve 89184
Gene 'Snooky' Young (tpt), Al Grey (tb), Frank Wess (as) and Eddie Davis (ten) replace Reunald Jones, Hughes and Graham
*New York, September 28 1957*

Count Basie and his orchestra, personnel including Thad Jones, Snooky Young, Wendell Culley, Joe Newman (tpt), Henry Coker, Al Grey, Benny Powell (tb), Marshall Royal, Frank Wess (as, fl), Billy Mitchell, Frank Foster (ten), Charlie Fowlkes (bar), Count Basie (p), Sonny Payne (d), Freddie Green (g), Joe Williams (vcl)
*New York, March 4 1958*
12794 **How Can You Lose** Roulette 4061
12795 **Five O'Clock in the Morning** Roulette 4061
12848 **Tell Me Your Troubles** (1) Roulette 4103
12849 **Hallelujah, I Love Her So** R52021
(1) Nat Pierce (p) replaces Basie
Same except add Harry Edison (tpt)
*Miami, Florida, May 21 1959*
**Five O'Clock in the Morning** Roulette (S)R52028
**Hallelujah, I Love Her So** Roulette (S)R52028

Count Basie and his Orchestra, personnel including John Anderson, Thad Jones, Joe Newman, Snooky Young (tpt), Henry Coker, Al Grey, Benny

Powell (tb), Marshall Royal, Frank Wess (as), Frank Foster, Billy Mitchell (ten), Charlie Fowlkes (bar), Count Basie (p), Eddie Jones (b), Sonny Payne (dr), Freddie Green (g), Joe Williams (vcl)

*Los Angeles, September 24 1959*

| | | |
|---|---|---|
| 14369 | **What Did You Win** | Roulette (S)R52033 |
| 14370 | **Cherry Red** | Roulette (S)R52033 |
| 14371 | **Baby, Please Come Home** | Roulette (S)R52033 |
| 14372 | **Every Day I Have the Blues** | Roulette (S)R52093 |
| 14373 | **Ain't No Use** | Roulette (S)R52093 |
| 14374 | **Shake Rattle and Roll** | Roulette (S)R52093 |
| 14375 | **Good Morning Blues** | Roulette (S)R52093 |
| 14376 | **Just A Dream** | Roulette (S)R52108 |
| 14377 | **Joe Sings the Blues** | Roulette (S)R52108 |

Count Basie and his Orchestra, Sonny Cohn replaces John Anderson (tpt), Add Dave Lambert, Jon Hendricks, Annie Ross (vcl)

*New York, May 26–27 1958*

| | | |
|---|---|---|
| 13062 | **Swingin' the Blues** | Roulette 4088, (S)R52018 |
| 13064 | **Li'l Darlin'** | Sonet (D)SXP2013 |
| 13065 | **Let Me See** | |
| 13066 | **Every Tub** | Rejected |
| 13067 | **Goin' to Chicago** | Rejected |
| 13068 | **M Squad Theme** | Rejected |
| 13069 | **Tickle Toe** | Rejected |

Same

*September 2–3 1958*

| | | |
|---|---|---|
| 13066 | **Every Tub** | Roulette (S)R52018, Sonet (D), SXP2014 |
| 13067 | **Goin' to Chicago** | Roulette 4088 0 (S)R52033, (S)R52050, (S)R52093, (S)R52111, A.P. WGM–4, Forum F(S)9034 |
| | **Tickle Toe** | Roulette (S)R52018 Sonet (D) SXP2013 |

Same

*New York, October 15 1958*

| | | |
|---|---|---|
| 13068 | **M Squad Theme** | Roulette 4109, Co(E), DB4262, Sonet (D)SXP2012 |
| 13197 | **Shorty George** | Roulette (S)R52018, Sonet (D)SXP2014 |
| 13198 | **Rusty Dusty Blues** | Roulette 4124, (S)R52062, (S)R52093, SSR8004, A.P. WGM–10 |
| 13199 | **Jumpin' at the Woodside** | Roulette 4124, (S)R52018, (S)R52057, SSR8003, (S)R512111 Sonet (D)SXP201 |

| | | |
|---|---|---|
| 13200 | **The King** | Roulette (S)R52018, A.P. WGM–4, Sonet (D)SXP2013 |

Count Basie (p, org), George Duvivier (b), Jimmy Crawford (d), Freddie Green (g), Joe Williams (vcl)
*New York, October 16 1958*

| | | |
|---|---|---|
| 13268 | **All of Me** | Roulette (S)R52021 |
| 13259 | **Ain't Misbehavin'** | Roulette (S)R52021 |
| 13260 | **The One I Love** | Roulette (S)R52021 |
| 13261 | **Dinah** | Roulette (S)R52021 |

Same
*New York, October 23 1958*

| | | |
|---|---|---|
| 13274 | **Memories of You** | Roulette (S)R52021 |
| 13275 | **Call Me Darlin'** | Roulette (S)R52021 |
| 13278 | **Sweet Sue, Just You** | Roulette (S)R52021 |
| 13279 | **Honeysuckle Rose** | Roulette (S)r52021 |
| 13280 | **If I Could be with You** | Rejected |
| 13281 | **I'll Always be in Love with You** | Roulette (S)R52021 |
| 13282 | **Baby, Won't You Please Come Home?** | Roulette (S)R52021 |

Same, Add Harry Edison (tp)

| | | |
|---|---|---|
| 13280 | **If I Could be with You** | Roulette (S)R52021 |
| 13472 | **Sometimes I'm Happy** | Roulette (S)R52021 |

Count Basie and his Orchestra, personnel including Sonny Cohn, Snooky Young, Thad Jones, Joe Newman (tpt), Al Grey, Henry Coker, Benny Powell (tb), Marshall Royal (clt, as), Frank Wess (as, ten, fl), Frank Foster, Billy Mitchell (ten), Charlie Fowlkes (bar), Count Basie (p), Eddie Jones (b), Gus Johnson (d), Freddie Green (g), Joe Williams (vcl)
*New York, January 23–24 1958*

| | | |
|---|---|---|
| | **Sent for You Yesterday** | Roulette (S)RB–1 |
| | **Boogie Woogie** | |

Sonny Payne replaces Gus Johnson
*September 9 1960*

| | | |
|---|---|---|
| | **Chains of Love** | Roulette (S)R52054 |
| | **Key to the Highway** | Roulette (S)R52054 |
| | **Keep Your Hand on Your Heart** | Roulette (S)R52054 |
| | **Confessing the Blues** | Roulette (S)R52054 |
| | **Lyin' Woman** | Roulette (S)R52054 |
| | **Mean Mistreater** | Roulette (S)R52054 |
| | **Tomorrow Night** | Roulette (S)R52054 |
| | **Night Time is the Right Time** | Roulette (S)R52054 |

| | | |
|---|---|---|
| | **Travelin' Light** | Roulette (S)R52054 |
| Add Sarah Vaughan (vcl) | | |
| 15286 | **If I were a Bell** | Roulette 4273 |
| 15287 | **Teach Me Tonight** | Roulette 4273 |

# *Bibliography*

Dance, Stanley, *The World of Count Basie,* Charles Scribner's Sons, New York, 1980

Horricks, Raymond, *Count Basie and His Orchestra,* Gollancz, New York, 1957

Pleasants, Henry, *The Great American Popular Singers,* Simon and Schuster, New York, 1974

Simon, George, *The Big Bands,* Schirmer Books, a division of Macmillan Publishing Co, New York, 1981

Stearns, Marshall, *The Story of Jazz,* Oxford University Press, New York, 1978

Travis, Dempsey J., *Autobiography of Black Jazz,* with an introduction by Studs Terkel, Urban Research Institute, Inc, Chicago, Ill, 1983

Williams, Martin, 'Horses in Midstream, Count Basie in the 1950s', in *Annual Review of Jazz Studies, 2,* edited by Dan Morgenstern, Charles Nanry, David A. Cayer, Transaction Books, New Brunswick, NJ, USA and London, England, UK

# Index